Philosophical Perspectives on
Existential Gratitude

Also available from Bloomsbury:

Four Views on the Axiology of Theism, edited by Kirk Lougheed
God's Action in the World, by Marek Slomka
Philosophical Hermeneutics and the Priority of Questions in Religions, by Nathan Eric Dickman
Why God Must Do What Is Best, by Justin J. Daeley

Philosophical Perspectives on Existential Gratitude

Analytic, Continental, and Religious

Edited by
Joshua Lee Harris, Kirk Lougheed,
and Neal DeRoo

BLOOMSBURY ACADEMIC
LONDON • NEW YORK • OXFORD • NEW DELHI • SYDNEY

BLOOMSBURY ACADEMIC
Bloomsbury Publishing Plc
50 Bedford Square, London, WC1B 3DP, UK
1385 Broadway, New York, NY 10018, USA
29 Earlsfort Terrace, Dublin 2, Ireland

BLOOMSBURY, BLOOMSBURY ACADEMIC and the Diana logo are trademarks of
Bloomsbury Publishing Plc

First published in Great Britain 2023
This paperback edition published 2024

Copyright © Joshua Lee Harris, Kirk Lougheed, Neal DeRoo and Contributors, 2023

Joshua Lee Harris, Kirk Lougheed and Neal DeRoo have asserted their right under the
Copyright, Designs and Patents Act, 1988, to be identified as Author of this work.

For legal purposes the Acknowledgments on p. viii constitute an extension
of this copyright page.

Cover image: Yosemite National Park in California, USA
© Mihai P/Getty Images

All rights reserved. No part of this publication may be reproduced or transmitted in any
form or by any means, electronic or mechanical, including photocopying, recording, or
any information storage or retrieval system, without prior permission in writing from the
publishers.

Bloomsbury Publishing Plc does not have any control over, or responsibility for, any third-
party websites referred to or in this book. All internet addresses given in this book were
correct at the time of going to press. The author and publisher regret any inconvenience
caused if addresses have changed or sites have ceased to exist, but can accept no
responsibility for any such changes.

A catalogue record for this book is available from the British Library.

A catalog record for this book is available from the Library of Congress.

ISBN: HB: 978-1-3502-8912-3
PB: 978-1-3502-8916-1
ePDF: 978-1-3502-8913-0
eBook: 978-1-3502-8914-7

Typeset by Deanta Global Publishing Services, Chennai, India

To find out more about our authors and books visit www.bloomsbury.com and
sign up for our newsletters.

To our teachers

Contents

Acknowledgments		viii
Introduction *Joshua Lee Harris*		1
1	Existential Gratitude: A Social-structural Account *Joshua Lee Harris*	13
2	Gratitude and Resentment: A Tale of Two Weddings *Graham Oppy*	31
3	Gratitude and the Human Vocation *Brian Treanor*	45
4	Generous Existence? Gift, Giving, and Gratitude in Contemporary Phenomenology *Christina M. Gschwandtner*	65
5	Gratitude for Life-force in African Philosophy *Thaddeus Metz*	89
6	On the Contingent Necessity of the World *Michael Almeida*	109
7	Existential Gratitude in Avicenna's *Metaphysics of the Healing* *Catherine Peters*	123
8	Lessons from Anti-natalism on God and Gratitude for Our Existence *Kirk Lougheed*	143
9	Thank *You*: William Desmond's Metaphysics of Gift and Ethic of Gratitude *Ethan Vanderleek*	163
Notes on Contributors		179
Index		181

Acknowledgments

This volume was made possible by the efforts of many beyond the named editors and contributors. We are grateful to the Bloomsbury editorial team, and especially Colleen Coalter and Suzie Nash, whose creativity and patience did much to help see things through to completion. We also thank our research assistants, Zahory Zapata and Erica Kath—Zahory for her rigorous and thorough literature review that gathered crucial momentum for the project; and Erica for her invaluable copyediting contributions. We also received support from the Canada Research Chair Secretariat via the Canada Research Chair in Phenomenology and Philosophy of Religion, and, finally, the project was funded by the John Templeton Foundation, Grant No. 61513.

Introduction

Joshua Lee Harris

In recent years there has been a resurgence of interest among social scientists and philosophers on the nature and effects of gratitude in human social life. Gratitude's reputation as the "quintessential positive trait" is well known among theorists and practitioners, and empirical studies do seem to show consistently that habitual expressions of gratitude uniquely correlate with increases in pro-social attitudes, strengthened relationships, emotional resilience, and other data points commonly associated with overall well-being (see, for example, Nezlek et al. 2017; Emmons and Stern 2013; Frederickson 2013; Wood et al. 2008; McCullough et al. 2002). In short, there seems to be considerable support for something approaching the Stoic view that gratitude is the "greatest of virtues" (see, for example, Cicero 1851).

While the bulk of this recent empirical research is geared toward understanding gratitude as an intersubjective phenomenon, some working in this area have noted the importance of "existential" or "cosmic" gratitude—that is, gratitude not for one gift or another but, rather, for one's *very existence* and/or *life as a whole* (Lacewing 2016; Roberts 2014; Emmons and McCullough 2004). When defined as such, the moral and spiritual exigence of existential gratitude is clearly recognized and lauded by most major religious traditions, and it is the object of admiration of many of the most influential philosophers in Western and non-Western traditions.

The chapters contained in this volume set out to consider this well-recognized but little understood phenomenon of existential gratitude from a wide variety of philosophical perspectives. The goal is to make progress in understanding existential gratitude by considering it under three different aspects. In Section 1, gratitude is considered insofar as it is a perennially and characteristically *human* phenomenon, central to the distinctive life of our species. In Section 2, gratitude is considered with special attention to the conditions under which existence itself might be construed as having a gift-like or otherwise gratitude-inducing character. Finally, in Section 3, gratitude is considered under a specifically religious aspect, with respect to our relationship to the divine.

In this chapter, we offer a brief topography of motivations for the importance of existential gratitude as a psychological, moral, and theological phenomenon. Then we outline some key criticisms leveled against the coherence and viability of existential gratitude as a constitutive feature of human moral striving. Finally, we introduce our chapters against this research background, drawing attention to ways in which philosophical progress on the issue can deepen our collective understanding of this multifaceted phenomenon.

1 Existential Gratitude in Contemporary Psychology

Gratitude studies are paradigmatic applications of "positive psychology," the contemporary subdiscipline of psychology that examines the subjective experiences, traits, and institutions associated with well-being (Seligman and Csikszentmihalyi 2000). Specifically, gratitude has been classified as a "strength of transcendence," since it is a trait (alongside others such as aesthetic appreciation, hope and spirituality) that "allows individuals to forge connections to the larger universe and thereby provide meaning to their lives" (Peterson and Seligman 2004: 519). Given the importance of purpose and a sense of meaning to general life satisfaction, consistent positive correlations between gratitude and well-being—especially in adults and adolescents (see, for example, Park and Peterson 2006)—should not come as a surprise.

Yet the connection between gratitude and a sense of transcendent purpose and meaning is even more intimate when we consider existential gratitude. And, as it happens, the recent development of the "Existential Gratitude Scale" (EGS) by Jans-Beken and Wong (2019) lends credence to the judgment that existential gratitude in particular may have a distinctive explanatory value in assessing resilience in contexts of suffering. The EGS developed by Jans-Beken and Wong is a thirteen-question questionnaire designed specifically to track participants' gratitude for their life as a whole—including phases and moments of both suffering and joy—as opposed to "dispositional" gratitude, which takes as its object only what is uncontroversially good. The EGS invites participants to respond to statements such as "I am grateful for my life even in times of suffering," and "I still feel bitter for all the bad experiences that have happened to me" (2019: 15). As these statements indicate, existential gratitude is marked by a positive recognition and responsiveness to one's existence or life *simpliciter*, as opposed to one or another benefit in particular. While gratitude in its dispositional and existential forms may go hand in hand in some cases, preliminary research using the EGS does seem to indicate that the two concepts may well come apart, especially when measuring the relative well-being of subjects in contexts of suffering.

The work of Emmons and McCullough (2004) on what they call "cosmic" gratitude lends further support to the value of distinguishing dispositional and existential forms of gratitude. They frame the discussion in terms of a dipolar "spectrum of gratitude," with *personal* gratitude on the one end and *transpersonal* gratitude on the other: "for one pole [for example], receiving a gift package from another person; for the opposite pole, a peak experience in the solitude of a mountain top" (2004: 285). While both exemplary experiences are similar in that they involve a recognition and positive responsiveness to goods received as blessings or gifts, once again the respective objects of gratitude differ starkly. While the case of personal gratitude involves an identifiable relationship with another person mediated by an exchange of gifts, the case of transpersonal gratitude (arguably) involves no such thing. On the contrary, although there is a sense in which the experience of the mountaintop itself is the blessing being recognized in the transpersonal case, Emmons and McCullough argue that the real point is different. In cases of transpersonal gratitude, they argue, there is something like "an overwhelming cosmic oneness, typically associated with a sense of 'I don't deserve this'" (285). To offer an admittedly liberal interpretation of these remarks, it is the fact that one is alive *in the first place* that is of concern here, rather than the discrete experience considered in isolation. In short, we suggest, such experiences can be understood as cases of what we are calling existential gratitude.

Finally, we would be remiss of course if we did not mention the psychological study of *religious* gratitude, since, among other reasons, religious modalities of gratitude may be the most obviously prescient for existential gratitude. In fact, as the study conducted by Rosmarin et al. (2011) demonstrates, distinguishing "religious" from "general" forms of gratitude can add variance to results when predicting mental well-being, if only due to the foundational role played by God (or something like God) as a universal benefactor. According to this line of reasoning, God or religiously directed gratitude increases what Emmons calls the "gratitude density" McCullough et al. 2002) of the subject, since one who is grateful in this sense is able to recognize and respond not just to human benefactors but also to the divine. The connection here is clear: a religious or spiritual sense that one's existence or life as a whole is given gratuitously to them by God (or something like God) is clearly a manifestation of existential gratitude.

Now of course this is a dreadfully incomplete precis of contemporary work in positive psychology on the phenomenon of existential gratitude. But perhaps it is enough to establish our thesis for the moment: namely, that there are identifiable empirical reasons for countenancing existential gratitude as a unique explanatory phenomenon—not just because of its remit as a concept but also because of its distinctive role in well-being. As these studies (among others) seem to show, there is value in identifying a psychological trait that is attentive to one's existence or life itself as a good.

2 Existential Gratitude in the History of Theology and Philosophy

Major world religions display a remarkable consistency when it comes to the centrality and necessity of gratitude as a civil and religious virtue. The religious and cultural economies of Greco-Roman antiquity feature "grace" (χάρις/*gratia*) as something like an essential principle for all forms of social reciprocity. Aristotle and Seneca, among others, famously leverage the ancient cultic reverence for the "Graces" as evidence for the vital role of graceful giving and grateful receiving in functioning societies, and the gods are repeatedly invoked as paradigmatic objects of gratitude (see, for example, Aristotle 2012, Bk. 5 and Seneca 1935, Bk. 1). For Seneca, especially, we understand interpersonal gratitude only to the extent that we understand the "first gift," which is nothing other than creation as such. For Seneca, the world need not be thus—or at all, for that matter—and the fact that it is nevertheless is the clearest sign of a grace to which gratitude is the necessary human response (Harris 2021). Therefore the earliest comprehensive treatments of gratitude clearly affirm what we are calling existential gratitude— not just because it is distinctive but also because it is *paradigmatic*.

Theologians and philosophers in the Abrahamic monotheisms develop the notion of existential gratitude in considerable detail—due in no small part to the development of doctrines of creation and contingent existence. As Seeskin points out (2006: 82) in his groundbreaking study, the great Jewish medieval philosopher Maimonides "regards existence as a gift. . . . [O]ffering thanks to God is not a hollow ritual but a legitimate response to a metaphysical truth." For the Islamic luminary Ibn Sīnā (Avicenna 2005: I.6-7), creaturely existence is *ğāʾiz al-wuğūd* or "possible existence," which is marked by its constitutive dependence upon the Necessary Existent (*wāğib al-wuğūd*). For Thomas Aquinas, existence (*esse*) is had by the creature by virtue of its "participation" in the divine, who is among other things subsistent existence itself (Aquinas 2012: Ia, q44). Broadly speaking, then, the conclusion that existence is a gift turns out to be an idiomatic rendering of a properly theoretical consensus shared by these traditions concerning their respective technical accounts of creation. The rational and moral appropriateness of existential gratitude can be understood as an implication of this line of reasoning, and therefore its spiritual exigence as recognized by all Abrahamic monotheisms should come as no surprise.

Remarkably, even unambiguously atheistic traditions of Mahāyāna Buddhism exhort adherents to be grateful to what is ultimate—even if what is ultimate is the Buddha as an embodiment of total and distinction-less emptiness (Eckel 1985). To have attained Buddhahood is after all a salvific condition in this tradition, and so there is a clear sense in which patterns of recognition of total gratuity and its accordingly appropriate response in gratitude is in fact appropriate—even if there is no personal agent responsible for this ultimate "gift."

Friedrich Nietzsche is another influential atheistic figure whose work features existential gratitude as centrally important. As Fox (2020) has shown convincingly, a key theme running throughout Nietzsche's prolific career is his conviction that a noble spirit must involve gratitude for artistic and natural beauty, and especially for the principle of all beauty, which is the principle of *life* (*Leben*). As he remarks memorably in the quasi-autobiographical *Ecce Homo* (2005: 9), "How could I not be grateful to my whole life?" One who is so disposed is not only grateful *for* life but also *to* it, that is, to affirm the beauty of the entirety of one's life and to avoid the spiritually crippling effects of resentment. Such a conviction surely counts as a romanticized exhortation to existential gratitude.

Of course this is only a snapshot of theological and philosophical accounts of the rational, moral, and spiritual urgency of existential gratitude. Indeed, it would be no easy task to distill a single definition that would clearly and univocally apply even just to the abovementioned traditions. Yet perhaps it is clear enough, even if only by family resemblance, that existential gratitude seems to evince an impressively universal scope across these otherwise widely divergent authors and their respective cultures of influence.

3 Philosophical Objections to Existential Gratitude

Now, given the apparently universal recognition and admonition of existential gratitude outlined earlier, it might seem like there is little for philosophers to do in advancing our understanding of the phenomenon of interest. Is existential gratitude just "common sense"? Not quite. As it happens, there are at least two core objections to existential gratitude as a moral or spiritual principle that are commonly recognized in contemporary philosophical literature.

The first objection concerns conceptual coherence. As Manela (2021) has noted, it is intuitively plausible as a matter of definition that a "benefit" by its very nature makes its beneficiary better off than he was before. But this is a potential problem for conceiving of one's existence or life as a benefit, since purported beneficiaries of life did not even exist prior to their "reception" of it, and being "better off" seems to require a prior state of being "worse off" before. But of course one must have existed before to have been worse off before. Therefore, at least on the assumption that gratitude is always gratitude for some benefit, there is something deeply strange about existential gratitude.

The second objection is the "Asymmetry Argument" advanced by Benetar (2005). This objection is closely related to the first, and in fact it might be construed as an exploration of the moral implications of the ambiguity identified in the first objection. According to the Asymmetry Argument, not only do we not have reason to think that existence or life is a benefit; we may actually have more reason to think of existence or life itself as a *harm*. This is because there is an asymmetry between pleasure and pain. That is, while the presence of pleasure and the absence of pain are obviously both goods, it is not obvious that the presence of pain and the absence of pleasure are both bad. In fact, argues Benatar (2006), it is better to characterize the absence of pleasure as neither bad nor good (rather than simply bad). Therefore any comparison of the respective merits of existing versus not existing must countenance the following asymmetry: to exist, one enjoys the good that is the presence of pleasure, but one must surely also face the positively bad outcome that is the presence of pain. By contrast, failing to exist in the first place involves the positive good of the absence of pain, but, crucially, it also involves the absence of pleasure, which is *neither bad nor good*. Assuming the inevitability of pain that accompanies every human life, then, at the very least this asymmetry of pain and pleasure presents a serious challenge to the position that existence or life is *inherently* beneficial. Indeed, Benetar's argument is not without precedent in the history of Western philosophy, as Schopenhauer's interpretation of tragedy demonstrates (e.g., Schopenhauer 1909: 328).

There are certainly more objections to consider when it comes to the viability of existential gratitude, but these two are especially worth mentioning here on account of their treatment in the chapters contained in this volume. In fact, encountering one or the other objection serves as something like a common thread running through each of the ensuing chapter contributions. Therefore, even if existential gratitude enjoys a remarkable level of universality across many eras and cultures, its coherence and moral appropriateness are not at all obvious.

4 Chapter Summaries

We conclude this brief introduction with summaries of the chapters contained in this volume.

In "Existential Gratitude: A Social-structural Account," Joshua Lee Harris argues that philosophical accounts of existential gratitude would be better served by appreciating what he calls the "social-structural" dimension of gratitude. Drawing upon Sally Haslanger's account of "social-structural" explanation, he argues that the appropriateness of gratitude is grounded in a distinctive social form of reciprocity—one in which the beneficiary finds herself positioned as the recipient of a benefit from a principle benefactor.

In his chapter, "Gratitude and Resentment: A Tale of Two Weddings," Graham Oppy argues that there is an important distinction between propositional expressions of gratitude and prepositional expressions of gratitude. Through a series of pointed examples, he suggests that there is a tension in the view that claims propositional expressions of gratitude can be understood as prepositional expressions of gratitude to God, while simultaneously denying that propositional expressions of resentment can be understood as prepositional expressions of resentment to God. Theists should refrain from connecting their propositional expressions of gratitude to prepositional expressions of gratitude to God. In order for the theist to be justified in such expressions, the object of gratitude needs to be part of God's original creative intent. This condition does not plausibly obtain in many of the typical cases for gratitude usually appealed to by theists.

Brian Treanor shows that the question of existential gratitude has direct implications for both philosophical anthropology and environmental thought. He begins by sketching a picture of gratitude, especially by distinguishing it from appreciation in terms of its relation to valuation and economic exchange. Then he shows that wild nature is uniquely able to elicit not just appreciation but also gratitude from us. From this basis he argues for two main claims: first, that human beings are uniquely "primed" for gratitude; and second, that one of the ways in which we can lean into this gratitude is by viewing the world as a place populated by (human and nonhuman) persons coexisting in a complex network of relationships, rather than as space containing impersonal things and dead matter that are valued only as "resources."

Christina Gschwandtner examines several key insights from the phenomenological tradition to question whether gratitude is a necessary (or beneficial) response to existence. First, she walks through two classical phenomenological investigations of givenness to challenge the idea that we ought to be grateful for our existence: Derrida's account of the necessarily economic nature of the gift calls into question the appropriateness of gratitude as a response to the gift, while Marion's phenomenology of givenness, by setting giving and being in opposition to each other, suggests that existence is not primarily what is given to us and that the proper response to God as the "giver of gifts" is, therefore, not existential gratitude but confession. Then she uses contemporary work in phenomenology to highlight how a robust phenomenology of gratitude would have metaphysical, ontological, theological, and ethical implications.

In his chapter, "Gratitude for Life-force in African Philosophy," Thaddeus Metz explores gratitude in the context of indigenous African philosophy of religion. According to Metz, there are four beliefs in this tradition that support the idea that we should be grateful to God for our existence. First, as with the Abrahamic faiths, this tradition affirms that there is a personal God who created all concrete objects in the universe. Second, everything that exists, both animate and inanimate objects, is imbued with an imperceptible energy known as life-force which ultimately comes from God. Third, the greater the life-force, the more final value a thing has, such that fourth, humans possess the highest degree of it any perceptible being on earth. Humans therefore have a dignity that nonhuman animals and inanimate objects lack. Being created with this kind of superlative, noninstrumental value justifies an attitude of gratitude for God.

In his chapter, "On the Contingent Necessity of the World," Michael Almeida argues that the most popular account of the metaphysics of theistic creation is theistic actualism. This is the view that everything that exists is part of the actual world. God's creative activity explains the existence of the actual world and actual persons. On theistic actualism, gratitude to God is the appropriate response for existence since it is an undeserved good. Almeida then considers an objection to gratitude on theistic actualism in the form of Peter van Inwagen's modal collapse argument, which entails that the world is self-explanatory and so gratitude isn't owed to God because of God's creative activity. Almeida then rejects this argument by suggesting that an ultimate explanation of everything that exists is consistent with the actual world being contingently necessary. That we exist necessarily is just a contingent fact which means that gratitude to God for our existence is appropriate.

In "Existential Gratitude in Avicenna's *Metaphysics of the Healing*," Catherine Peters explores some key ambiguities surrounding the appropriateness of existential gratitude in the work of Avicenna. With special reference to the central Avicennian distinction between possible and necessary existence and its application to the context of existential gratitude and divine munificence, she argues that Avicenna is committed to the apparently paradoxical conclusion that God cannot *receive* gratitude from his creatures, even though creatures are morally and spiritually bound to offer it.

In his chapter, "Lessons from Anti-natalism on God and Gratitude for Our Existence," Kirk Lougheed draws connections between the emerging philosophical literature on anti-natalism and the theist's claim that we ought to be grateful to God for our existence. After briefly explaining why gratitude for our existence is an appropriate response to God, Lougheed outlines five different arguments for anti-natalism. This is the view that it is (almost) always all things considered wrong to procreate. While Lougheed does not defend any of these arguments, he observes that if any of them are sound, they constitute a defeater to the theistic claim about gratitude to God for our existence. Furthermore, if any of the arguments for anti-natalism are sound, they demonstrate that God could not be justified in creating humans in our particular world. As this would pose a new route to atheism, theists need to engage with the arguments for anti-natalism.

Finally, Ethan Vanderleek argues alongside William Desmond and others that we should construe the being of finite existence as a gift from a personal giver, and that the appropriate response to this gift is gratitude understood in ontological, metaphysical, ethical, and religious ways. Because finite beings do not include their own reason for existence, he argues, we should understand them as necessarily in relation to the infinite being that makes them be. This relation is characterized by a gift: being is given to finite beings by a personal giver. He then shows that the rational response to this gift/giver is gratitude, most deeply an "ontological gratitude" that permeates every part of our finite being as gifted. Vanderleek concludes, again following Desmond, by showing that both ethics and prayer are birthed from this prior metaphysical and ontological gratitude.

A picture that emerges from these chapters demonstrates the uniqueness and complexity of existential gratitude. That is, despite its remarkable universality and importance, there are surprisingly difficult problems associated with its conceptual coherence and practical viability. Therefore, we hope that this volume can make a unique contribution to this most central moral and spiritual concern phenomenon.

References

Aristotle (2012). *Aristotle's Nicomachean Ethics*, trans. R. Bartlett and S. Collins. Chicago, IL: University of Chicago Press.

Aquinas, T. (2012). *Summa theologiae: Secunda Secundae 92–189*, trans. L. Shapcote. Lander, WY: Aquinas Institute.

Avicenna (2005). *The Metaphysics of the Healing*, trans. M. Marmura. Provo, UT: Brigham Young University Press.

Benatar, D. (2006). *Better Never to Have Been: The Harm of Coming into Existence*. Oxford: Oxford University Press.

Cicero (1851). *The Orations of Marcus Tullius Cicero* (Vol. III), trans. C. Young. London: George Bell & Sons.

Eckel, M. (1985). "Gratitude to an Empty Savior: A Study of the Concept of Gratitude in Mahāyāna Buddhist Philosophy." *History of Religions*, 25 (1): 57–75.

Emmons, R. and M. McCullough, eds. (2004). *The Psychology of Gratitude*. Oxford: Oxford University Press.

Emmons, R. and R. Stern (2013). "Gratitude as a Psychotherapeutic Intervention." *Journal of Clinical Psychology*, 69 (8): 846–55.

Fox, J. (2020). "Gratitude to Beautiful Objects: On Nietzsche's Claim That the Beautiful 'Promises Happiness.'" *Journal of Nietzsche Studies*, 51 (2): 169–87.

Frederickson, B. (2013). "Positive Emotions Broaden and Build." *Advances in Experimental Social Psychology*, 47, 1–53.

Harris, J. (2021). "The Human Arts of Graceful Giving and Grateful Receiving." *Renovatio: The Journal of Zaytuna College* 5 (1): 11–15.

Jans-Beken, L. and P. Wong (2019). "Development and Preliminary Validation of the Existential Gratitude Scale (EGS)." *Counseling Psychology Quarterly*, 34 (1): 1–15.

Lacewing, M. (2016). "Can Non-Theists Appropriately Feel Existential Gratitude?." *Religious Studies*, 52: 145–65.

Manela, T. (2021). "Gratitude." In E. Zalta (ed.), *The Stanford Encyclopedia of Philosophy*. https://plato.stanford.edu/archives/win2021/entries/gratitude/.

McCullough, M. E., R. A. Emmons, and J.-A. Tsang (2002). "The Grateful Disposition: A Conceptual and Empirical Topography." *Journal of Personality and Social Psychology*, 82:112–27.

Nezlek, J. B., D. B. Newman, and T. M. Thrash (2017). "A Daily Diary Study of Relationships Between Feelings of Gratitude and Well-Being." *The Journal of Positive Psychology*, 12 (4): 323–32.

Nietzsche, F. (2005). *Nietzsche: The Anti-Christ, Ecce Homo, Twilight of the Idols: And Other Writings*. Cambridge: Cambridge University Press.

Park, N. and C. Peterson (2006). "Character Strengths and Happiness among Young Children: Content Analysis of Parental Descriptions." *Journal of Happiness Studies*, 7: 323–41.

Peterson, C. and M. Seligman (2004). *Character Strengths and Virtues: A Handbook and Classification*. Oxford: Oxford University Press.

Roberts, R. (2014). "Cosmic Gratitude." *European Journal for Philosophy of Religion*, 6 (3): 65–83.

Rosmarin, D., S. Pirutinsky, A. Cohen, Y. Galler, and E. Krumrei (2011). "Grateful to God or Just Plain Grateful? A Comparison of Religious and General Gratitude." *The Journal of Positive Psychology*, 6 (5): 389–96.

Schopenhauer, A. (1909). *The World as Will and Idea*, trans. R. Haldane and J. Kemp. London: Kegan Paul, Trench, Trübner and Co.

Seeskin, K. (2006). *Maimonides on the Origin of the World*. Cambridge: Cambridge University Press.

Seligman, M. and M. Csikszentmihalyi. (2000). "Positive Psychology: An Introduction." *American Psychologist*, 55 (1): 5–14.

Seneca (1935). *Moral Essays Volume III: De Beneficiis*, trans. J. Basore. Cambridge, MA: Harvard University Press.

Wood, A. M., J. Maltby, R. Gillett, P. A. Linley, and S. Joseph. (2008). "The Role of Gratitude in the Development of Social Support, Stress, and Depression: Two Longitudinal Studies." *Journal of Research in Personality*, 42: 854–71.

Existential Gratitude

A Social-structural Account

Joshua Lee Harris

1 Introduction

Thanks to the influence of positive psychology, there has been a renewal of interest in the phenomenon of what is sometimes called "existential" gratitude (EG), that is, gratitude for one's life or existence *as a whole*, as opposed to gratitude for one particular benefit or another. EG seems to be verifiable across contemporary religious and cultural traditions, which in turn has led social scientists to consider whether and to what extent it might be possible to conceptualize the phenomenon in such a way as to capture its distinctiveness and universality.

I hope to contribute to this conceptual project by intervening in a debate about the *appropriateness* of EG. According to Roberts (2014), EG is appropriate only on theism. This is because gratitude generally is an emotion experienced in the recognition of a benefit conferred by a personal benefactor, and such a personal benefactor in cases of EG could only be available on theism. Roberts's account of EG satisfies the theoretical *desideratum* of distinctiveness, but (as I will argue) it is disappointing when it comes to accounting for the apparent universality of EG.

By contrast, Lacewing (2015) defends a more inclusive account of EG—one that is grounded in the recognition of the *undeserved* goodness of one's life/existence. For Lacewing, the *desideratum* that is the distinctiveness of EG lies in the fact that life/existence is a good we could not possibly deserve—regardless of whether the benefit in question is owed to a personal benefactor or not. Lacewing's account is more inclusive because it is well positioned to include nontheists. However, Lacewing's etymological justification for his position is a bit thin, and it arguably fails to do justice especially to the data that are the centrality and significance of EG across cultures.

My thesis is that the accounts offered in this debate would be better served by appreciating what I call the "social-structural" dimension of gratitude generally and therefore also EG. In other words, I argue that the appropriateness of gratitude is structured not primarily in facts about the intentional states of individuals or benefits—not as objects of analysis in their own right, at least. Instead, drawing upon Sally Haslanger's (2016) account of "social-structural" explanation, I argue that the appropriateness of gratitude is structured by a distinctive *social form* of reciprocity—one in which the beneficiary finds herself *positioned* as the recipient of a benefit from a principal benefactor. Therefore, EG is grounded in one's being so positioned with respect to some such principle with respect to one's life/existence (personal or not). Such an account performs nicely when it comes to the aforementioned *desiderata* of distinctiveness (since apparently similar intentional states are not so structured) and universality (since such conditions of reciprocity are pervasive in known cultures historical and contemporaneous).

I begin by offering a brief recap and evaluation of the Roberts-Lacewing debate. Then I sketch out my alternative, social-structural account of gratitude in general by drawing on Haslanger's work. Finally, I apply these ideas to an account of EG, reflecting on what I take to be the theoretical advantages of my account vis-à-vis Roberts and Lacewing.

2 The Roberts-Lacewing Debate

2.1 Roberts

In his influential essay entitled "Cosmic Gratitude," Roberts considers the phenomenon of "transpersonal" or "cosmic" gratitude in the work of David Steindl-Rast. According to Steindl-Rast, we should distinguish between (a) *thankfulness*, which is "in terms of giver, gift, and receiver"; and (b) *gratefulness*, which he describes as the "integral element of the experience of universal wholeness" (2004: 286). In contrast to thankfulness, argues Steindl-Rast, gratefulness does not require the tripolar structure of benefactor, gift, and beneficiary, and therefore it does not even require that the *dative object* (i.e., the one *to whom* I am grateful) is a *personal agent*. In short, when it comes to cosmic or transpersonal gratitude—"gratefulness," in Steindl-Rast's terms—one can be grateful without having *anyone* to be grateful *to*.

Roberts develops his own view first and foremost by rejecting this position: "I suspect that if one tried to do completely without personifying concepts, the description would fail plausibly to describe a kind of gratitude" (73). If there is no one to be grateful *to*, then there is no gratitude at all, and this is because the very logic of gratitude involves the following tripolar, "to-for" structure: "*A is grateful to B for C*. . . . A beneficiary construes *himself* as beholden to a *benefactor* for a *benefit*" (82). Whereas for Steindl-Rast this tripolar structure was only a feature of a *species* of gratitude (i.e., "thankfulness," as distinct from "gratefulness"), for Roberts it is an essential feature of gratitude. Thus even the admittedly more mystical and less discretely definable experience of cosmic gratitude must have a personal agent as its dative object: namely, God (or some person like God).

But why is Roberts so committed? Is this dispute simply a matter of terminology, or does his insistence upon the tripolar structure of gratitude a philosophically substantive position? As it happens, there is good reason to think that the latter is in fact the case. The core reason he offers in defense of this position concerns the abovementioned theoretical *desideratum* of distinctiveness. That is, without the tripolar structure of gratitude, there is no way to distinguish cosmic or EG from other "transcendent emotions" such as joy, relief, and wonder. "Gratitude has the to-for structure. Other emotion types in the neighborhood of gratitude do not have it, for example, . . . the simple joy at the existence of the world that [Steindl-Rast] sometimes takes to be gratitude" (76). So, while he is certainly willing to grant the empirical claim that the transcendent or cosmic emotional states that Steindl-Rast identifies (see, for example, Steindl-Rast 1984) do in fact exist, Roberts argues that we need to be able to distinguish such states from gratitude. And the distinguishing feature of gratitude he proposes is precisely this tripolar structure: benefactor, gift, and beneficiary.

Roberts's position has an interesting implication for our thesis about EG—one that he recognizes and admits: namely, that EG must be construed in theistic terms. Again, this is because EG is gratitude for life and/or existence *as such*, and the only one who could plausibly be thought to be bestow such a gift is God (or something like God).[1] Only theists can feel EG appropriately.

2.2 Lacewing

Now it is this very implication that occasions Lacewing's article, "Can Nontheists Appropriately Feel EG?" (2016)—a question he answers in the affirmative. According to Lacewing, to say that nontheists are somehow unable to experience EG without identifying a personal agent as a dative object seems to fly in the face of ordinary language and perhaps even common sense. "[S]he was grateful for a moment's quiet after looking after the kids all morning, he was thankful to find a stream on a hot day. These are constructions that do not normally raise the question of to whom one is grateful" (149). Is it really the case that such instances of gratitude are somehow *mistaken*? If they do not involve a personal dative object, Roberts must say so.[2] Yet, continues Lacewing, "this can't be a correct linguistic analysis . . . such phrases do not change their meaning depending on whether they are uttered by theists or atheists!" (149). Such a theoretical implication—namely, that such instances of gratitude are somehow "mistaken"—is a sort of *reductio* for the theory itself, and this is because such phrases gain their meaning in the first place from the ordinary experiences and language used to describe them. But if we do not need a personal dative object for gratitude generally, then, reasons Lacewing, neither do we need one for EG.

But recall that what was motivating Roberts's account in the first place was the theoretical *desideratum* of distinctiveness. That is, the reason we needed a personal dative object—and indeed the entire tripolar structure of benefactor, gift, and beneficiary—was to give EG its due as a *distinctive* transcendent emotion. EG is not quite the same as joy, relief, or wonder, after all. Therefore if Lacewing is going to deliver on his more inclusive account of EG, he is responsible for offering an alternative distinguishing feature.

And it is precisely this distinguishing feature that Lacewing offers in his emphasis on the *gratuitousness* of gratitude:

> We gain some clue to whether gratitude must always be *to* something by considering its origins and closely related words. Thus "gratitude" connects to "grateful," "gratuitous," "gratuity," "gratify," "gracious," and "grace." . . . But the root of all of them is *gratus*, which means both "pleasing" and "thankful". . . . [T]he root of "gratitude" lies in a Latin term that does not specify the response as necessarily to a giver, rather than just to an undeserved good. (148–9)

Lacewing leverages this brief etymological excursus to distinguish gratitude from other related emotions in a way that does not require a personal dative object. As the Latin root *gratus* indicates, what makes gratitude different from joy, relief, or wonder is the experience of some good *insofar as it is undeserved*: "In joy, happiness, and so on, the *goodness* of the good is salient; . . . In gratitude, it is the *undeserved* nature of the good that is particularly salient, that it originates outside oneself, not flowing from one's efforts, achievements, or value" (149). On this account, it is clear why mothers can be truly grateful for a moment's quiet, hikers for a stream on a hot day, and indeed nontheists for their life or existence:

namely, because in each case the experiencers are experiencing and recognizing undeserved goods.

Thus the terms of the dispute are set: Roberts argues that gratitude in general—and EG in particular—is essentially tripolar. Lacewing rejects this, arguing that the tripolarity is accidental, and that the undeservedness is essential.

2.3 Initial Evaluation

How ought we to adjudicate this debate? Are there clear evidentiary criteria for siding with either Roberts or Lacewing, or are we simply at the mercy of the incommensurability of their respective intuitions? As it happens, I do think that we can make intellectual progress here, and that a promising way to do so is to return again to the abovementioned theoretical *desiderata* of universality and distinctiveness. That is to say, to the extent that we can account for *both* of these theoretical *desiderata*, we will have made progress in understanding EG.

With this in mind, we can return to Roberts. As we have seen, his account performs quite well with respect to distinctiveness. The essential tripolarity of gratitude offers a clear path for distinguishing EG from other transcendent emotions such as joy and wonder. However, when it comes to universality, there are indeed some awkward implications: namely, that nontheists are simply "mistaken" when they characterize relevant experiences as instances of EG.[3] Indeed, beyond the cases mentioned by Lacewing, it is unclear how Roberts might account for recent developments in the empirical literature up to and including the so-called Existential Gratitude Scale,[4] not to mention centuries of nontheist religious and philosophical reflection on the subject (see, for example, Eckel 1985). Now of course this is nothing like a knockdown argument against Roberts's position, but if there were an account of EG that could handle such universality, such an account would be preferable. Overall, it seems that Roberts's account of EG performs admirably in terms of distinctiveness but not in terms of universality.

By contrast, Lacewing's account provides a neat and tidy explanation for the universal scope of EG. Because EG is essentially a matter of recognizing and responding to the gift that is one's life or existence insofar as it is gratuitous or undeserved, it is no surprise that even nontheists should document their own experiences accordingly.

But how does Lacewing's account perform in terms of distinctiveness? On the one hand, we do have a more or less clear way to distinguish EG from joy or wonder in the aspect of underservedness. And perhaps this is enough to mark out a unique extension for the concept. Yet extensional adequacy is only one part of crafting a good definition.[5] There are also intensional considerations. If a definition is extensionally adequate only at the cost of omitting essential features of the phenomenon identified, then we have reason to doubt that definition. As it happens, Lacewing's account of EG seems to suffer from precisely this malady.

Recall that a key component of Lacewing's justification for his account was his brief etymology of gratitude, the centerpiece of which is the Latin term *gratus*. Because *gratus* in itself implies nothing about givers of gifts, so the argument goes, neither do we need to assume as much when it comes to gratitude.[6] But the brevity of this particular etymological observation conceals problems that become clear when more context is given.

While it is obviously true enough to say that *gratus* is an etymological root for the English term "gratitude," it is misleading to reference the adjectival Latin term without the context of its nounal correlate, *gratia*. Indeed, once we do, it becomes impossible to avoid the context of reciprocal gift-giving and receiving. As Leithart (2014: 20) puts the matter in a helpful summary of the Roman notion of *gratia* (and its Greek predecessor, χάρις),

> [F]rom Homer to Seneca . . . gratitude was understood as the closing curve of a circle that began with a gracious gift, and it was common sense that the circle would be closed by an in-kind gift in response to a favor or a gift. Ancient society was constituted by multiple circles of reciprocity, the first of which is the circle formed by gifts and gratitude between gods and human beings.

Ancient texts overwhelmingly point to the circular reciprocity of gift and gratitude as an essential feature of *gratia*.[7] Indeed, as a remarkable testament to the intimate links between gratitude and gift-giving, in the ancient world both the act of giving and the response of thanks were considered forms of *gratia*—no special terms were assigned to distinguish the "sides" of the exchange.[8] In short, it is this unique mode of circular reciprocity that is the focal point of *gratia*— not the individual psychology of one who happens to be enjoying undeserved goods.[9] Any etymology of gratitude—or of the Latin *gratus*, for that matter— misses what is fundamental to the extent that it fails to integrate such context. Therefore, to the extent that Lacewing's justification fails to do so, there is reason to think that his account of EG is missing something essential.

Again, what is needed is an account of EG that performs well in terms of both universality and distinctiveness, not just extensionally but intensionally as well. In the following sections, I will set out to do just that.

3 The Social-structural Dimensions of Gratitude

We have already mentioned that the ancient term *gratia*/χάρις is unintelligible without social practices of gift exchange, and that any account of gratitude that takes its etymology seriously would have to integrate this fact somehow. In the earlier sketch of the Roberts-Lacewing dispute, we saw that Lacewing's account of gratitude as appreciation for undeserved goods seems to come up short here. Roberts's account of gratitude as essentially tripolar (involving benefactor, gift, and beneficiary) seems to do better on this front. However, notably for what follows, it is important to see that *both* Roberts and Lacewing fundamentally agree on the "proximate genus" of gratitude as a transcendent *emotion*, that is, a psychological state or disposition of individuals.[10] That is, while they disagree on the *content* and perhaps also the *syntactical structure* of gratitude, the two philosophers are agreed when it comes to identifying *what sort of thing* gratitude is in the first place: namely, a psychological state enjoyed by individuals.

I think we should reevaluate this overly psychologistic conception of gratitude in general, and EG in particular, by integrating its proper social dimension. That is to say, a better performing theoretical account of gratitude (and EG) may be available on the condition that we recognize it as a *positioned* phenomenon, and thus a *part* of a properly social form of reciprocity. It is this insight—that gratitude is a part of a social form of reciprocity considered as an object in its own right—that will allow us to make progress in terms of our theoretical *desiderata*. Therefore it is to this end that I will borrow from Sally Haslanger's notion of social-structural explanation.

4 Social-structural Explanation in General

Haslanger (2016: 114) observes that "sometimes it is good and useful to explain the behavior of a thing by explaining the behavior of something of which it is a part, if it is a part whose behavior is constrained by other parts of the whole." This is true of physical and biological systems generally, but it is the particular phenomenon of individual persons intending and acting within *social*-structural wholes that interests Haslanger most immediately. Referencing an example drawn from the work of Garfinkel (1981), she considers different possible responses to the following question: namely, "Why did Mary get an A [on her final exam]?" Absent the context of the social structure in which Mary's exam is a part, it might make sense to answer by referencing qualities of Mary, that is, her diligence, thoughtfulness, or originality.

But consider the difference that is made when we *do* learn something about the abovementioned social structure:

> Suppose that, in a class I am teaching, I announce that the course will be "graded on a curve," that is, that I have decided beforehand what the overall distribution of grades is going to be. Let us say . . . that I decide that there will be one A, 24 Bs, and 25 Cs. The finals come in, and let us say Mary gets the A. (Garfinkel 1981: 41)

It should be obvious that, given this information about the social structure in which Mary's exam is a part, explanations that merely reference Mary's diligence, thoughtfulness, or originality can no longer be adequate. While it might be true that Mary's exam is evidence of all of those things inasmuch as she is an individual student in a general sense, any good explanation of her getting an A must reference the fact that she is getting *the* A; that is, there must be a reference to the grading curve structure of which the exam is a part. Without referencing this social-structural whole, there is no adequate explanation of the phenomenon. Mary got the A not merely—and maybe not even primarily—because of her diligence, thoughtfulness, or originality; rather, Mary got the A because she outperformed all forty-nine of her peers on the curved final.

Haslanger goes on to buttress her account of social-structural explanation by distinguishing "triggering" from "structuring" causes. It is impossible, of course, to account for Mary's A without referencing Mary's act of writing the exam (along with its attendant qualities). Following Dretske (1988), Haslanger labels this a *triggering* cause of the phenomenon, since it is Mary's concrete, individual act of writing the final (and its qualities) that triggers the chain of events that leads to her getting the A. Yet, as we have seen, there is a second type of cause that is responsible for the outcome: namely, the *structuring* cause that is the curved grading structure in which Mary's exam is a part. While of course the curved grading structure does not write the exam for Mary, it nevertheless plays a critical role in the explanation insofar as it "constrains" or "canalizes" (Haslanger 2016: 129) the activity of the individuals involved. Without this structuring cause, Mary's A does not exist.

Haslanger goes on to develop a fuller account of social structure, but for our purposes the point has been made: namely, at least some phenomena are best explained by referencing social-structural wholes in which the phenomena themselves are parts. In short, there are structuring and triggering causes. As we turn back to our phenomenon of interest, EG, I think there is good reason to think that something similar is going on. That is to say, while it is good and useful to speculate about the qualities of EG as a psychological state of individuals, we are missing something crucial if we fail to identify the social-structural whole in which it is a part. In other words, just as it was inadequate to reference Mary's diligence, etc., on its own, it may also be inadequate to limit our account of EG to qualities of individual psychological states.

5 A Social-structural Account of Gratitude Defended

The account of EG I want to defend here is of course rooted in prior considerations of gratitude generally. And what I want to suggest is that gratitude generally is a positioned response to the form of social reciprocity that we might loosely call gift exchange. That is, while it is correct to identify gratitude as a psychological state of individuals with attendant qualities, it is important also to identify those qualities as "constrained" or "canalized" by the social structure of gift exchange. Once we do so, in fact, I argue that the resulting account of EG will be more resilient in the face of theoretical challenges affecting Roberts and Lacewing.

Specifically, there are three essential theses concerning gift exchange I want to identify to help motivate the account: (1) gift exchange is a structuring cause of gratitude; (2) gift exchange is distinct from other social forms of reciprocity; and finally (3) that gift exchange is "total" rather than partial phenomenon. These three theses are drawn respectively from three of the most influential theorists of gratitude in Western philosophy: Seneca, Thomas Aquinas, and Marcel Mauss.

5.1 Seneca: Gift Exchange as a Structuring Cause

In Book II of his magisterial *De Beneficiis*, undoubtedly the most important ancient text on the subject of gratitude, Seneca borrows a suggestive analogy for the process of gift exchange:

> I wish to use Chrysippus's simile of the game of ball, in which the ball must certainly fall by the fault either of the thrower or of the catcher; it only holds its course when it passes between the hands of two persons who each throw it and catch it suitably. . . . This is just what we ought to do in conferring benefits. . . .

> [J]ust as some spiteful ball-players purposely put out their companion, of course to the ruin of the game, which cannot be carried on without entire agreement, many men are of so depraved a nature that they had rather lose the presents which they make than be thought to have received a return for them.... [Y]et how much better and more kindly would it be if they tried to enable the others also to perform their parts. (Seneca 1935, II.17.3)

In this passage Seneca's immediate concern is the suitability of gift-giving—specifically with respect to how much or how little one ought to give. But for my purposes what is interesting here is the analogy of the ball game, which, as Griffin (2013: 44) observes, portrays gift exchange as an emergent process that requires givers and receivers (or throwers and catchers) to respond organically to one another so as to "fulfill its function of social cohesion."[11] That is, for Seneca, what is important in gift exchange is not the individual qualities of the giver, gift, or receiver. Indeed, he explicitly rejects that gifts must or even should be impressive or that receivers must have ample means to return in kind. Instead, what is important is the active maintenance of the "game," that is, the emergent process of social reciprocity, in which the "players" *perform their parts*. This is why it is so disastrous for givers or receivers to be overly concerned with their individual honor or status, according to Seneca: namely, such that inward focus threatens the "ruin of the game." There is an emergent process of social cohesion at work here—one that cannot happen without "having extended consent" (*qui non potest, nisi consentitur, extendi*).

We should note how seamlessly this Senecean insight fits with our discussion of Haslanger's concept of social-structural explanation. While it might be true at an individual level that a beneficiary's feeling of (for example) undeserved appreciation may *trigger* his grateful response of thanks, his return gift, etc., the *structuring* cause of the relevant intentions and actions is the specific form of reciprocity that is the process of gift exchange. The "whole" (process of gift exchange) gives shape to the "parts" (benefactors, gifts, and beneficiaries), and in doing so the former plays a key role in the explanation of the latter. Therefore, on this Senecean model, absent the structuring cause, the purportedly essential properties of gratitude would be arbitrary.

Again, this is not to say that the process of gift exchange is a *triggering* cause of gratitude any more than a ball game is the triggering cause of a ball's motion when thrown. However, if Seneca is right, then this process does play an essential role in the explanation of gratitude in the mode of a structuring cause. In Haslanger's terms, the social process of gift exchange "constrains" or "canalizes" the psychological phenomenon that is gratitude. Therefore, to understand the emergent features of gift exchange as a (social-structural) object of analysis in its own right is to better understand gratitude. In Aquinas, I suggest, we have precisely such an analysis of these emergent features.

5.2 Aquinas: Gratitude as a Social Form

Aside from Seneca's treatment in *De Beneficiis* there is probably no more influential treatment of gratitude in Western philosophy than in Question 106 of the *Secunda Secundae Pars* of Aquinas' *Summa theologiae*. For our purposes, it is a fascinating sequence of objection and reply that is most important. Whereas Aquinas takes the affirmative position that gratitude (*gratia*, notably) is indeed a "special" virtue that is distinct from others such as justice and charity, he does consider an objection to his position:

> [P]roportionate repayment belongs to commutative justice. . . . But graces are returned as repayment. Therefore the return of graces, which belongs to gratitude, is an act of justice. Therefore gratitude is not a special virtue, distinct from other virtues. (Aquinas 1906, IIa-IIae, Q. 106, A. 1, *Obj.*)

According to this objector, gratitude is not really distinct from commutative justice, the virtue by which fellow members of a community render what is due to one another. (*S.th.* IIa-IIae, Q. 61, A. 1). In both cases, the important thing is that graces or benefits are *returned*, and thus there is no reason to assign a special status to gratitude as something distinct in kind from commutative justice.

Aquinas' response is telling, especially for our guiding question concerning the distinctive features of gift exchange as a structuring cause of gratitude:

> Proportionate repayment belongs to commutative justice when it answers to the legal debt; for instance when it is contracted that so much be paid for so much. But the repayment that belongs to the virtue of grace or gratitude answers to the moral debt, and is made spontaneously. Hence gratitude is less graceful when coerced.

What is notable about this response for our purposes is the way in which gratitude is distinctive: namely, as a mode of "repayment" (*retributio*). Whereas commutative justice is "equalized" according to some mediating objective element (e.g., in terms of an amount of money paid for a good or service), gratitude is "made spontaneously" (*sponte facit*)—which is to say, without the obligation to equalize a return gift objectively. If anything, in fact, as he goes on to say in a later article, ideally a grateful response is supposed to offer "more" than one was given initially (IIa-IIae, Q. 106, A. 6). The difference here concerns the nature of the "debt" in each case: whereas justice concerns "legal" debt, gratitude concerns "moral" debt—that is, the mode of reciprocity that is proper to gift exchange.[12]

The upshot of this analysis for our purposes is the *structuring* cause of gift exchange as a mode of social reciprocity. Like Seneca, Aquinas understands gratitude first and foremost as *part* of the structural whole that is gift exchange, that is, a mode of social reciprocity that proceeds according to moral rather than legal debt. This is why he is concerned first and foremost to distinguish gratitude from justice rather than, for example, joy or appreciation. If someone is grateful, it is first and foremost because he is *positioned* as a beneficiary in a unique mode of reciprocity. What makes it different from justice primarily is not just one quality or another of the beneficiary's individual psychological state; rather, it is the structuring cause of the "game" being played: namely, the process of gift exchange.

5.3 Mauss: The Totality of Gift Exchange

But there is one final feature of gift exchange that is relevant for our social-structural account of gratitude: the notion of a "total social fact," drawn from Marcel Mauss's classic treatment of gift exchange (2006: 100). This concept arises out of Mauss's influential study of the nature and role of gift exchange in Melanesian, Polynesian, and North American Indigenous tribal cultures. It is relevant for our purposes because it helps to illuminate the all-encompassing nature of gift and gratitude in human social life, thereby providing a context of application for a similarly foundational notion of EG.

According to Mauss, gift exchange is an example of a total social fact because it is "at the same time juridical, economic, religious, and even aesthetic and morphological" (2006: 101). That is to say, in the abovementioned cultures, the act of giving and receiving gifts extended far beyond familiar relations between friends and family and into the foundations of civic and religious life. To receive a gift was to initiate a relation of reciprocity that imposed obligations of honor and esteem on beneficiaries—regardless of whether or not those beneficiaries welcomed their "gifts" in the first place.[13] This fundamentally asymmetrical relation of benefactor with respect to beneficiary comes to characterize the common mode of reciprocity between leaders and subjects (95), wives and husbands (39), and gods and human beings (20).

Further, and importantly for our thesis, Mauss identifies ways in which the dynamics of gift exchange so identified still permeate the social life of developed Western orders: "A considerable part of our morality and our lives themselves are still permeated with this same atmosphere of the gift, where obligation and liberty intermingle.... Things sold still have a soul. They are still followed around by their former owner, and they follow him also" (83–4). This is true at least to the extent that there is a sense of moral exhortation attached to benefits received spontaneously—regardless of whether there is a known and/or identifiable benefactor or not.[14]

This is what Mauss's study of gift exchange as a total social fact adds to the picture: namely, the widespread human tendency to understand themselves as *positioned* as beneficiaries across various domains of social life. Therefore, without diminishing the importance of gratitude's emotional dimension, once again gift exchange as its structuring cause cannot be ignored. To be grateful is (at least) to respond *as a beneficiary*, and as Mauss observes, human beings are prone to do so in many social modalities.

5.4 Conclusions: Summarizing the Account

I have argued that gratitude is, among other things, a positioned response in a form of reciprocity we call gift exchange. Therefore, to better understand the emergent features of gift exchange is to better understand gratitude. In particular, three features of gift exchange are especially salient:

1. Gift exchange serves as a "structuring cause" of gratitude in that the requisite psychological qualities of a grateful person arise in a role-structured way, that is, as a beneficiary.
2. Gift exchange as a form of social reciprocity operates according to the "rule" of *moral* rather than *legal* debt. Whereas legal debt concerns the equalization of an objectively measured benefit, gratitude involves no such equalization.
3. Finally, gift exchange is a "total social fact," which is to say that this particular form of reciprocity is recognizable in many, if not all domains of social life.

With these features of gift exchange in mind, we can better appreciate the social-structural dimension of gratitude in general. And it is against this background that we turn again to EG.

6 EG Reconsidered

If it is true that gratitude in general is a positioned response within a social form of reciprocity, then so also is EG. That is to say, EG is the principle of a positioned response to the gift that is one's existence or life as a whole. So, while this account can happily accommodate the usual (individual) psychological dimensions of gratitude, the proposed innovation is the social-structural dimension of gift exchange. In short, I am suggesting that one is existentially grateful to the extent that one "plays the part" of beneficiary with respect to the gift that is one's existence or life as a whole.

Such an account of EG offers some important explanatory benefits that are visible when considered in light of the Roberts-Lacewing debate.

6.1 Benefits of the Account

6.1.1 *Universality*

As we have seen, the theoretical deficiency of Roberts's account of EG was its inability to account for its apparently universal scope. Because the "tripolar" grammar of gratitude demands a personal dative object—and because the only plausible candidate for such a personal dative object in EG is God—EG can only be appropriate on theism. However, given how many nontheists claim to experience EG, Roberts is left with the awkward conclusion that they are all somehow "mistaken" about their own experiences.

An account of EG that is attentive to its social-structural dimension is not so committed. On the contrary, on the proposed account, what matters is not whether the principle benefactor is a person or not; instead, what matters is whether the existentially grateful person is structurally positioned as a beneficiary in a form of reciprocity that does not demand equal repayment. While such an account can surely countenance gift exchanges involving a personal benefactor—perhaps even paradigmatically—it need not exclude those that do not. A social-structural account of EG can include someone like the Stoic Seneca, who, notably, uses the terms "God," "the gods," and "Nature" more or less interchangeably (Burton 1906). It can even include outright atheists such as Friedrich Nietzsche, who advocate gratitude *for* one's life and *to* the (a personal) principle of Life (*Leben*) as the centerpiece of his aesthetic philosophy (Fox 2020). Again, this is because what matters on the proposed account is whether one recognizes one's life as a gift incurring a "moral" rather than a "legal" debt. In short, it is to "play the game" (to use the Senecean metaphor) of gift exchange with respect to one's life. Given gratitude's status as a "total social fact," then, it is no surprise on this account that human beings understand themselves to have experienced EG so universally, theist or not.

6.1.2 Distinctiveness

We have also seen that, while Lacewing's account of gratitude as mere appreciation for undeserved goods can account for the apparently universal scope of EG, it is less impressive when it comes to distinctiveness. There needs to be some accounting for the deep and intimate connections between gratitude and χάρις/*gratia*, that is, that "circular reciprocity" of gift exchange that marks out gratitude's origins in Western culture. A mere appreciation for undeserved goods in general is too thin to capture this essential dimension of gratitude.

In fact, it is this incorporation of reciprocity that is perhaps the most obvious benefit of my proposed social-structural account of gratitude. Because gift exchange is foregrounded as a structuring cause of the emotional, intellectual, and moral dimensions of gratitude, the ancient origins of gratitude are better preserved, and gratitude retains its distinctiveness not just extensionally but also intensionally, that is, with its essential features included. Such an account is simply much more faithful to the intellectual and material history of gratitude as a human phenomenon.

6.2 Unifying

Beyond these two *desiderata* of universality and distinctiveness, there is another reason to prefer my social-structural account of gratitude to the respective accounts of Roberts and Lacewing: namely, its ability to *unify* the respective intuitions of the two rival theories. That is to say, when we appreciate the role of gift exchange as a structuring cause of the individual psychology of gratitude, we can *explain* the intuitions behind Roberts's notion of tripolarity and Lacewing's notion of appreciation of undeserved goods.

With respect to tripolarity, the point is clear enough. There is indeed a benefactor-gift-beneficiary relation syntax implied in grateful intentions, just as Roberts suggests. What the notion of a structuring cause of reciprocity offers in addition, however, is the historically grounded reason for this tripolarity. Gratitude simply does not make sense without reciprocity, and so it is necessary to be attentive to the specific kind of reciprocity that is at work in the phenomenon. Without this structural dimension of gratitude, Roberts's notion of tripolarity runs the risk of being an arbitrary condition for "real" gratitude.

Further, with respect to appreciation of undeserved goods, once again the nature of the reciprocity of which gratitude is a response does an admirable job explaining why this would indeed be important for the grateful individual. After all, the specific kind of reciprocity that structures the intensions of grateful people is not mediated by the equalization of benefits. The logic of gift reciprocity is that of moral rather than legal debt, and thus both gift and gratitude are *gratis*—that is, without the compulsion of an objectively measurable return gift. Once again, the idea here is that gift exchange as a structuring cause of gratitude explains the intuition: gratitude does involve the appreciation of undeserved goods, since that is part of the nature of a gift in the first place.

7 Conclusion

For these reasons I have argued that my proposed social-structural account of gratitude is theoretically preferable to the comparatively individualistic accounts of Roberts and Lacewing. Gratitude is rooted in *gratia*, that form of benevolent reciprocity that is free of measured equalization. When we recognize this reciprocity as a structuring cause of gratitude, we can better appreciate and account for the universality and distinctiveness of EG. As Seneca would have it, we are existentially grateful when we are *enabled to play our part* in returning the gift that is our existence or life as a whole.

Notes

1. One may of course object to this and reference instead one's parents as the proper dative objects of one's life. While this is of course true in a proximate sense, existential gratitude is concerned with the ultimate benefactor of life, that is, someone responsible for *all* conditions of one's existence.
2. Or, rather, Roberts (2014: 76) must say that there is a sort of implied dative object from which the locution is derived.
3. As Roberts says (2014: 82), "in casual discourse people sometimes say they are grateful when they are only glad, that is, when no benefactor is plausibly denoted."
4. The Existential Gratitude Scale or EGS (Jans-Beken and Wong 2019) is designed to measure the tendency to give thanks for all things, including especially tough times in one's life. Importantly, the EGS considers "a nonreligious/secular meaning to spirituality. Spirituality overlaps with religiousness with respect to belief in the mystical, transcendental reality, and affirmation of meaning and purpose amid suffering and death. However, spirituality does not require religiousness" (3).

5   For a discussion of the role of intension and extension in definitions, see Gupta (2021).
6   Lacewing cites Bertocci and Millard (1963) as fellow travelers when it comes to emphasizing the gratuitous dimension of gratitude as its essential feature.
7   For an extended discussion of the reciprocity implied in χάρις/*gratia* in ancient literature, see Vidal (2014).
8   As Leithart notes (2014: 90), the Latin term *gratitudo* does not emerge regularly in Latin texts until the age of medieval Scholasticism.
9   This is not to say of course that matters of individual psychology are wholly unrelated to ancient notions of χάρις/*gratia*. In fact, as we will see later, on the contrary, *gratia* was also a matter of moral and even aesthetic psychology. But the point is that the aforementioned circular reciprocity provides the essential context for all of these "downstream" effects on individuals.
10 Defining emotions in general is matter of considerable contemporary philosophical dispute (Scarantino 2018), but for my purposes what is important about emotions is that they are had by individual subjects.
11 For Seneca (*De Beneficiis*, IV.18.2-4), it is precisely this "fellowship [*societas*] "that has given to [humankind] dominion over all creatures. . . . Take away this fellowship, and you will sever the unity of the human race [*unitatem generis humani . . . scindes*] on which its very existence depends."
12 As he remarks in a later article (IIa-IIae, Q. 106, A. 5), "since gratitude regards the favor inasmuch as it is bestowed gratis, and this regards the disposition of the giver, it follows again that repayment of a favor depends more on the disposition of the giver than on the effect."
13 Obviously this comes with serious dangers, as Mauss observes (2006: 76) in a memorable aphorism: "The gift is therefore at one and the same time what should be done, what should be received, and yet what is dangerous to take."
14 Mauss identifies (2006: 15) the moral and spiritual presence of the benefactor in the gift given as *hau* in Maori law: "Even when it has been abandoned by the giver, it still possesses something of him. Through it the giver has a hold over the beneficiary just as, being its owner, through it he has a hold over the thief."

References

Aquinas, T. (1906). *Opera omnia iussu impensaque Leonis XIII P. M. edita, Summae theologiae*. Rome: Leonine Commission.

Bertocci, P. and R. Millard (1963). *Personality and the Good*. New York: David McKay Company.

Burton, H. (1906). "Seneca's Idea of God." *The American Journal of Theology*, 13 (3): 350–69.

Dretske, F. (1988). *Explaining Behavior: Reasons in a World of Causes*. Cambridge, MA: MIT Press.

Eckel, M. (1985). "Gratitude to an Empty Savior: A Study of the Concept of Gratitude in Mahāyāna Buddhist Philosophy." *History of Religions*, 25 (1): 57–75.

Fox, J. (2020). "Gratitude to Beautiful Objects: On Nietzsche's Claim That the Beautiful 'Promises Happiness.'" *Journal of Nietzsche Studies*, 51 (2): 169–87.

Garfinkel, A. (1981). *Forms of Explanation: Rethinking the Questions in Social Theory*. New Haven, CT: Yale University Press.

Griffin, M. (2013). *Seneca on Society: A Guide to De Beneficiis*. Oxford: Oxford University Press.

Gupta, A. (2021). "Definitions." In Edward N. Zalta (ed.), *The Stanford Encyclopedia of Philosophy*. https://plato.stanford.edu/archives/win2021/entries/definitions/.

Haslanger, S. (2016). "What is a (Social) Structural Explanation?" *Philosophical Studies*, 173 (1): 113–30.

Jans-Beken, L. and P. Wong (2019). "Development and Preliminary Validation of the Existential Gratitude Scale (EGS)." *Counseling Psychology Quarterly*, 34 (1): 1–15.

Lacewing, M. (2016). "Can Non-Theists Appropriately Feel Existential Gratitude?" *Religious Studies*, 52: 145–65.

Leithart, P. (2014). *Gratitude: An Intellectual History*. Waco, TX: Baylor University Press.

Mauss, M. (2006). *The Gift*, trans. W. Halls. London and New York: Routledge.

Roberts, R. (2014). "Cosmic Gratitude." *European Journal for Philosophy of Religion*, 6 (3): 65–83.

Seneca (1935). *Moral Essays Volume III: De Beneficiis*, trans. J. Basore. Cambridge, MA: Harvard University Press.

Scarantino A. and R. de Sousa (2018). "Emotion." In Edward N. Zalta (ed.), *The Stanford Encyclopedia of Philosophy*. https://plato.stanford.edu/archives/sum2021/entries/emotion/.

Steindl-Rast, D. (1984). *Gratefulness, the heart of Prayer: An Approach to Life in Fullness.* Mahwah, NJ: Paulist Press.

Steindl-Rast, D. (2004). "Gratitude as Thankfulness and as Gratefulness." In R. Emmons and M. McCullough (eds.), *The Psychology of Gratitude*, 282–90, Oxford: Oxford University Press.

Vidal, D. (2014). "The Three Graces, or The Allegory of the Gift A Contribution to the History of an Idea in Anthropology." *Hau: Journal of Ethnographic Theory*, 4 (2): 339–68.

2

Gratitude and Resentment

A Tale of Two Weddings

Graham Oppy

1

I am pleased that the sun shone on my wedding day. Given that it was midwinter in Melbourne, it would not have been surprising if it had rained all day. Indeed, most of the week either side of my wedding day was dismal.

It is not just that I was pleased that the sun shone on my wedding day. Many other people—friends and relations—were pleased for me that the sun shone on my wedding day. I was—and they were—happy that the sun shone on my wedding day. I was—and they were—grateful that the sun shone on my wedding day.

Many of my friends and relatives are religious. No doubt, if asked, some of them would have claimed to be grateful to God for making the sun shine on my wedding day. Further, if asked, some may well have said that, in order to make sense of others' being grateful that the sun shone on my wedding day, it had to be that those others were grateful to God for making the sun shine on my wedding day. After all, to whom else would it even make sense to be grateful for making the sun shine on my wedding day?

I think that it is a mistake to run together being grateful that the sun shone on my wedding day and being grateful to God for making the sun shine on my wedding day. The *propositional* expression of gratitude—"being grateful that p"—is one member of a family of propositional expressions—"being happy that p," "being pleased that p," "being glad that p," "being relieved that p," etc.—whose truth need not depend upon the truth of an appropriately related *prepositional* expression of gratitude—"being grateful to S for Φ-ing."

Certainly, in my own case, given my naturalistic proclivities, I have no inclination to link my claim about what pleases me, or makes me happy, or makes me glad, to any claim about gratitude to God for performing particular actions. But, further, I suspect that many monotheistic religious believers will make a similar assessment: in a range of cases like the case that I have been considering, they, too, will have no inclination to like their claims about what pleases them, or makes them happy, or makes them glad, to claims about gratitude to God for performing actions directed toward *their* particular pleasure, or happiness, or gladness.

There have been recent attacks, on the idea that there is propositional gratitude, in the works of Roberts,[1] Manela,[2] and others. Indeed, Manela[3] goes so far as to say that there is an emerging consensus that analyses of the concept of gratitude should be concerned only with prepositional gratitude. However, it seems to me that Rush[4] provides a satisfying response to these critics and, in particular, to their claim that propositional gratitude cannot be properly distinguished from propositional happiness, propositional pleasure, propositional gladness, propositional relief, and the like. For the purpose of this chapter, I am happy to invite those who do not share my enthusiasm for propositional gratitude to take me to be arguing for claims conditioned on the assumption that the notion of propositional gratitude is in good order.

2

A year after my own wedding, one of my cousins was married in Melbourne in midwinter. This time, it was a very wet day. Two sets of wedding guests did not make it to the wedding because they were involved in traffic accidents caused by the treacherous condition of the wet roads. The traffic accidents were minor: there was damage to the cars, but no injuries to anyone traveling in the cars. Nonetheless, the accidents, and the absence of the wedding guests involved, were not things that pleased or gladdened those involved in the wedding. On the contrary, many of the guests were displeased that rain poured down on my cousin's wedding and prevented some other invited guests from attending. Many of the guests were unhappy that rain poured down on my cousin's wedding and prevented some other invited guests from attending. Many of the guests were resentful that rain poured down on my cousin's wedding and prevented some other invited guests from attending.

Unsurprisingly, as with my wedding, many of the guests at my cousin's wedding are religious. But, if we had asked them, would they have claimed to resent God for making the rain fall heavily on my cousin's wedding day? It seems no stretch of ordinary language to suppose that they were resentful that rain poured down on my cousin's wedding. It was hardly fair that, while the sun shone on my wedding day, my cousin's wedding day was one on which it poured with rain. However, if you suppose that, in order to make sense of guests' being resentful that it poured with rain on my cousin's wedding day, it had to be that they resented someone who made the rain fall heavily on my cousin's wedding day, then what option would there be other than to suppose that they resented God for making the rain fall heavily on my cousin's wedding day? (Perhaps some might think to excuse God by insisting that it was the Devil who made the rain fall heavily on my cousin's wedding day. However, it seems to me that those among the guests who take this proposal seriously would equally have resented God's allowing the Devil to make it rain heavily on my cousin's wedding day.)

I want to say the same thing about resentment that I said previously about gratitude. The *propositional* expression of resentment—"being resentful that p"—is one member of a family of propositional expressions—"being unhappy that p," "being displeased that p," "being sad that p," "being upset that p," etc.—that need have nothing to do with the *prepositional* expression of resentment—"being resentful to S for Φ-ing." In my own case, given my naturalistic proclivities, I have no inclination to link my claim about what displeases me, or makes me unhappy, or makes me sad, to any claim about resenting God for performing particular actions. But, in this case, it seems to me that monotheistic religious believers are almost uniformly going to agree: they, too, have no inclination to like their claims about what displeases them, or makes them unhappy, or makes them sad, to claims about resentment to God for performing actions directed toward *their* particular displeasure, or unhappiness, or sadness.

3

Some may be inclined to deny that there are propositional expressions of resentment while nonetheless accepting that there are propositional expressions of gratitude. However, it seems to me that there are many considerations that speak against this view. I shall discuss only some of them here.

First, it should be noted that there is no evident difference in the relevant linguistic data. It is not in doubt that people do say things of the form "I am grateful that p" and "I am resentful that p." Whatever initial inclination we have to take what people say at face value, we have the same initial inclination in both cases. Moreover, there is no evident difference in the frequency of the usage of expressions of these forms that might point to a reason for taking only one of these kinds of expressions at face value. In particular, there is no evident difference in the frequency of the use of expressions of these forms that indicates greater comfort with expressions of the form "I am grateful that p" than with expressions of the form "I am resentful that p" that is not simply a reflection of greater comfort with expressions of the form "I am pleased that p," "I am happy that p," and "I am glad that p" than with expressions of the form "I am displeased that p," "I am unhappy that p," and "I am sad that p."

Second, it should be noted that there are many kinds of cases of resentment that are recognized across the disciplines—in, for example, literature, philosophy, and psychology—that it is hard to construe as anything other than examples of propositional resentment. In some of these cases, perhaps, we might suppose that the resentment is directed toward a specific, nonindividual actor: a group, a corporation, an institution, a community, a nation, and the like. But, often enough, in these kinds of cases, the most that we could suppose is that the resentment is directed toward "them" or "the man." And in some of these cases, even that kind of identification of a focus for the resentment seems to be lacking. As MacLachlan notes,[5] among the things that a person might resent, there are all of the following: being trapped or locked into a difficult and unrewarding job; needing and receiving care, and being vulnerable in ways that come with that territory; witnessing long-term change in your neighborhood or to other locations that you treasure for their beauty or history; observing general decline in manners, reciprocal social connection, personal grooming, and fashion; noting the increasing prevalence of people whose dress codes are utterly impenetrable to you; and so forth. Resentments of some of these kinds might be based in group identification, or long-term historical claims, or observations of receipt of benefits based in historical injustice, or ill-directed resentment, or incomprehension of your prior resentment on the part of those to whom it is properly directed, and so on.

Third, it should be noted that there is nothing in credible evolutionary accounts of the origins of our reactive attitudes that would plausibly indicate the postulated asymmetry between propositional gratitude and propositional resentment. Prepositional gratitude and prepositional resentment have obviously useful roles in coordinating the behavior of members of small groups whose members are responsive to prepositional gratitude and prepositional resentment. A general tendency, within a group, for more or less shared responses of gratitude when one member does something to benefit one or more of the other members in the group, and for more or less shared responses of resentment when one member does something to injure one or more other members in the group, given what it feels like to be the object of such gratitude and such resentment, encourages intragroup beneficence and discourages intragroup infliction of injury. The step from prepositional gratitude and prepositional resentment to propositional gratitude and propositional resentment is plausibly a much later development, perhaps while humans are still living in relatively small groups, or perhaps only when humans are living in much larger groups. Either way, it is hard to see any reason to suppose that the step is any harder, or any less plausible, in one case than it is in the other.

Fourth, if it were to turn out that there are asymmetries in the use of expressions of propositional gratitude and propositional resentment, but only on the part of active participants in monotheistic religions, then that would tell us something interesting about participants in monotheistic religions, but it would not tell us anything of further significance about expressions of propositional gratitude and propositional resentment. While an asymmetry in the use of these expressions on the part of active participants in monotheistic religions might skew overall figures, the ready explanation in terms of pollution by prior theory would undermine the need for any further explanation.

While there is doubtless more to be said on this topic, I think that it is fairly safe to conclude that there is no deep, neutral, independent asymmetry in the use of expressions of propositional gratitude and expressions of propositional resentment that might lead us to take only the former at face value. The reasons that we have for thinking that there really are expressions of propositional gratitude carry over to reasons for thinking that there really are expressions of propositional resentment.

4

Even if it is accepted that there are expressions of propositional gratitude, some might think to claim that, while propositional expressions of gratitude are tied to prepositional expressions of gratitude, propositional expressions of resentment are not similarly tied to prepositional expressions of resentment. I think that there is something uncomfortable in this position. That is, I think that there is something uncomfortable in a position that (a) holds that propositional expressions of gratitude are tied to prepositional expressions of gratitude, but (b) denies that propositional expressions of resentment are tied to prepositional expressions of resentment.

In the previous sections, I listed a bunch of cases in which it seems plausible to say that, while someone is resentful that p, there is no S for which it is true that that one resents S for relevantly Φ–ing (e.g., bringing it about that p). But there are corresponding cases in which it seems no less plausible to say that, while someone is grateful that p, there is no S for which it is true that that one is grateful to S for relevantly Φ–ing (e.g., bringing it about that p).

A person might be grateful that they are not trapped or locked into a difficult and demanding job; that they do not need and receive care and so are not vulnerable in ways that come with that territory; that they are not witnessing long-term change in their neighborhood or in other locations that they treasure for their beauty and history; that they are not observing general decline in manners, reciprocal social connection, personal grooming and fashion; that they are not noting the increasing prevalence of people whose dress codes are utterly impenetrable to them; and so forth. Lest it be worried that those examples were all negative, we can also note that a person might be grateful that they are living in more enlightened times; that, at least so far, their children are making a decent fist of finding their way in the world; that, where they live, there is a centuries-old tradition of protecting the speech of those who dissent from the dominant religion of the community/city/province/nation in which they live; and so on.

Apart from the weight of cases, one might also think to add that it is very hard to see why it would have come about that, while propositional expressions of gratitude are tied to prepositional expressions of gratitude, propositional expressions of resentment are not tied to prepositional expressions of resentment. In particular, we might look at other expressions of our reactive attitudes, both negative—disapprobation, indignation, guilt, shame, pride—and positive—approval, delight, (some species of) love, esteem, honor, pride. In my estimation, there is no other pair of expressions of reactive attitudes in which we find the asymmetry that is being mooted in the case of gratitude and resentment.

5

Even if it is accepted that there are expressions of propositional resentment, and that it is generally true that expressions of propositional resentment are tied to expressions of prepositional resentment, some may be inclined to suppose that it is not true that propositional expressions of resentment are tied to prepositional expressions of resentment to God, while nonetheless supposing that propositional expressions of gratitude are tied to prepositional expressions of gratitude to God.

I think that, quite apart from the difficulties discussed in the preceding two sections, there is something uncomfortable in a position that (a) holds that propositional expressions of gratitude are tied to prepositional expressions of gratitude to God, but (b) denies that propositional expressions of resentment are tied to prepositional expressions of resentment to God.

Return to the case of my wedding. Even though it was midwinter, there were dozens of weddings that took place in Melbourne on that day. In order for me to be grateful to God for making the weather fine on my wedding day, it seems that I need to think that God make the weather on my wedding fine *for me*. Suppose that, in fact, God was indifferent whether my wedding day was fine, but set on ensuring that someone else—married on the same day in the same weather conditions—enjoyed fine weather. In that case, I have no particular reason to be grateful to God for the fine weather on my wedding day. After all, the fine weather was in no way connected to its being my wedding day. At most, I have reason to be grateful *that* my wedding happened to fall on the same day as the wedding of the person who really did have reason to be grateful to God for the weather on his wedding day. Of course, we do not need to suppose that God was set on ensuring that someone else—married on the same day in the same weather conditions—enjoyed fine weather. For all we know, God may have been perfectly indifferent about the weather in Melbourne on that day or any other day. Perhaps we have reason to be grateful that God had reason to create in the way that God did without having any reason to be grateful to God for creating as God did.

In order to explore the question of what kinds of gratitude to God, for doing certain kinds of things, are appropriate, it may help to distinguish different views that have been taken on God's creative activities.

Suppose, first, that Leibniz is right: there is a best universe, and, when God creates, God creates that best universe. On this view, it seems that, with respect to the weather on my wedding day, I have reason to be grateful that the best universe is one in which the sun shone on my wedding day, and I have reason to be grateful that God made the best universe. But it does not seem right to say that I have reason to be grateful to God for making the sun shine on my wedding day. After all, I have no reason to suppose that the shining of the sun on my wedding day played a role in making our universe the best universe. Perhaps our universe is the best *despite* the fact that the sun shone on my wedding day. For all I know, I have no reason at all to be grateful to God for making it the case that the sun shone on my wedding day. (Matters are no better if we add to the Leibnizian account that God *must* create the best. Perhaps they are worse. It still seems that I have no reason to suppose that the shining of the sun on my wedding day played a role in making our universe the best universe. And, given that God would have created the best universe whether or not the sun shone on my wedding day, it is hard to see why I do not merely have reason to be grateful that God had to create the best universe.)

Suppose, next, that Plantinga—following Molina—is right: if God creates, God chooses the best universe that it is open to God to create, where that choice is constrained by God's prior knowledge of how indeterministic causes will play out. On this view, it seems that, with respect to the weather on my wedding day, I have reason to be grateful that the best universe that it was open to God to create is one on which the sun shone on my wedding day, and I have reason to be grateful that God did make the best universe that it was open to God to make. But it does not seem right to say that I have reason to be grateful to God for making the sun shine on my wedding day. After all, I have no reason to suppose that the shining of the sun on my wedding day played a role in making our universe the best universe. Perhaps our universe is the best *despite* the fact that the sun shone on my wedding day. For all I know, I have no reason at all to be grateful to God for making it the case that the sun shone on my wedding day. (Matters are no better if we amend this account so that God must create the best of the universes that it is open to God to create. In this case, it is quite clear that God would have created the best universe whether or not the sun shone on my wedding day. So, it seems, at most I have reason to be grateful that God had to create the best universe.)

So far, we have considered accounts on which God *instantiates* a universe: God chooses from a range of universes which one to actualize. There are alternative accounts on which God merely *initializes* a universe: God chooses an initial state and laws, and there is a subsequent indeterministic evolution of the universe whose course is not known in advance to God. For example, on typical versions of open theism, God creates the initial state of the universe and the laws knowing only the range of possible ways in which the universe could unfold. Suppose, as seems hard to rule out, that when God initialized our universe, it was not determined that my wedding day would be sunny. Suppose, further—as also seems plausible—that there was no subsequent point in the evolution of our universe at which God intervened to ensure that my wedding day would be sunny. In this case, while it seems that I have reason to be grateful that God created the laws and initial state that God created, and while I also have reason to be grateful that God did not intervene to bring it about that it was not sunny on my wedding day, I have no reason to be grateful to God for making the sun shine on my wedding day. For all I know, given that God initialized the universe, I have no reason to be grateful to God for making the sun shine on my wedding day because there was no point at which it was part of God's creative intent that the sun shine on my wedding day.

Suppose, instead, that God's instantiation of our universe follows more classical lines: God's creative activities include both conserving the universe in existence and concurring with everything that happens. In this case, too, it seems that I have reason to be grateful that the universe that God has made is one in which the sun shines on my wedding day, and I have reason to be grateful that God conserves that universe in existence, and I have reason to be grateful that God concurs with the sun's shining on my wedding day. But none of that adds up to a reason to be grateful to God for making the sun shine on my wedding day. Indeed, for all I know, it may have been a matter of complete indifference to God whether the sun shone in Melbourne on that particular day. Perhaps, for all I know, it is always—or nearly always—a matter of complete indifference to God what the weather is like in Melbourne. (Some might think that this would help to explain the weather in Melbourne.) For all I know, given this more classical version of initialization, I have no reason to be grateful to God for making the sun shine on my wedding day because there was no point at which it was part of God's creative intent that the sun shine on *my* wedding day.

So far, I have made a prima facie case for thinking that we have reason to be skeptical that propositional expressions of gratitude must be tied to corresponding prepositional expressions of gratitude to God. It seems that I can be grateful that the sun shone on my wedding day without being grateful to God for making the sun shine on my wedding day. But perhaps there are theists who will want to deny this: perhaps there are theists who will insist that it can only be the case that the sun shines on *my* wedding day if it is part of God's creative intent that the sun shine on *my* wedding day.

It seems plausible to suppose that theists who take that line will be committed to a more general claim of the following form: *if God makes it the case that p, then it is part of God's creative intent that p*. Given this general claim, it is true that, if God makes it the case that the sun shines on my wedding day, it is part of God's creative intent that the sun shine on my wedding day. And then, if it is true that I am grateful *that* God made it the case that the sun shone on my wedding day, it is plausible that I should also be grateful *to* God for making it the case that the sun shone on my wedding day.

There are at least two reasons why this looks like a difficult road to take. Return to the case of my cousin's wedding. We have already noted that if we are going to give anyone the credit for making it pour on my cousin's wedding, then it is going to be God who gets that credit. But, if we insist that, given that God made it the case that it poured with rain on my cousin's wedding, it was part of God's creative intent that it pour with rain on my cousin's wedding, what attitude should we suppose that it is appropriate to take toward God's creative intent that it pour with rain on my cousin's wedding? On the one hand, it seems to me very implausible to claim that we should be grateful to God for making it the case that it poured with rain on my cousin's wedding. And, on the other hand, it seems to me to be not implausible to claim that we should be resentful to God for making it the case that it poured with rain on my cousin's wedding.

The idea that we should be grateful to God for everything that God has made the case—even where those things that God has made the case are no part of God's creative intent—seems to me to be an appalling claim. Consider the Boxing Day Tsunami. On any of the accounts of God's creation that we considered earlier, the Boxing Day Tsunami is something that God made the case. But I do not think—and I do not think that I will be alone in thinking—that we should not suppose that we should be grateful to God for the Boxing Day Tsunami. It seems very plausible to think that gratitude toward someone for doing some particular thing is warranted only if what that one does is beneficial to those who are grateful. It is inhuman to suppose that we should be grateful for disasters like the Boxing Day Tsunami because it is inhuman to suppose that the Boxing Day Tsunami was beneficial to humanity. The Boxing Day Tsunami was a disaster. Nearly a quarter of a million people died. About one third of those killed were children. More than 100,000 were injured, and 1,750,000 people were displaced. Many ecosystems were damaged, some beyond repair. Many people will carry the resulting psychological trauma with them until they die. No one should be grateful to God for the Boxing Day Tsunami. It would be evidence of horrid pathology for someone to claim that we should be grateful to God for the Boxing Day Tsunami.

If we suppose that the Boxing Day Tsunami was part of God's creative intent, then it seems to me that, if there is a reactive attitude that is appropriate to God's making it the case that the Boxing Day Tsunami occurred, then that proper reactive attitude cannot be weaker than resentment. If the Boxing Day Tsunami was part of God's creative intent, and if God made it the case that the Boxing Day Tsunami occurred, then it seems perfectly proper that we should be resentful that God made it the case that the Boxing Day Tsunami occurred. Arguably, this is seriously to understate matters. If the Boxing Day Tsunami was part of God's creative intent, and if God made it the case that the Boxing Day Tsunami occurred, we should be horrified and appalled that God made it the case that the Boxing Day Tsunami occurred. Nonetheless, even if it is understated, it is also true that we should be resentful that God made it the case that the Boxing Day Tsunami occurred.

While, of course, there is no proportionality between the Boxing Day Tsunami and the rain on my cousin's wedding, the upshot of the discussion is clear. On the assumption currently in play—namely, that if God makes it the case that p, then it is part of God's creative intent that p—if there is an appropriate reactive attitude toward God for the rain at my cousin's wedding, that attitude is resentment. It would be absurd to insist that we should be grateful to God for making it rain on my cousin's wedding; the rain at my cousin's wedding did not benefit anyone involved in the wedding. Moreover, it is reasonable to insist that we should be resentful to God for making it rain on my cousin's wedding; the rain at my cousin's wedding was harmful to some, and not beneficial to others, involved in my cousin's wedding.

The conclusion that I draw from the immediately preceding discussion is that theists should not suppose that it can only be the case that the sun shines on my wedding day if it is part of God's creative intent that the sun shine on my wedding day. Instead, theists should suppose that it may perfectly well be the case that the sun shines on my wedding day even though it is no part of God's creative intent that the sun shines on my wedding day. But then, I think, theists should suppose that I can be grateful that the sun shone on my wedding day without being grateful to God for making the sun shine on my wedding day. That is, even theists should suppose that there is no general connection between their propositional expressions of gratitude and prepositional expressions of gratitude to God. While that might seem like a bit of a cost, I think that it is also true that even theists should suppose that there is no general connection between their propositional expressions of resentment and prepositional expressions of resentment to God. It was fine for the monotheistic guests at my wedding to say that it was unfair that it was raining so heavily on my cousin's wedding day; in saying that, they were not even implicitly committing themselves to the claim that they resented God for making it rain so heavily on my cousin's wedding day.

6

There are various loose ends left in the preceding discussion. I conclude by tying some of them.

First, while I have argued that theists should suppose that there is no general connection between their propositional expressions of gratitude and prepositional expressions of gratitude to God, I have not argued that theists must eschew all prepositional expressions of gratitude to God. For all that I have argued here, it may be perfectly proper for theists to be grateful to God for particular things that God has done for them. What matters, on the line that I have taken in this chapter, is whether theists (properly) suppose that particular things that God has done that have benefited them were part of God's creative intent, that is, part of what motivated God to create the particular universe that God has created. If that condition is satisfied, then prepositional gratitude might be justified; else, not. (Hunt argues that prepositional gratitude to God can never be appropriate.[6] I take no stance on this argument here.)

Second, the emphasis that I have placed on the distinction between propositional and prepositional gratitude has important consequences for recent claims that have been made about the importance of gratitude in a well-lived life. In the very large recent literature on the benefits of practicing gratitude, the distinction between propositional and prepositional gratitude is typically entirely overlooked.[7] Many proposals in connection with practicing gratitude—gratitude journals, gratitude jars, gratitude rocks, gratitude trees, gratitude ambles, gratitude reflections, gratitude flowers, and so forth—are focused squarely on propositional gratitude (though all may incidentally involve prepositional gratitude). Some proposals emphasize that there is value in other things—gratitude emails, gratitude visits, sincere direct expressions of gratitude to particular people—that are obviously expressions of prepositional gratitude. But it is quite clear that there is nothing in this literature that suggests that you cannot get the alleged benefits of practicing gratitude solely by practicing propositional gratitude. I am skeptical that this is right; I suspect that it is much better for you to spend quality time with those who love and appreciate you than it is to keep a gratitude journal. However, I confess that this is just speculation on my part.

Notes

1 Roberts (2014: 65–83).
2 Manela (2018: 623–44; 2019).
3 Manela (2019).
4 Rush (2020: 1191–211).

5   McLachlan (2010: 422–41).
6   Hunt (2020: 1–18).
7   For a review at the more professional end of this literature, see Jans-Beken et al. (2019: 743–82).

References

Carr, David, ed. (2014). *The Psychology of Gratitude*. Oxford: Oxford University Press.

Helm, Bennett. (2017). "Love." *Stanford Encyclopedia of Philosophy*. https://plato.stanford.edu/entries/love/

Hunt, Marcus William. (2020). "Fitting Prepositional Gratitude to God is Metaphysically Impossible." *International Journal for Philosophy of Religion*, 88: 1–18.

Jans-Beken, Lilian, Nele Jacobs, Mayke Janssens, Sanne Peeters, Jennifer Reijnders, Lilian Lechner, and Johan Lataster. (2019). "Gratitude and Health: An Updated Review." *The Journal of Positive Psychology*, 15 (5): 743–82.

Katz, Leonard D. (2016). "Pleasure." *Stanford Encyclopedia of Philosophy*. https://plato.stanford.edu/entries/pleasure/

Lacewing, Michael. (2016). "Can Non-Theists Appropriately Feel Existential Gratitude?" *Religious Studies*, 52 (2): 145–65.

Manela, Tony. (2018). "Gratitude to Nature." *Environmental Values*, 27: 623–44.

Manela, Tony. (2019). "Gratitude." *Stanford Encyclopedia of Philosophy*. https://plato.stanford.edu/entries/gratitude/

McAleer, Sean. (2012). "Propositional Gratitude." *American Philosophical Quarterly*, 49 (1): 55–66.

McLachlan, Alice. (2010). "Unreasonable Resentments." *Journal of Social Psychology*, 41 (4): 422–41. https://philarchive.org/archive/MACURv1

Prinz, Jesse J. (2004). *Gut Reactions: A Perceptual Theory of Emotion*. New York: Oxford University Press.

Roberts, Robert C. (2014). "Cosmic Gratitude." *European Journal for Philosophy of Religion*, 6 (3): 65–83.

Roberts, Robert C. and Daniel Telech, eds. (2019). *The Moral Psychology of Gratitude*. New York: Rowman & Littlefield.

Rush, Michael. (2020). "Motivating Propositional Gratitude." *Philosophical Studies*, 177 (5): 1191–211.

Schwarze, Michelle. (2020). *Recognizing Resentment: Sympathy, Injustice, and Liberal Political Thought*. Cambridge: Cambridge University Press.

Stockdale, Katie. (2013). "Collective Resentment." *Social Theory and Practice*, 39 (3): 501–21.

Strawson, Peter. (1962). "Freedom and Resentment." *Proceedings of the British Academy*, 48: 1–25.
Taylor, Jacqueline. (2019). "Resentment, Empathy and Indignation." *HUMANA.MENTE Journal of Philosophical Studies*, 12 (35): 1–17.
Wallace, R. Jay. (2019). "Trust, Anger, Resentment, Forgiveness: On Blame and Its Reasons." *European Journal of Philosophy*, 27 (3): 537–51.

3

Gratitude and the Human Vocation

Brian Treanor

1 The Gift of Wild Berries

Robin Wall Kimmerer describes the mental maps of her childhood as sprinkled with strawberry patches. She remembers the small white flowers with the yellow button of pistils, scattered among the grass in late spring. How she would lie beside the patches on summer days, waiting for them to ripen, and how, when they were ripe, she could often smell them before seeing them.

> Even now . . . finding a patch of wild strawberries still touches me with a sensation of surprise, a feeling of unworthiness and gratitude for the generosity and kindness that comes with an unexpected gift all wrapped in red and green. "Really? For me? Oh, you shouldn't have." After fifty years they still raise the question of how to respond to their generosity. Sometimes it feels like a silly question with a very simple answer: eat them.[1]

Here, Kimmerer draws our attention to the experience of apprehending reality as a gift. However, my concern in what follows is not primarily apprehending the gift-nature of reality, which has generated significant scholarship in recent decades.[2] My concern, rather, is to think through what the gift-nature of reality tells us about ourselves and our role in the wider world.

I'll begin by considering appreciation, which is, in its fullest sense, a particular form of love. But appreciation is also tied to the appraisal of value, the fixing of prices in the marketplace; and so appreciation is not quite gratitude, which is focused on the gift in a decidedly noneconomic manner. Therefore, the second section seeks to disambiguate these two perspectives by considering whether and how gifts can exist in an economy. Having sketched an image of gratitude, I then move on to suggest that nature—particularly wild nature—is an arena in which, if we are observant, appreciation and gratitude are more clearly and consistently elicited from us. Wild nature confronts us with an otherness that is inhuman without being anti-human, and an environment that is essentially noneconomic. Consequently, the appreciation we feel for wild nature primes us, so to speak, for gratitude. Finally, I consider two related claims regarding our gratitude for the natural world. First, that appreciative-love might be unique to, or at least distinctive of, human beings, that humans are made for gratitude. And, second, because gifts suggest givers and recipients, that one of the ways in which we can prepare ourselves to experience reality as a gift is to view it in personalist terms: as a place populated by persons—both human and nonhuman—coexisting in a complex network of relationships, rather than as space containing impersonal things and dead matter, the *telos* of which is our extraction and manipulation.

2 From Need to Appreciation

In her chapter on "the gift of strawberries," Kimmerer does not actually use the word "love" to describe her feeling about wild strawberries, though the sentiment fairly drips from her prose (and she does speak of her father's "love" for them). Kimmerer is more focused on what strawberries taught her about relationships and economics—two subjects to which we will return later—as well as about gratitude. Nevertheless, while I will bring us back to thinking about gratitude, there is good reason to begin with love, because we'll see that the latter helps us to understand the former.

It's difficult to know where to begin when thinking through a subject as important and so thoroughly considered as love. Plato's *Symposium*, Aristotle's *Nicomachean Ethics*, the Song of Songs, the *Bhagavad Gita*, Augustine's *Soliloquia* and *De Beata Vita*, Kierkegaard's *Works of Love*, Dante's *Divina Commedia*, Abelard and Heloise, works by Sappho, Li Po, Rumi, Shakespeare, Blake, Keats, Shelly, Austen, Proust, Scheler, Neruda, and Kundera—accounts of love are so numerous that any attempt to list them, must less consider them, would be comically incomplete.

Nevertheless, if we are to begin, we have to start somewhere; and one could do worse than to start with C. S. Lewis's *The Four Loves*. Less emotionally charged than some literary or poetic expressions, less analytic than certain philosophical classics, marked and occasionally constrained by Lewis's own idiosyncrasies, *The Four Loves* nevertheless offers a clear and compelling account of love that is recognizable to many people.

The structure of the book follows the traditional philosophical practice of distinguishing between different types of love, with chapters devoted to *storge* (affection), *philia* (friendship), *eros* (intimate or romantic love), and *agape* (disinterested love or charity). However, in addition to reflecting on these classical types of love, we can distinguish between what we might call different "modes" of love, as well as the experiences or realities to which they are a response, for love is always, in some measure, a response to a call.

Lewis first draws our attention to the difference between "need-love" and "gift-love." "The typical example of Gift-love would be that love which moves a man to work and plan and save for the future well-being of his family which he will die without sharing or seeing; [and an example of Need-love], that which sends a lonely or frightened child to its mother's arms."[3] Thus, need-loves are generally a response to something we experience as a lack; and they are rooted in an awareness of and desire for the thing or things that would alleviate the deficit in question. We feel love for water when we are thirsty. Or, in Lewis's example, we feel a love for those who protect us or comfort us when we are in need of protection or comfort. Gift-love, in contrast, is about giving rather than receiving and so is unrelated to the experience of need or lack. We experience gift-love as desire to give gratuitously to the object of our love. So, we might experience gift-love in caring for others, or in helping to satisfy their desires, wants, or needs. Because gift-love is more or less disinterested, we dispense such love without the need for thanks or recognition offered in return. We give, gratuitously, simply out of love for the other.

Lewis further observes that love is generally tied to pleasure; and pleasure, like love, comes in various forms.[4] For example, there is pleasure associated with the satisfaction of needs. These need-pleasures, like need-loves, are inextricably tied to the experience of a lack. When we are hungry, we love and desire food that might alleviate that hunger; and when we eventually consume that food, we experience the pleasure of satiating our hunger. A truly hungry person pays little attention to the quality of the food. This is true to such a degree that hunger can make even unpalatable food pleasurable to eat. As the saying goes, hunger is the best sauce. Similarly, although Lewis does not dwell on it, there is certainly a kind of pleasure associated with giving. There is no one genuinely motivated by gift-love who does not also take pleasure in seeing the object of their love receive the gift.

All this seems straightforward enough; but it causes Lewis to recognize the existence of another kind of pleasure that he calls the pleasure of appreciation. The experiences that give rise to appreciative-pleasure are, no doubt, as diverse as the people who experience it; but there are certain commonalities: our inability to induce the experience; the feeling of being overwhelmed; the peace and sufficiency of the moment; wonder; and gratitude.

I've been visiting Yosemite for more than forty years. I even lived there for a while. Much of that time was spent climbing, and I've climbed El Capitan several times—in spring, summer, and autumn, with friends and alone, over slow, multiday campaigns and in relatively quick ascents. However, despite that familiarity, the impact of seeing El Cap as I exit Wawona tunnel and enter the Valley on highway 41 has never lost its potency. Its bulk, literal and metaphorical, imposes itself on the viewer. It dominates the landscape and the skyline, seeming to blot out half the sky from the meadow at its base. It testifies to an inhuman spatial and temporal scale. Its constancy—relative to human life—is bewildering, unsettling, and reassuring at once. Touching, seeing, or even thinking about El Cap evokes memories of warm granite, the cool updraft of wind in the afternoon, autumn sunsets from bivouac ledges, and the splendid isolation of finding oneself alone on a sea of granite thousands of feet above the valley floor. I'm aware of and grateful for its presence, the brute fact of its existence, even when I'm far away. And my experience of this kind of appreciation is far from unique.

Annie Dillard writes of a girl, blind since birth, who, when her sight was restored, described a tree as full of light, and another who, after a difficult two-week adjustment from her sight-restoring surgery, was overcome by astonishment, repeatedly exclaiming, "Oh God! How beautiful!"[5] How can we capture that naive wonder? Dillard herself struggles to see the world with this kind of appreciation and gratitude; but the harder she tries, the more she finds herself observing and analyzing. Eventually, she gives up, stops trying to force the experience, and goes about her business.

> Then one day I was walking along Tinker Creek thinking of nothing at all and I saw . . . the backyard cedar where the mourning doves roost charged and transfigured, each cell buzzing with flame. . . . Gradually the lights went out in the cedar, the colors died, the cells unflamed and disappeared. I was still ringing. I had been my whole life a bell, and never knew it until at that moment I was lifted and struck.[6]

Dillard was able to experience wonder and appreciate the full presence of the tree only when she stopped trying. She emphasizes both her lack of control over the situation, paradoxically both disorienting and profoundly reassuring, as well as her feelings of participation and belonging. In another example, poet Charles Simic imagines the sorrow of a Roman citizen exiled to the far north, trapped in an alien world, among "barbarous" people, endlessly petitioning the capital for forgiveness so he can return to the Eternal City. The culture, or lack thereof, the environment, and even the stars seem to abuse and mock him.[7] But, in the final stanza, the tone changes; Simic imagines the heartache and frustration of the exile quieted in a moment in which he recognizes and appreciates the stark beauty of his surroundings. Here, the beauty of nature—even nature that is otherwise experienced as indifferent, threatening, or cruel—is enough to soothe, perhaps even compensate for, the harsher aspects of life. It elicits a feeling of reverence rooted in the recognition and appreciation of something that is intrinsically good.

These examples, and countless others like them, illustrate that appreciative-pleasure is profoundly different from need-pleasure. Appreciative-pleasure does not come about as a consequence of satisfying a need, nor is it the result of giving a gift to one's beloved; it arises spontaneously and, in a sense, indifferently with respect to our desire. Appreciative-pleasure cannot be scheduled like the need-pleasure of eating lunch. It always comes upon us as something of a surprise, as in the case of Simic's exile. In fact, when we try to schedule it or force it, appreciative-pleasure often eludes us. Insofar as I anticipate and expect to be blown away by the view of El Capitan, treat it as something that *will* happen, something I can control or program, the experience never quite lives up to the expectation (though it never truly disappoints). But when I'm distracted enough not to plan on being awestruck, as if it is something I am owed, I'm often rewarded with something I could not have predicted, despite my familiarity with the Valley: a rising moon over Half Dome; some particular arrangement of light playing across the stone; the fiery setting sun illuminating Horsetail Falls. Revelation cannot be scheduled or predicted. This is because appreciative-pleasure is not about having something, which we might be able to achieve through our actions but, rather, about being in the presence of a goodness that we cannot bring about and to which we can only bear witness. Need-pleasures are associated with alleviating an experienced deficit or absence, and they are inextricably connected to receiving something that is good-for-me; but appreciative-pleasure is associated with recognizing something that is good-in-itself. Consequently, appreciative-pleasure is not really about receiving at all, at least not in the sense of possession, and certainly not in the sense of use or consumption. It is, to be redundant, about appreciation, perhaps even gratitude.

We can differentiate between these pleasures based on either, or both, their concern (the agent or the object) or their temporal focus (the past or the present). Lewis observes that "when Need-pleasures are in question we tend to make statements about ourselves in the past tense," as when I assert, after slaking my thirst, that "I really needed that." The focus is on *myself* and the experience of pleasure is *in the past*. But "when appreciative pleasures are in question we tend to make statements about the object in the present tense."[8] "The Grand Canyon of the Tuolumne is wonderous." Here the focus is on the *entity that elicited or called me to appreciation*, and the appreciation takes place *in the present*, even in instances when I am not in the immediate presence of the object. When I am no longer thirsty, I take no pleasure in water; but even when I am not in Yosemite, I have a deep and abiding appreciation for it. We can experience appreciative-pleasure for—and even, in a certain sense, the presence of—things that are removed from us in space (e.g., children who have left home for college, friends or family on other continents) or time (e.g., having seen El Capitan at some point in the past). Indeed, a person can feel appreciative-pleasure for something she has not directly experienced, and may never directly experience, simply on the basis of hearing about it or seeing some image of it. The collections in the Louvre, Rijksmuseum, and Uffizi. Silence at Epidaurus. Sunrise at Bagan. The oceanic expanse of the Pacific from "Point Nemo." A Saola, Sumatran Rhino, or Amur Leopard. The gypsum hair and flowers in the Chandelier Ballroom of Lechuguilla Cave. The "stellar nursery" in the Horsehead Nebula. One or more of these examples will strike a chord for most people and, practically speaking, a list of similar examples would be endless.

What is important about appreciative-pleasure is that it reminds us of an exceptional, and often overlooked, form of love: "In the Appreciative pleasures, even at their lowest, and more as they grow into the full appreciation of all beauty [and goodness], we get something that we can hardly help calling *love* and hardly help calling *disinterested*, towards the object itself."[9] In the case of need-love, we desire something because it will alleviate some experienced lack—thirst, hunger, loneliness—and only insofar as it helps to alleviate a lack. A person who has drunk her full neither desires nor loves water.[10] But in the case of appreciative-pleasure and appreciative-love, we feel that it is we who owe something to the object in question, that appreciation of it is right and just.[11] This is a manifestation of love to which we feel *called* in a particular way. We lay claim to the objects of need-pleasure, but the objects of appreciative-pleasure make a claim on us.

2.1 What Makes Appreciative-love Exceptional?

First, it helps us to focus on the present. Need-love is always fixated on the future or the past. When a person is very thirsty, all she can think about is the drink that will alleviate her thirst, which, as not present, is obviously (she hopes) in the future. And, once a need has been satisfied, all one is left with is a memory, highly attenuated, of the need and the desire to satisfy it. But it's just the opposite with appreciative-love, which, because it is the result of being in the presence of profound beauty or goodness, keeps us rooted in the present. In the grip of appreciative-love, we are not thinking about what we were doing the day prior, or scheming about how we can get more of it in the future. Therefore, the experience is often accompanied by a sense of the sufficiency of the moment, a feeling that other needs and desires are somehow insignificant, or at least relatively insignificant.

In *To the Lighthouse*, Virginia Woolf writes of a dinner planned and prepared by Ms. Ramsey, in which the food, the people, the setting, and the conversation all come together just so, creating a moment that "partook . . . of eternity."[12]

> [She felt] a coherence in things, a stability; something . . . is immune from change, and shines out . . . in the face of the flowing, the fleeting, the spectral, like a ruby; so that again tonight she had the feeling she had had once today already, of peace, of rest. Of such moments, she thought, the thing is made that endures. This would remain.[13]

Of course, such moments do not last. Like everything else temporal, they slip away. But the feeling of appreciative-love does not evaporate in the way need-love does as it slips into the past. Although we know such moments cannot last in the order of temporalty, we also feel that there is something "eternal" about them. In appreciative-love, we experience the goodness of a thing; and although the thing passes away, the goodness does not. The eternity of the moment is in the appreciation. And that, says Ramsey, "is enough."[14]

3 From Appreciation to Gratitude

Working from Lewis, our focus so far has been on appreciative-love; but appreciation is, perhaps, not yet gratitude. To appreciate something is to recognize and take enjoyment in its good qualities; it is rooted in valuation, stemming from the Latin *appretiare*, "to appraise or set a price on." But also "to appropriate to the self" or "to purchase or buy." Gratitude implies something more; it is not merely the recognition of goodness, or even the enjoyment of it, but in addition feeling thankful for it—from *gratitudo*, related to *gratus*: "thankful," "dear," "beloved." I don't want to make too much of the etymology, which can become a kind of prop for continental philosophy; and much of what Lewis has to say about appreciation points straight to gratitude and thankfulness.

Nevertheless, we should be mindful when the odor of the marketplace—and therefore of economy, exchange, and perhaps even appropriation—clings to appreciation. This is because we associate gratitude, not with the marketplace or reciprocal exchange but, rather, with gifts, gratuitous and superfluous, and thankfulness, all of which has a distinctly anti-economic spirit.

Let's return to the berry patch with Kimmerer. A gift, she says, "comes to you through no action of your own, free, having moved toward you without your beckoning. It is not a reward; you cannot earn it, or call it to you, or even deserve it. And yet it appears. Your only role is to be open-eyed and present."[15] This seems to resonate well with what we've said about appreciative-love and the things that elicit it. We cannot schedule the experience or anticipate its arrival. When we go to a museum, or a church, or to nature expecting to be overwhelmed by the glory, "nine times out of ten nothing will happen."[16] Nevertheless, the gifts are there, waiting for our senses, and our sensibilities, to become sensitive to them. It is, as Kimmerer and others note, a matter of learning to see.[17] If you've ever been hunting for mushrooms with a mycologist or an experienced forager, you've had the experience of staring blankly at a forest floor on which your partner sees—as if by magic—mushrooms strewn everywhere. They are, apparently, right there, in front of your face; but you can't see them until you learn how to look. So too with beauty: "[t]here is just as much beauty visible in the landscape as we are prepared to appreciate,—not a grain more."[18] And, consequently, Annie Dillard exhorts us to a certain kind of unfocused attention: "Beauty and grace are performed whether or not we will or sense them. The least we can do is try to be there."[19]

But Kimmerer also argues that gifts "establish a particular relationship, an obligation of sorts to give, to receive, and to reciprocate."[20] And, later, "a gift is something for nothing, except that certain obligations are attached."[21]

> From the viewpoints of the private property economy, the "gift" is deemed to be "free" because we obtain it free of charge, at no cost. But in the gift economy, gifts are not free. The essence of the gift is that it creates a set of relationships. The currency of the gift economy is, at its root, reciprocity. In Western thinking, private land is understood to be a "bundle of rights," whereas in a gift economy property has a "bundle of responsibilities" attached.[22]

Some philosophers will object to the claim that gifts are part of an "economy" that "obliges" one to respond.[23] If the recipient of a gift is obliged to reciprocate, doesn't that make the "gift" something very like a "purchase"? Something we obtain in exchange for something we give? It reminds us uncomfortably of parsimonious people who keep track of the value of birthday and Christmas gifts, so they can be sure to purchase similarly priced gifts in return. In those cases, what is going by the name of "gifting" seems much more like bartering, but with an insincere hug and a party, just an economic transaction with the money eliminated as a medium of exchange. And when I barter for something, it's no longer a gift. Isn't a real gift *completely* gratuitous? Given without thought, expectation, or desire for return? Doesn't the very idea of exchange or compensation tarnish the spirit of the gift?

We must admit that there is something to this objection, which Kimmerer herself recognizes in distinguishing between gifts and commodities.[24] When appreciation retains too much of the spirit of appraisal, valuation, exchange, and balancing accounts, it loses the feeling and character we associate with gratitude, much less love. This is why, when it comes to love, we often speak of things as being "priceless" or "beyond"—superior to, other than—value. That's one of the errors of utilitarianism. I "love" coffee, and I *love* my wife; but it is nonsensical to ask how much coffee could compensate me for the loss of my wife.

3.1 How Should We Behave in the "Gift Economy" Kimmerer Speaks of?

Appraisal, assessing value, is the common response when we emphasize the *economy* of "gift economy." It helps us to sustain and strengthen a mutually beneficial and reciprocal relationship. In one of Kimmerer's examples, a person harvests sweetgrass sustainably to make use of it and, in so doing, fosters the health of the sweetgrass by preventing overcrowding and encouraging growth: a symbiotic, economic exchange. We can tell that this is an economic responsibility because one of the rules is "never take more than half."[25] The precise percentage of a sustainable, honorable harvest might be different depending on whether we are speaking of sweetgrass, black ash, or pine martens; but the point is we are counting, measuring, assessing, and appraising with the goal of preserving— perhaps even earning or deserving—a reciprocal relationship.

But, when we emphasize the *gift* of "gift economy," our response ought to be different. A gift, as Kimmerer rightly notes, cannot be earned. And so the proper response here is not appraisal, so I can calculate how much to give back (i.e., pay), but gratitude, which exists outside the economy. Gratitude is not about a sustainable, mutually beneficial harvest; it is about joy and celebration and thankfulness. There may be a ritual gesture of exchange, as when, in Kimmerer's tradition, one sprinkles tobacco leaf or recites the "Thanksgiving Address"; but those are more about recognition and less about payment. Appraisal is sorting out just how many strawberries to pick; gratitude is taking joy in their beauty and sweetness. The response to the *gift* of strawberries is, as Kimmerer observed at the outset, *eat them*. Joyfully. Thankfully. Appraisal is a response to the call "we sustain each other, let's keep it that way." Gratitude is a response to the call "see the wonder of the world," or "isn't life good," or perhaps even "I love you."[26]

There is nothing wrong with the economy, so long as we keep it in its place. The world is arranged so that we can only live in it by exchange, a material give and take that ought to be sustainable and appropriate. I fully endorse Kimmerer's description of a healthy economic relationship with the world and our fellow creatures. But the giftedness of the world is something we should acknowledge as distinct from our participation in economic symbiosis with it, if only in theory. We could, for example, imagine a sustainable, reciprocal relationship in a fully technological world, one in which our relationship with food, clothing, shelter, and even culture is one of impersonal manufacturing. The replicators of the Star Trek universe, which assemble things at the molecular or subatomic level—uncertainty abounds, as it is science fiction, but basically "out of thin air"—could conjure me ripe strawberries as easily as hot Earl Grey tea. There might be pleasure in eating such food, but there would be little wonder, joy, or gratitude for the strawberries so produced. In the real world, of course, Kimmerer is perfectly correct that we cannot extract the gift from the economy, something she knows both as a biologist and as member of the Citizen Potawatomi Nation. Strawberries evolved to be attractive and tasty so that they are pleasing to see and to eat, so that animals, including me, will consume them as part of mutually beneficial and reciprocal relationship. I get delicious strawberries, and the plant gets its seeds dispersed and fertilized. In such a relationship, joy serves mutual flourishing and, in a qualified sense, gratitude serves to fuel and maintain the economy.

4 Gratitude, Naturally

Where and how do we experience appreciative-love and gratitude? In many places and in many ways assuredly, from the common and familiar to the monumental or exceptional. Looking at what is no doubt the most common experience of love, we can, and ought to, feel appreciative-love toward other people, especially those close to us—to love them for who they are, simply for existing, distinct from the ways in which they contribute to our own well-being, independent of their interaction with us in any way. However, in our relationships with other people, appreciative-love is deeply entangled with gift-love and need-love. I hope to love my wife appreciatively, that is, to appreciate her being, not what she represents to me or does for me, independent of our shared life together. But the fact is, it is difficult to abstract the goodness of her being from my experience of it over decades in which we have fulfilled each other's needs (emotional, intellectual, physical, social, spiritual, etc.) and during which we regularly expressed that love with gifts (generally nonmaterial).

Next, consider nature as an object of love. Obviously, nature also fulfills many of our needs—again, physical, emotional, spiritual, and so on; and in some cases it may, again, be difficult for us to disentangle need-love from appreciative-love. However, there are experiences of nature that confront us with a species of otherness that makes attending to appreciative-love somewhat easier.

> Our village life would stagnate if it were not for the unexplored forests and meadows which surround it. We need the tonic of wildness.... At the same time that we are earnest to explore and learn all things, we require that all things be mysterious and unexplorable, that land and sea be infinitely wild, unsurveyed and unfathomed by us because unfathomable. We must be refreshed by the sight of inexhaustible vigor, vast and Titanic features, the seacoast with its wrecks, the wilderness with its living and its decaying trees, the thundercloud, and the rain which lasts three weeks and produces freshets. We need to witness our own limits transgressed, and some life pasturing freely where we never wander.[27]

There is the otherness of the garden, or the meadow, or the sheltered cove, otherness in which it might be more difficult for us to see clearly the independence of the world from human designs and concerns. But there is also the otherness of the deep forest, or the high mountains, or the open ocean, where the indifference to our interests is abundantly clear. *Wild* nature—nature that resists us and pushes back against us, insisting on its independence and freedom—is where we feel most easily and instinctively the presence of something that is larger than our individual concerns, larger than all human concern, something that bursts the bounds of any human scale, something more constant and enduring than we can quite grasp.[28] We recognize the independence and indifference of wild nature precisely in its "uselessness" to us. Although we draw on it to satisfy our needs, and too often abuse it in doing so, experiences of wild nature remind us, powerfully, that nature does not exist to satisfy our desires—material, aesthetic, or spiritual.[29] It exists in and for itself, above and beyond the particular cares of any of its creatures.[30]

However, at the same time, we experience nature, even wild nature, as our home—something of which we are also a part, a greater whole to which we belong and contribute, and which therefore cares for us and our particular role in it as much as it cares for the role of any of its other constituents. We find ourselves appreciating beauty, experiencing wonder, and contemplating mysteries in ways that lead us to conclude—even when we have difficulty explaining our reasoning—that nature and wildness are profoundly *good*. Nature, *qua* wild, is not good for any human purpose; it is good in itself. And, insofar as we experience and recognize this goodness, we feel ourselves confronted, as Lewis describes, with something that elicits, even requires, our appreciation. As he explains in his own idiom: "nature gave the word glory meaning for me. I still do not know where else I could have found one.... And if nature had never awakened certain longings in me, huge areas of what I can now mean by the 'love' of God would never, so far as I can see, have existed."[31] The glory of nature often leaves people, theists and atheists alike, with the feeling that we owe nature our appreciation, that appreciation of it is right and just; and in some instances, we find ourselves drawn toward something that can only be called adoration.[32]

Another special aspect of nature is its honesty. In a letter to his former student, Bede Griffiths, Lewis speculates about obedience and dutifulness, using nature as example: "I think that this is one of the causes of our love of inanimate nature, that in it we see things which unswervingly carry out the will of their Creator, and are therefore wholly beautiful."[33] There is good reason to question Lewis's use of "inanimate" here; but we could express a similar sentiment in terms more congenial to an animate view of the world. One of the reasons we perceive nature to be good and beautiful is because of its honesty. In nature, things are themselves rather than striving to be something else. Nature is beautiful because of its unwavering fidelity to and expression of the real.

The "elemental mysteries" that captivated Scottish author Nan Shepherd led her to a lifetime of communion with nature in her beloved Cairngorms. She writes of one mountain spring:

> Water, that strong white stuff, one of the four elemental mysteries, can here be seen at its origins. Like all profound mysteries, it is so simple that it frightens me. It wells from the rock, and flows away. For unnumbered years it has welled from the rock, and flowed away. It does nothing, absolutely nothing, but be itself.[34]

In being honest and forthright about itself, nature asks nothing less of us: "everything in nature invites us constantly to be what we are."[35] Unlike society, which, as we know, demands all kind of things of people—arbitrary things, contradictory things, inconstant, changeable things—nature accepts us for who and what we are, asking nothing other than that we be what we are and behave as good creatures.

Every creature has a niche and role, an appropriate way of interacting with other beings in the world. We might even say that every being has a *vocation*, a calling to be authentically what it is.[36] What is the human vocation? What does it mean to be a good human creature? Many things, surely. Most obviously it means remembering that we are creatures, not the Creator, animals, not almighty architects. The world and the myriad wonderous things in it are good in themselves. They do not exist solely for our use or, worse, abuse. Of course, because we exist in an interdependent web of being, and because there are interlocked and conflicting interests in that web, we find ourselves in a situation in which using and consuming other beings is a necessity. But, as Kimmerer points out, there is a difference between honorable and dishonorable participation in the web of life. So, on the most basic level, be respectful and have restraint. This seems obvious enough, and there are warnings—crop failures, droughts, extinctions, climate change—when we fail to behave as we should.

But there is another aspect to the human vocation, one that is perhaps properly distinct to being a *human* creature: gratitude. While it is true that beauty and grace are present whether or not we attend to them, it's also true that our perception, experience, and appreciation of them adds something to the world that would not be there without us. We are, as far as we can tell, the only beings who respond to the world with appreciative-love, the only beings that can express disinterested gratitude for the goodness of things. All living beings have desires and pursue goals. All living beings use things and, presumably, feel something positive when they achieve their ends. But we are the only beings who, in addition to desiring things in the world, can also give thanks for them. Many beings are capable of need-love; we are capable of appreciative-love and gratitude. This, then, is the distinctively human vocation—or, at least, an essential part of it—to love the world and give thanks for it, for the bare fact that things are rather than are not, and for the miracle that we are here to bear witness to the beauty. Something is *added* to the world by our gratitude that would not be there if there was no one to bear witness:

> A certain kind of consciousness interacts with the mountain-forms to create this sense of beauty. . . . It is something snatched from non-being, that shadow which creeps in on us continuously and can be held off by continuous creative act. So, simply to look on anything, such as a mountain, with the love that penetrates to

its essence, is to widen the domain of being in the vastness of non-being. *Man has no other reason for his existence.*[37]

5 Nature, Personally

Of course, if we are able to shift our perception of nature to experience it—at least in certain moments—as a true gift, it is natural to start thinking about relationships. A gift seems to imply something like a giver and recipient, which in turn raises the question of what kinds of beings might play these roles.

Hermeneutics has long held that each language frames a particular way of seeing the world. If we can't speak about something—that is, if we don't have words with which to express ourselves—we can't really understand or even see it clearly; and if we cannot experience or understand something, it generally remains unspoken. Kimmerer claims that about 30 percent of the words in the English language are verbs, while about 70 percent of Potawatomi words are verbs.[38] As a consequence, many of the things that English thinks nominally (e.g., this is a mountain), Potawatomi thinks verbally (e.g., this is being a mountain). And this nominal-verbal difference marks a profound shift in the way of seeing and experiencing the world: "A bay is a noun only if water is *dead*. When *bay* is a noun, it is defined by humans, trapped between its shores and contained by the word. But the verb *wiikwegamma*—to be a bay—releases the water from bondage and lets it *live*."[39]

English distinguishes between the living and the nonliving differently than Potawatomi, and differs with respect to where it locates personhood. Kimmerer relates a debate that took place between some of her biology students.[40] One student observed that using the third person pronoun "it" implies the land is simply an object, nothing more than "natural resources" for our consumption. Another student points out that to use "he" or "she" would be to engage in anthropocentrism. Aside from being inappropriate, this is disrespectful to nonhuman animals: "We shouldn't project our perceptions on to them. They have their own ways—they're not just people in furry costumes." But, wonders the first student, while they are not "humans," might they still be "persons"?

This distinction is precisely the point. And it evokes for us not only the Potawatomi traditions that inform Kimmerer's prose (as well as her work as a biologist, botanist, and plant ecologist); it also points toward a rich, if understudied, tradition in Western philosophy: personalism. Most philosophers, if they have heard of personalism at all, will understandably associate it with

Emmanuel Mounier, Max Scheler, or Karol Wojtyła (who became Pope John Paul II). However, personalism is not a formal school or tradition of philosophy; it is merely a term of resemblance—sometimes only vague or superficial resemblance—for philosophers who emphasize the "person" in their work. The foci of some personalists may overlap only partially with others or might not overlap at all.

Most personalists have relatively little to say about nature and the more-than-human world, and what they do say tends to reinforce a strict "humans are persons and non-humans are non-persons" binary. For example: "Whenever we say that man is a person, we mean that he is more than a mere parcel of matter, more than an individual element in nature, such as is an atom, a blade of grass, a fly or an elephant.... Man is an animal and an individual, but unlike other animals or individuals."[41] However, there are examples of "personalism" that extend personhood, implicitly or explicitly, to the more-than-human world.

Martin Buber describes two "primary words" through which we can relate to the world: I-It and I-Thou. When we adopt the attitude of I-It, we engage things as objects and experience them as such. Under the influence of I-It, we *experience* things but do not *relate* to them; we engage in a monologue rather than a dialogue and, consequently, are really only relating to ourselves. In contrast, when we adopt the attitude of I-Thou, we participate in a dialogue with authentic existence. As a dialogue, I-Thou is a genuine relation, and it changes both participants. In an I-Thou relationship, the Thou affects me and I affect it. Crucially, Buber is clear in saying that I-Thou is a global attitude or way of being that is a possibility when relating to things, humans, and spiritual beings.[42]

But perhaps the most explicit proponent of a personalist view of nature is Czech philosopher Erazim Kohák, who recognizes what is at stake in extending our view of personhood.

> Whatever may seem true in the simplified human environment of the cities, [in the forest, under the starry sky] the ultimate metaphysical question stands out in profound simplicity. Shall we conceive of the world around us and of ourselves in it as *personal*, a meaningful whole ... or shall we conceive of it and treat it, together with ourselves, as *impersonal* ... ? Is *person* or is *matter in motion* the root metaphor of thought and practice? That answered, all else follows.[43]

This egalitarian personalism is not a panpsychism attributing rational agency to all reality. The personhood of the natural world

> is not contingent on the attribution of any set of traits. Nor is the overwhelming sense of the clearing as a "society of persons," as structured by personal relations,

a function of any alleged personality traits of boulders and trees. It is, far more, an acknowledgement of the truth, goodness, and unity of all beings, simply because they are, as they are, each in his own way. That is the fundamental sense of speaking of reality as personal: recognizing it as a Thou, and our relation to it as profoundly and fundamentally a moral relation, governed by the rule of respect.[44]

It is not coincidental that here, as in Kimmerer and Buber, the idea of *relationship* is front and center. Under this brand of personalism, the natural world is not something we can hold before us as dead matter, meaningless except for its extrinsic value to us. It is, rather, a community of personal realities with whom we are in relationship. And we have a distinctive role within this community. Just as other beings have distinctive capacities or aptitudes for photosynthesis, the pollination of certain plants, hibernation, or metamorphosis, humans have distinctive traits that mark their particular form of being. One of those is the capacity for appreciation and gratitude, the possibility of giving thanks for the being of the world and the things in it. Viewing reality in relational and personalist terms, we are forced to recognize that all beings both take from and give to the world.[45] Something will be lost from the world if and when Chinook salmon no longer complete their remarkable anadromous life cycle with a 2,000-mile swim from the Bering Sea upstream into the interior of Canada along the Yukon River; and something uniquely good will be lost from the world—and, as far as we know, the cosmos—when human beings are no longer here to witness it, appreciate it, and give thanks for it.[46] Or when, out of insensitivity, we fail to do so.[47]

Notes

1. Kimmerer (2013: 23).
2. See note 23 for some examples.
3. Lewis (1960: 1).
4. Lewis (1960: 11).
5. Dillard (2007: 31).
6. Dillard (2007: 36).
7. Simic (1990: 23).
8. Lewis (1960: 12–13).
9. Lewis (1960: 16).
10. Of course, in lived experience different forms of pleasure and love—need, gift, appreciation—are often intermingled in complex ways. When a person is hungry,

she will experience need-love for food that will alleviate her hunger and take pleasure in consuming it; however, if she is fortunate enough to have access to good food, and if her hunger does not overwhelm her and cause her to eat too quickly and thoughtlessly, she can also experience love for the quality of the food and take pleasure in it. Similarly, a person who is not thirsty and who therefore does not feel need-love for water might still, on reflection, be able to experience appreciative-love for the bare fact of water, for its being, and for what it makes possible (i.e., life).

11 Lewis (1960: 14).
12 Woolf (2013: 114).
13 Woolf (2013: 114).
14 Woolf (2013: 73).
15 Kimmerer (2013: 23–4).
16 Lewis (1960: 22).
17 For an extended discussion of learning to see otherwise, see my Treanor (2021), especially chapter five, *Amor Mundi*.
18 Thoreau (1996: 58).
19 Dillard (2007: 10).
20 Kimmerer (2013: 25).
21 Kimmerer (2013: 27).
22 Kimmerer (2013: 28).
23 For some sense of the debate, see: Caputo and Scalon (1999), Derrida (1992), and Marion (2002). Kimmerer herself recognizes that a true or complete "gift economy" is in some way a dream (see Kimmerer 2013: 28–30).
24 Kimmerer (2013: 26).
25 Kimmerer (2013: 157).
26 Kimmerer struggles, later in her book, to articulate just how we could respond or give back to the earth in anything like reciprocal measure to what we've been given. She acknowledges that the significance of the "gift" or "exchange" of tobacco is spiritual rather than material and mentions one elder who says directly that "gratitude is our only responsibility" (Kimmerer 2013: 238). Here, and in the following pages, she and her students imagine different ways of "paying back" the earth; but these "payments," while well-intentioned are vague, unequal in value, or both. I suspect that Kimmerer is struggling with precisely the distinction this chapter tries to point out: the response to the *gift* of the gift economy (i.e., gratitude) is different than the response to the *economy* of the gift economy (i.e., sustainable use).
27 Thoreau (2004: 317–18).
28 I will use "nature" to name a certain kind of nonhuman otherness, an otherness that emphasizes the difference between the spontaneous and the choreographed, the evolved and the manufactured, the unconstrained and the regulated. Such

a conception affirms that humans—one type of animals evolved on this planet among others—are "natural" beings, in the sense that there is no sharp ontological break between humanity and the rest of the world; but it also recognizes the degree to which humans can live in "unnatural" ways, by meaningfully separating themselves from the rest of reality so constituted. There is a difference between "humans as creatures among fellow creatures" and "man as the measure of all things." When hybridization occurs between closely related species in the wild, or when evolution exerts its gentle pressure on species over the course of eons, the change is *natural*. When humans insert a gene from a fish into a tomato to increase its resistance to frost, it is *unnatural*. I will use "wild" or "wilderness" to point to parts of nature distinguished by their resistance to human control or modification, nature that resists us and imposes itself on us, nature that, rather than being bent to accommodate our wishes, forces us to accommodate ourselves to it. In both instances, nature and wildness, I am making a distinction that admits of degrees rather than a binary or absolute difference; things can be more or less natural, more or less wild.

29 Of course, as in the case of nature, my wife's life is bigger than her life with me. Some of her interests are indifferent to me. Most obviously, all the interests she had before she met me and, should I predecease her, many of the interests she will have after I die. Additionally, there are all the aspects of my wife's being and all her interests that remain mysterious to me, even after more than three decades together. In this sense, she remains "wild" to me. And happily so. As Thoreau observes, "all good things are wild and free" (Thoreau 2010: 25). The point is not that appreciative-love only happens in the context of nature; it is that, because of the *inhuman* otherness of nature, we can see our appreciation of it, independent of its relationship to us, more clearly.

30 It is true that nature does provide for us, collectively and individually. If it did not, what would? But nature is not teleologically or hierarchally organized so as to cater to human needs and wants. Likewise, anthropogenic climate change may well destroy the world that humans have evolved to live in over the past 10,000 years; but it cannot destroy nature itself.

31 Lewis (1960: 20).

32 As T. S. Eliot has it: "You are not here to verify, / Instruct yourself, or inform curiosity / Or carry report. You are here to kneel" (Eliot 1943: 51). Thus, perhaps the relevant distinction is between, on the one hand, a way of being in the world that experiences it not only as personal, on which more below, but also as *sacred*—shot through with meaning, and worthy of our respect—and, on the other hand, a way of being that treats the world as if it were *profane*, meaningless, interchangeable, a mere object for our (ab)use.

33 Zaleski and Zaleski (2015: 250).

34 Shepherd (2011: 23).

35 Erlich (1985: 84).
36 Remember that, earlier, I claimed that all love is, in some sense, a response to a call (*vocare*).
37 Shepherd (2011: 102). Emphasis mine. "We are here to witness," writes Annie Dillard, "that is why I take walks: to keep an eye on things," that is, to keep an eye out for the extraordinariness in the ordinary (Dillard 1982).
38 Kimmerer (2013: 26). The source for these data is not given; and any claim like this is highly questionable. One might, at best, hazard a guess; but any estimate would be highly speculative given that there is no exhaustive count of the total number of English words, that so many English words are loan words, that there are differences between spoken English and written English, that there are significant regional variations in usage, and so on. "Corpus analysis" can tell us the percentage of different parts of speech in any particular body of work. For example, one corpus analysis of Thoreau's *Walden* finds about 19 percent of the total word count comprised of nouns, and about 15 percent comprised of verbs, which would complicate the claim that English is a "noun-based" language ("Foray's [*sic*] into parts of speech." http://infomotions.com/blog/2011/02/forays-into-parts-of-speech/. Accessed August 2, 2021). But the use of nouns and verbs in *Walden*, or any other work, can't be extrapolated to English as a whole. Another study pegs English nouns at 37 percent of word-tokens (Hudson 1994). The range of these estimates suggests the difficulty of the problem. Nevertheless, Kimmerer's core point seems plausible: English implies much of the nonhuman world is comprised of things or objects, while Potawatomi implies that that world is animate and full of (nonhuman) persons.
39 Kimmerer (2013: 55).
40 Kimmerer (2013: 57).
41 Maritain (2012: 66).
42 Buber (1958: 7).
43 Kohák (1987 [1984]: 125).
44 Kohák (1987 [1984]: 128).
45 For her part, Kimmerer is astounded, and saddened, by the fact that her students can enumerate many of the ways in which humans negatively impact nature but are wholly unable to describe positive interactions between humanity and nature (Kimmerer 2013: 6).
46 "On the level of the act [i.e., what we do] rather than merely the fact of being human [i.e., anthropocentric exceptionalism] we can say that humans are worth the cost of their sustenance because they are the beings capable of doing good" (Kohák 1987 [1984]: 99).
47 The development of this chapter included field work under the auspices of a research permit issued by Yosemite National Park and the National Park Service (Erin Stackle and Benjamin C. Llu primary permit recipients).

References

Buber, Martin. (1958). *I and Thou*, trans. Ronald Gregor Smith. New York: Macmillan Publishing.

Caputo, John D., and Michael J. Scalon, ed. (1999). *God, the Gift, and Postmodernism.* Bloomington, IN: Indiana University Press.

Derrida, Jacques. (1992). *Given Time: I. Counterfeit Money*, trans. Peggy Kamuf. Chicago, IL: University of Chicago Press.

Dillard, Annie. (1982). *Teaching a Stone to Talk*. New York: HarperCollins, 90 and 91.

Dillard, Annie. (2007). *Pilgrim at Tinker Creek*. New York: HarperPerennial.

Eliot, T. S. (1943). "Little Gidding." In *Four Quartets*, 49–59. New York: Harcourt Brace & Company.

Erlich, Gretel. (1985). *The Solace of Open Spaces*. New York: Penguin.

Hudson, Richard (1994). "37% of Word-Tokens are Nouns." *Language*, 70 (2): 331–9.

Kimmerer, Robin Wall. (2013). *Braiding Sweetgrass*. Minneapolis, MN: Milkweed.

Kohák, Erazim V. (1987 [1984]). *The Embers and the Stars*. Chicago, IL: The University of Chicago Press.

Lewis, C. S. (1960). *The Four Loves*. London: Harcourt Brace & Co.

Marion, Jean-Luc. (2002). *Being Given*, trans. Jeffrey L. Kosky. Stanford, CA: Stanford University Press.

Maritain, Jacques. (2012). *Christianity and Democracy and The Rights of Man and Natural Law*. San Francisco, CA: Ignatius Press.

Shepherd, Nan. (2011). *The Living Mountain*. Edinburgh: Cannongate.

Simic, Charles. (1990). "The North." In *The Book of Gods and Devils*, 23. Boston, MA: Mariner Books.

Thoreau, Henry David. (1996). *Autumnal Tints*. Bedford, MA: Applewood Books.

Thoreau, Henry David. (2004). *Walden*. Princeton, NJ: Princeton University Press.

Thoreau, Henry David. (2010). *Walking*. Sheffield, MA: Cricket House Books.

Treanor, Brian. (2021). *Melancholic Joy: On Life Worth Living*. London: Bloomsbury.

Woolf, Virginia. (2013). *To the Lighthouse*. Dublin: Roads.

Zaleski, Philip and Carol Zaleski. (2015). *The Fellowship: The Literary Lives of the Inklings*. New York: Farrar, Strauss and Giroux.

4

Generous Existence?
Gift, Giving, and Gratitude in Contemporary Phenomenology

Christina M. Gschwandtner

The most important and most influential twentieth-century voice on the topics of human existence and "being as such" is, without doubt, Martin Heidegger. The German term "Dasein," which achieved such notoriety with *Being and Time*, is usually employed in German simply to mean *existence* and is used in that sense by several earlier phenomenologists, such as Hedwig Conrad-Martius, Max Scheler, and even Husserl himself. In fact, this is also its meaning in Heidegger, although he restricts its use to human existence, while others employ it much more broadly for any sort of existence.[1] At least in *Being and Time*, there is little sense that humans ought to be grateful for existence. We are "thrown" into the world without our choice; we find ourselves there among others in a world and an environment not created by us, a world in which we are often not at home.[2] This deep discomfort with our existence, the sense of not "fitting" into the world, makes us anxious for our existence, dreading our annihilation and anticipating our death.[3] Human existence, for the Heidegger of *Being and Time*, does not elicit gratitude but angst. This primordial dread is exacerbated by an overwhelming but indefinable sense of guilt that smites our conscience in the awareness of our "nihilating" (or negligible, *nichtig*) finitude.[4] We can only "own" our existence decisively by resolutely embracing our finitude and living deliberately toward our death. Although Heidegger claims over and over again that his analysis carries no ethical or normative connotations, that it is purely descriptive of primordial human existence, it is hard to escape the impression that our existence is a burden that we can only assume through a radically individual, virile "taking charge," rather than by grateful receptivity.[5]

Interestingly, Heidegger's often vastly overstated "turn" shortly after the publication of *Being and Time*, which left that great work incomplete and to some extent even abandoned the task of unveiling the question of Being (*Sein*) via human existence (*Dasein*), is maybe more than anything characterized by a shift in tone. Not only does his writing become far more poetic and less philosophical, not only does he emphasize "thinking" over philosophizing, but he associates this thinking (*Denken*) precisely with gratitude, or at least with the activity of thanking (*Danken*).[6] Influenced by Meister Eckhart and other mystical approaches (including conversations with Japanese thinkers), Heidegger's later writings counsel a more peaceful *Gelassenheit* (equanimity or letting go) in the face of existence, including the ravages of technology and the threat of a potential third world war.[7] Still concerned with the question of Being, which he never abandoned, he no longer tries to grasp it via resolute human efforts of owning oneself but instead suggests that Being "gives" (*es gibt Sein*), a play on the auxiliary verb "to give" employed in German to mean "there is."[8] Being reveals itself generously and we receive it in gratitude, no longer to own it but to witness to its manifestation, especially in art and poetry. This is not, strictly speaking, a gratitude for or on behalf of existence, but it comes close. It does not constitute, however, a full analysis of gratitude as a phenomenon or a description of its particular phenomenality.

While this later Heideggerian elusive emphasis on gratitude was maybe less influential, the notion of giving, or more precisely of the gift, entered phenomenology with a vengeance in French philosophy in the wake of Marcel Mauss's anthropological study of gift-giving in indigenous societies.[9] It seems there is hardly a Francophone philosopher who does not speak of the gift sooner or later.[10] These discussions of the gift, however, are curiously short on extensive reflections on the topic of gratitude and that for a very particular reason. Based on Mauss's study and especially the example of the potlatch, the gift was early on accused of a kind of violence, of being inscribed in an economic system of reciprocal exchange that would place the recipient under an obligation, undoing the very notion of gift-giving and hence making gratitude impossible, superfluous, or, at best, rather manipulative. Furthermore, sometimes giving is even interpreted in opposition to existing or as its undoing. The present contribution will consider three "installments" of thinking about the gift in light of or in opposition to existence before drawing out some implications for the phenomenon of gratitude: first, Jacques Derrida's critique of the economy of the gift, second, Jean-Luc Marion's phenomenology of givenness, and, third, Anthony Steinbock's phenomenological consideration of the interpersonal dimensions of giving and loving.

1 Derrida and the Economy of the Gift

Derrida considers the topic of the gift in several contexts, most famously in *Given Time* and *Gift of Death*. Following on Mauss, he suggests that gift-giving is always inscribed in an economic relation of exchange: a gift calls forth a counter-gift or recompense of some sort, even if it is simply the expectation of gratitude.[11] Through such reciprocity, gratitude or a return gift becomes an obligation and thus undoes the connotations of gratuitousness and generosity in the gift that are such an essential part of its meaning. This leads to his claim that the gift is "the impossible," a claim he also makes about other phenomena, some of them related to the gift, such as forgiveness, hospitality, the democracy to come, and so forth. This does not mean—as it is often misunderstood to imply—that there can never be any gifts or that gift-giving by definition cannot occur, but rather that the gift, like forgiveness and hospitality, includes a structural impossibility in its very meaning. That is to say, it is essential to the phenomenon of the gift, part of its very nature or definition, that it be characterized by abundant generosity and thus cannot demand or expect a return of any kind. To give freely without reciprocity or recompense lies in the very meaning of the idea of a gift and as soon as such reciprocity intervenes, as it always necessarily does, the purity of the gift is compromised. The gift is "the impossible" because its very definition demands an impossible purity that is undone by its exercise, by any actual giving of gifts.[12] A gift without connotations of ownership is impossible, because if I do not own it, I cannot give it away. Yet if gift-giving is about property exchange, then it has been absorbed in an economy, and the abundant generosity or pure gratuity essential to gift-giving has been erased. So, the claim is not that no one can give a gift, but that what is given is not simply a "gift" (in the most technical sense of that term), but already also part of an economy of exchange: the gift given is not purely a "gift," but always a mix of gift and exchange, of gratuitous generosity and expectation of recompense in some form. The same is the case for hospitality: its very notion implies a free welcome without any restriction whatsoever and yet it is structurally constitutionally impossible to practice such completely free welcome, because one cannot welcome if one no longer has a home over which one exercises at least some ownership, necessarily implying restrictions on hospitality.[13]

In *Gift of Death* Derrida explores this first in terms of Kierkegaard's analysis of the biblical story of Abraham's "sacrifice" of Isaac, which he finds characterized by the essential "secret" that Abraham can divulge to no one, then in terms of the injunction in the Sermon on the Mount to give one's gifts "in secret" so that one hand would not know what the other is doing (or giving).¹⁴ He wonders whether this truly erases the expectation of reward, as the biblical text seems to imply, or whether instead the earthly economy of giving and rewarding has been replaced by a higher, "heavenly" economy, in which this apparently free and generous giving is "rewarded" by the "Father in heaven" who sees everything and thus acknowledges the gift. If one still acts with the promise of a (final) reward, is one truly giving generously, selflessly, without expectation of recompense? Derrida does not simply conflate these two economies, as he is often interpreted as doing, but he does certainly question whether it is possible for gift-giving to escape notions of reciprocity or economic exchange altogether. He suggests—as he also does for notions of forgiveness, hospitality, democracy, and cosmopolitanism—that the meanings of gift, giving, and gratitude in our society cannot be understood without their profound Judeo-Christian roots, that these terms, even when they are employed in non-Western contexts, are always already informed and maybe burdened by their heritage, by the particular connotations they have acquired in centuries of Christian use in the European West.¹⁵

This raises serious questions about something like a gratitude for existence. Would it impose obligations that involve our very being in a relation of exchange? Would it institute a quasi-economic circularity, maybe at a higher level, if existence is seen to be granted by the divine? Does the idea of *having* to be grateful for our existence make us beholden to God or our parents in some problematic way that undoes the very notion of gratitude, which surely ought to be offered freely, *gratis*, rather than under constraint? What about the notions of grace (*gratia*) and their particular theological history in the Christian West, which underwrite and ground our notion of gratitude?¹⁶ What would it mean to be grateful for an act of grace or for the gracious? These are the sorts of questions Derrida might raise about the idea of gratitude in light of his reflections on the gift.

Interestingly, Paul Ricœur in his discussion of forgiveness at the end of his monumental *Memory, History, Forgetting* challenges Derrida's interpretation of the gift, arguing that not all connotations of reciprocity or mutuality must involve economic exchange and that gratitude may well escape the sort of recompense or retribution Derrida always sees at work in gift-giving.¹⁷ What Mauss describes in Polynesian societies, so Ricœur points out, is an economic exchange that raises the stakes with each exchange and thus always imposes an obligation on the recipient to give back *more* than was received. This does indeed, even in Ricœur's view, annul the gift-character of giving, reducing it to mere economic exchange with all its connotations of possession, obligation, and return. Yet, a giving among friends is not like this. When a gift meets the response of gratitude, no counter-obligation of further giving is imposed; the cycle of "exchange" ends here. It is mutual rather than "upping the ante" in a way that requires further economic labors. The friend does not give to impress or overwhelm, and by receiving a gift gratefully one acknowledges the other's friendship rather than fulfilling an obligation or manipulating the situation for further goods. Thus the genuine phenomenon of the gift escapes the logic of economic exchange. When such economic obligations are generated by the giving, we are not really dealing with the phenomenon of gift-giving at all. (Ricœur goes on to show that, similarly, forgiving, while difficult, is not impossible.) The question is, of course, whether gratitude for existence can be said to be mutual in this nonobligatory sense.

In both Derrida and Ricœur, giving and forgiving are closely connected, as their etymology also shows (in French: *le don* and *le pardon*). Derrida focuses initially on such expressions as giving one's time and "giving death" (*donner la mort*, the French expression both for killing and for suicide). Yet from Jankélévitch's seminal study of forgiveness onward, forgiving is taken as bestowing a gift.[18] While Derrida points to the structural and logical similarity of giving and forgiving that both imply a kind of excess that is undone by the actual practice (e.g., when one requests that the other change or be properly remorseful before one can grant forgiveness),[19] Ricœur instead interprets forgiveness as a gift of "unbinding" in which the actor is separated from his or her (evil) actions and released for new activity.[20] Their focus is almost exclusively on the phenomenon of the act of giving, examining its nature and possibility of appearance, much more rarely on the response of receiving. Even when that response is the focus, as in some of the reflections on forgiveness, its difficulty and structural inadequacy are under examination, rather than gratitude as a phenomenon. Indeed, gratitude often seems suspect, as if such a response were to take away something from the phenomenon of giving, especially its dimension of generosity. Although there is no sustained reflection on either gratitude or existence in Derrida, his account has been so influential that it largely sets the stakes within which the topic of giving and receiving is examined. In terms of the present topic, it raises serious questions about the appropriateness of gratitude as an obligatory response to any giving, including or maybe especially that of life.

2 Marion and the Phenomenology of Givenness

Although Marion's initial writings about givenness and the generous and kenotic dimensions of love precede Derrida's *Given Time* and *Gift of Death*, much of his explicit discussion of the gift responds to Derrida and tries to escape the aporia he sees Derrida outlining regarding the impossibility of the gift.[21] This is clearest in his early "Sketch of a Phenomenological Concept of Gift," later revised into Part II of *Being Given*, but Derrida's claims are also less obviously behind some of the discussions of the gift, sacrifice, and forgiveness in Marion's *Negative Certainties*.[22] Marion wants to show not only that the gift is possible and that it can escape the connotations of economic exchange, but also to develop a notion of giving and givenness that would escape ontology, thus what he sees as the constraints of being and existence, precisely in the Heideggerian sense. Both— admittedly related—claims are made partly to permit a phenomenology and theology freed from "metaphysical" constraints in a quasi-kenotic abandon of abundant giving. This is not to say, as many suspect, that God is always the giver behind all phenomena for Marion, but it does pattern the giving of all genuine gifts on the divine generosity.[23]

Marion's phenomenology of givenness is developed as a richer, wider, deeper, more generous version of Husserl's and Heidegger's phenomenologies, one that would overcome their phenomenological restrictions that, so Marion claims, think of phenomena in terms of objects or beings, respectively. Marion draws on Husserl's notion of *Gegebenheit*, that is, the "given" of phenomena, to argue that phenomena are not first of all objects to be constituted in Husserl's sense or the being by which one might be called in Heidegger's sense, but are "givens" in the sense of gifts.[24] Marion plays on the ambiguity of the French *se donner* that can have both passive and reflexive or reciprocal connotations and can mean both "being given" and "giving oneself" (although the latter translation predominates in the English primary and secondary literature).[25] There is thus an essential generosity in phenomenality itself; phenomena "give themselves" to us before they "are" or appear as objects. This means for Marion that they are not under our control, that they cannot be anticipated or manipulated in advance, that one cannot prepare for them, and that they always come as a surprise, suddenly, by dazzling and overwhelming us.[26] All phenomena, especially the most saturated or most abundant ones, thus manifest, in some sense, as gifts and not merely as "objects" in Husserl's or "beings" in Heidegger's sense.[27]

Marion makes this explicit by drawing clear parallels between giving and the gift. The gift, he argues, can be given without succumbing to economic exchange, if the poles of the supposed gift exchange are eliminated, that is to say, if either giver or recipient or gift-object is unknown, absent, or not involved in some fashion.[28] If the gift cannot be returned, it is no longer subject to reciprocal exchange. This is the case, for example, for such phenomena as giving to an enemy who will refuse to acknowledge the gift or the giver, thus suspending the recipient, receiving an inheritance from an unknown giver, thus suspending the giver, or offering a symbolic gift like a ring or time where the object is not the gift itself but merely "stands in" for it, thus suspending the gift itself. If one of the poles of the gift exchange is suspended in this way, economic relations no longer apply: "This result allows us first of all to define the properly phenomenological sense of the gift—namely, that it owes nothing to any anthropological or sociological model . . . to win the figure of the gift, we must take our direction from givenness, and not from economic exchange between real terms."[29] Setting aside at least one of the terms of exchange—either giver or recipient or gift-object—allows the process of giving to emerge fully as a phenomenon.[30] If it is described in terms of economic exchange, the gift is misunderstood in its phenomenality. Instead it must be understood against the horizon of givenness.[31] Marion thinks it especially important to disassociate the gift from any principle of sufficient reason, that is to say, a gift is always of an abundance that exceeds and undoes any kind of coordinates of rationality or sufficiency.[32]

In a subsequent analysis Marion is less sure that this analysis allows the gift to escape reciprocity fully, and he instead suggests that only in the phenomena of sacrifice or forgiveness does the (initial) gift appear fully, so to say in retrospect or in abeyance or by returning upon itself.[33] He appeals to Abraham, to King Lear, and to the parable of the prodigal son as examples. In the sacrifice of Isaac, Abraham acknowledges that Isaac was initially given as a gift and is not his possession. Thus the sacrifice makes "visible" God's gift of Isaac in a way that had been forgotten by Abraham until then. Furthermore, by ultimately refusing Isaac as a sacrifice, God

> does not thereby refuse to acknowledge the gift offered by Abraham; he accepts the sacrifice all the more, understood this time in the strict phenomenological sense of abandonment. By sparing Isaac, henceforth recognized (by Abraham) as a gift (from God), God regives Isaac to Abraham, gives him a second time, presenting a gift by redounding [*don par une redondance*], which consecrates it definitely as a gift henceforth shared and, ultimately, transparent between the giver and the recipient.[34]

Sacrifice makes visible the giver for the first time.

Forgiveness, instead, reveals the recipient. King Lear's appeal to forgiveness of his daughter Cordelia finally recognizes and acknowledges the gift of love she initially gave him, although he did not recognize it at the time and spurned it (i.e., did not receive it).[35] The prodigal son's returning for the father's forgiveness first acknowledges the initial overwhelming gift of love offered by the father, which the son had not recognized but had instead turned into a possession by demanding his inheritance (lit., the "ousia" or "being" of the father).[36] Thus the gift and its generosity become visible and fully manifest only via these later phenomena that are subsequent to the gift and in some fashion double it or return it upon itself: "The gift cannot at the same time be possessed and manifest itself." That is, one must renounce "possession of the gift in order to see the process of givenness, or more exactly, in order to allow givenness to show itself as its own process."[37] The emphasis is throughout on the abundant self-giving of the gift or the phenomenon, although Marion does mark the appropriate response as one of radical receptivity.[38]

Like the gift or the self-givenness of the phenomenon, this receptivity is fundamentally kenotic in character. This emerges especially in Marion's account of the phenomenon of love, which consists for him in radical mutual self-abandonment to the other.[39] But it also characterizes his broader description of the proper receptivity to what is given, especially to the saturated phenomenon. This abundant, rich, bedazzling, overwhelming, surprising phenomenon is given in such excess and self-abandonment that it becomes almost impossible to "bear up" under it, that is, to receive it with the sort of resistance that would make it fully visible, thus allowing it to manifest as such. Marion repeatedly compares such receptivity to the immense abundance and generosity of givenness to the genius of the artist who can "see" something in the realm of the "unseen" (*l'invu*) and—for example, by rendering it in a great work of art—make it visible to others by adding a new phenomenon to the world.[40]

He also often stresses the abundant abandonment of the self-giving of the phenomenon, especially in more theological contexts.[41] The Eucharist is a phenomenon that shows itself fully only by giving itself entirely from itself; its very phenomenality is characterized by the abandon of abundant giving.[42] The gift of God cannot be seen because it is fully manifest only through Christ's self-sacrifice on the cross. "The giver, givenness, and the given itself are only illuminated if the insistence of being decreases, that is to say, only if the given gives itself up to givenness and only to the extent of this abandon(ment)," as is the case for Christ's self-abandonment to the point of death.[43] The Eucharist must be recognized as the gift par excellence, because "the more the gift is emptied of itself to the point where it is reduced to a minimal presence, the more the giver appears there in the superabundant light of givenness."[44] As the gift is given in radically kenotic fashion, so the only appropriate response to this gift must be total abandonment of self to the other.

Most important for our present concern, as evident already obliquely in the foregoing, is the fact that Marion resolutely sets giving and being in opposition to each other. Questions of ontology, including those of existence (divine or otherwise), are, for Marion, metaphysical in their very nature, and it is this precise metaphysical restriction he seeks to overcome. The generosity of giving and especially of loving escapes ontological restraints; they are outside concerns about being or existence and suspend them. This claim characterizes Marion's work from beginning to end; it is made already before *God without Being* (in fact, Marion voices it even in an interview he gave as a young student in his early twenties) and is still at play in his most recent work, such as the Gifford Lectures *Givenness and Revelation*.[45] In the crucial, but unfortunately so far untranslated, early work on Descartes' "white theology," Marion censures the late medieval and early modern moves to apply univocal language to the divine and the human.[46] This is the case especially for ontological language, for example, by employing the notion of existence or being in the same way for God and for everything else. But Marion applies it not only to the insufficiency of proofs for God's existence or any description of the divine in terms of being. The phenomenology of givenness provides "relief" to metaphysical theology and philosophy precisely because it frees them from their obsession with questions of being and existence.[47] God becomes manifest or revealed, most profoundly in intra-trinitarian self-givenness.[48] The Holy Spirit in particular manifests the given gift (Christ) and the process of giving (from the Father).[49]

He also makes similar claims about human beings. Melancholia or the experience that all is vain, for example, strikes being and existence with irrelevance; we no longer care about "being" in any form.[50] More positively, love similarly undoes any connection or obsession with existence: "Only love does not have to be."[51] The rationality of love and givenness suspends the (metaphysical) rationality of being, existence, and sufficient reason.[52] To define the human as an object or a being is to eliminate our humanity.[53] He again equates the economic and the ontological in this context: "Thus, the economic interpretation of the fact that I am remains a limited and contradictory prescription, so that the (quidditative) definition of man in general that it decrees appears all the more like a perfectly illegitimate proscription of who I am," because it "accomplishes the eclipse of the *who* by the *what* (quiddity)" in the sense of Heidegger's notion of *Vorhandenheit* (i.e., in the sense of an object).[54] Our humanity can only be safeguarded if we vouch for a crucial incomprehensibility and indefinability at the very heart of the human. We must receive ourselves as gift and indeed as creation via our likeness to the divine, in the way in which a painting is referred to by the name of its artist.[55] The human cannot be captured in terms of presence or existence, but only as a "likeness of the invisible."[56] What God has created cannot be interpreted as a "being"; creation is not "presence-at-hand" in Heidegger's sense.[57] God must instead be confessed as the "giver of gifts"; creation appears or manifests not as a collection of entities or existences but as an abundant gift.[58] Relying on Augustine, for Marion the appropriate response to this gift is confession rather than gratitude per se.[59] We must respond in love and self-abandonment, but not necessarily in gratitude, which would be impossible in any case, given the abundance of the gift to which it would have to respond.[60] The self must receive itself as a gift, which sets aside its obsession with existence and place: "God gives place to what cannot yet receive because it is not yet there, not having by itself and for itself either a *here* or a *there*, either *self* or *Being*." Thus, "the question of my Being falls under the gift, before ontology fixes and freezes it in an illusory persistence."[61] I find myself always already given, as gift or gifted, but unable to respond or receive in due measure.[62] Gratitude, thus, remains fundamentally and by definition impossible. Despite Marion's emphasis on the abundant generosity of the Creator's giving, this is not a discussion about the existence given in creation; instead, being and giving are read in opposition to each other. Marion's account should at the very least make us hesitate to associate giving and existence too quickly.

3 Steinbock and Giving as Interpersonal Loving

Anthony Steinbock criticizes both Derrida and Marion in his recent *It's Not about the Gift*, which traces various accounts of givenness and of the gift. Ultimately, it is "not about the gift" for him, because it is instead about the interpersonal relation within which the gift appears: "The 'subject' does indeed not give or receive a gift because it's not about the subject and it is not about aiming at a gift; rather, it concerns the interpersonal nexus in which a gift appears as such and can only appear as such."[63] He judges Heidegger as incapable of thinking about loving in the context of giving and accuses Michel Henry's account of life and forgetfulness of idolatry.[64] Interestingly, Henry probably comes closest to something like a relationship between the gift and existence, because it is Life that gives everything for him.[65] Steinbock argues, however, that the lack of individuation in Henry's account makes him incapable of interpreting acts of mercy or charity as occurring in the context of relations with others. He is also unable to articulate an account of the divine as self-giving love. Steinbock's summary of Derrida and Marion acknowledges the usefulness of their respective descriptions but suggests that they concern only a limited version of the gift and do not ultimately go far enough. He interprets Marion as going beyond Derrida, as outlining a way in which the economic exchange Derrida criticizes as always characteristic of gift-giving could be suspended at least to some extent. Marion thus provides a phenomenological description of the gift that escapes at least some of Derrida's criticism but is still too focused on the gift itself rather than the way in which giving concerns relations between persons.

Steinbock draws on Maimonides for an alternative approach. He outlines various "degrees" of giving that can be ascertained in Maimonides, the lowest of which correspond to Derrida's description of the gift. Slightly higher stages or forms of gift-giving he interprets as achieving Marion's suspension of economic reciprocity and as bracketing giver, recipient, or gift-object in a somewhat similar fashion by stressing the ideas of giving anonymously or without knowing the recipient. Maimonides goes beyond this, however, to an even higher level where gift-giving becomes interpersonal. The first of the three stages of this highest level "attempts to preserve the process of gift-giving while short-circuiting the structure in which shame or embarrassment might emerge."[66] The second stage of this level gives because of the requirement of "good deeds" (*mitsvah*), which is itself an expression of a religious command and thus presumes a relationship with the Holy One. Gift-giving thus finally becomes simply an expression of my love for God and the other. It is, then, no longer the gift that matters but the loving relation of which it is an expression. This highest stage finds its culmination in enabling the other to pursue a full life (rather than relying on my charity), thus it designates "the interpersonal relation that is oriented toward the liberation of other persons."[67] The concern is no longer with the gift but with loving as such.

Like the other thinkers examined here, Steinbock focuses in this text almost exclusively on the activity of giving and less on the phenomenon of receiving. Yet some hints on what that would entail can be ascertained from his description of humility, both in the first chapter of the book on giving and in his slightly earlier and more comprehensive analysis of what he calls the "moral emotions," such as pride, shame, repentance, hope, trust, or love.[68] Moral emotions are emotions that have an interpersonal dimension, that are in some way characteristic of living in the world with others or possibly even in response to others. They are not necessarily normative in any predetermined fashion, but "creative of interpersonal structures," something that surely can also be said of gratitude.[69]

Gratitude is, without doubt, an interpersonal emotion, inasmuch as it implies response to another and is offered to another. Steinbock distinguishes between moral emotions of self-givenness (such as pride, shame, and guilt), of possibility (such as repentance, hope, and despair), and of otherness (such as trust, loving, and humility). Gratitude is not one of the emotions under explicit consideration in this book, but his analysis is certainly relevant to it, and one might extrapolate implications for gratitude from his description of humility.

For example, his distinction between "founding" and "founded" emotions might suggest that while humility is a founding emotion because it concerns the core of the self and exists independently, gratitude is a "founded" emotion inasmuch as it is about a particular experience rather than the very being of the self and requires the giving and receiving of the gift to appear.[70] Yet just as in humility, in gratitude "I do not focus on myself" but "am too engaged in the reception of what is given to be concerned with myself."[71] In this respect, gratitude might be seen to require some elements of humility. In the context of his discussion of giving, Steinbock also focuses on humility, rather than generosity or gratitude, because they seem to imply an obligation and thus can be seen to have negative effects.[72] Humility is an emotion that is necessary for loving and can serve as the pathway to it. He distinguishes between an "experience of disequilibrium," as is the case for surprise, "diremptive experiences" that throw me "back on myself before another," such as shame, and moral emotions that open me toward another.[73] Humility is in this third category: Steinbock stresses that "humility is not only related to the way in which something is accepted or received, but it is also a way in which I receive myself in and through being other oriented and the way in which I receive Myself as having been given to myself prior to being able to choose myself."[74] Gratitude presumably would also fall into the third category inasmuch as it is oriented toward the other.

Steinbock identifies humility as a "religious" emotion, albeit not in a strictly confessional or theological sense.[75] While this might not be the case for ordinary, everyday gratitude, it might apply to the idea of being grateful for existence, if existence is taken as being granted by the divine or some (even nonreligious) cosmic giver. Similarly, while gratitude in the narrow sense may not "give me to myself" in a particular way or be directed at "the personal core of the individual," as Steinbock claims for humility, gratitude for existence would be much more fundamentally concerned with the self.[76] What Steinbock says about humility surely also applies to gratitude: "humility is relational and reveals me to Myself as not self-grounding." This is "expansive and interpersonal such that I accept myself from another, as accepting the givenness from another and the contributions from others to what I do and to who I am."[77] Gratitude, however, seems slightly more limited than humility, which is a more fundamental emotion, inasmuch as it affects who I am, while it is possible for gratitude to be limited to a particular situation, the concrete giving of a gift. Unlike humility, then, gratitude might not be as essentially connected to loving, which may explain why it can become a sort of obligation in some contexts, especially in those to which Derrida's account alludes. As regards their temporality, gratitude confirms the structure of expectation in a way that humility does not; that is to say, while humility expects nothing, especially no gratitude for one's acts, gratitude responds to a specific act of giving and thus "returns" it in some way, although this need not be sinister in the way in which Derrida at times seems to imply.[78] How might these preliminary extrapolations be pushed even further via a fuller phenomenological analysis of gratitude?

4 Conclusion: The Phenomenon of Gratitude

If in light of these seminal treatments of the gift, one were to investigate more fully the phenomenon of gratitude specifically, what might one suggest about its phenomenality? How does gratitude appear or manifest as a phenomenon? And would the specific gratitude for *existence* manifest in the same way as other kinds of gratitude? What is the "nature" or "essence" (i.e., the *Wesen*) of gratitude, not in the sense of an idealist notion of some elusive core abstracted from particular instantiations, but in the sense of distinguishing its nature or structure of appearing from that of other emotions or acts? Describing it as a phenomenon would surely reveal its interpersonal and responsive nature, even more fully than we could ascertain from extrapolating on Steinbock's account. Gratitude is generated by a prior something, usually a gift or given, even if no object is involved. That is, one could be grateful for another's help, time, kindness, consideration, and so forth. Gratitude has a specific target; one is grateful *for* something. Yet, gratitude responds not just to the "thing" that is given but to the person who gives it; it is thus other-directed in its very nature. Gratitude occurs in the context of, results from, maintains, and cultivates relations with another, but maybe in a more limited sense than loving, which is a more fundamental and more pervasive attitude to the other. Although gratitude may often manifest as a feeling or emotion, it is usually expressed concretely, often in words of thanks, sometimes in bodily acts such as an embrace or handshake, at times in other acts, such as doing something for someone out of gratitude for a prior service or gift. Gratitude is also characterized by a temporal delay: one expresses gratitude *after* receiving a gift. Even anticipatory gratitude assumes that the gift will have been given. The phenomenon of gratitude thus appears with the temporality of a directedness to the past.

The nature of gratitude as a phenomenon might emerge even more clearly if it is compared to other, similar or opposing, phenomena. Accordingly, although they are often linked in some way, gratitude is different from generosity in that it is a phenomenon of receiving rather than a phenomenon of giving, as one might designate generosity. Gratitude differs from its opposite, ingratitude, by recognizing or acknowledging a gift; it thus requires both the "knowledge" that a gift has been given and the posture of acknowledgment (which is partly why in some cases gratitude can come to feel obligatory or contrived), while ingratitude ignores the gift or possesses it without acknowledgment—maybe even without awareness—that it has been given as a gift. In this respect, one might say that gratitude has both an epistemic and a moral dimension: knowing that a gift has been given and assuming a particular posture toward it or, rather, its giver. Gratitude appears as an "affirmative" rather than a "rejecting" emotion, not just in the sense that it is generally felt as "positive" in a way that ingratitude appears as negative, but that it lies in its nature to affirm and respond to what has been given, while ingratitude rejects or ignores it, is incapable of affirming it or unwilling to do so.

Gratitude also changes the posture of the one who offers it. It is not a supplicating phenomenon in the way in which requesting a gift, such as an act of charity, might be, although it can be wrapped up with it, if gratitude is expected as response to the offering. That is, gratitude implies a kind of deference, the acknowledgment of a certain kind of "passivity" in response to the one who has performed the act of giving. The posture is receptive but in a way that allows at least an element of activity via the expression of gratitude. In that respect, the emotion or act can be experienced as a way to "even out" the debt that receiving the gift might seem to have incurred, to reciprocate the generosity of the other in some form, to put oneself in a relationship of response to the other that is not mere deference even if it acknowledges what the other has done for me. Gratitude is thus connected with humility and maybe also tempered by it, although it also opens itself to the possibility of humiliation, to the posture of receiving "charity." In this latter respect, it can appear as ambivalent, and Derrida's warnings are apposite also in regard to the phenomenon of gratitude.

What would it mean to apply this to one's existence? Can one or should one be "grateful" for existence? It would imply at the very least that existence must be understood as something given by someone or even as a sort of gift from someone. From whom? God? One's parents?[79] If God gives existence one would have to understand the world as creation, as wholly given by a divine giver. This could be an ontological or metaphysical claim, but it might also be a psychological or even normative claim, an issue of the posture one ought to take toward one's existence. On purely phenomenological terms it is not clear that there is anything in the phenomenality of existence, as existence, that requires experiencing it as a gift, but obviously this is hard to ascertain given that it is not a phenomenon among others but the phenomenon that makes the experience of all other phenomena possible in principle. Existence, as Heidegger might say, is a more than primordial phenomenon; it is the phenomenon—or maybe even the phenomenality—that grounds even the most primordial phenomena by enabling them to assume these particular structures. Nevertheless, existence certainly has at least some elements of givenness, even on purely phenomenological grounds, in the sense that it cannot be produced by oneself. One does not put oneself into existence, does not choose existence, does not even pick out a particular existence, although one could choose to end one's existence or to alter its structures at least to some extent. Surely Steinbock is right that accepting a gift requires humility and thus experiencing one's entire existence as such a gift could induce a fundamental humility to all of life. Yet, the stance this existence might entail would to a large extent depend on whether one experiences life as a gift or as a burden: Is it something granted generously and experienced as filled with comforts and joys or are we thrown into it, even "condemned" to it, and existence thus a cruel joke?[80]

Thus one might also ask what it would mean to feel *gratitude* for this existence one has ostensibly been given. The givenness of existence would have to be experienced as less than arbitrary, as not purely contingent, as having at its roots a kind of causality that ought to be acknowledged, that should be returned to someone in some fashion. Accordingly, in this case existence would have to manifest as not simply given but as given intentionally, given by another to whom one ought to respond. Life itself would also have to take on a more intentional character; it would be experienced not as mere happenstance, not as pure fate or luck, but instead as an existence given as a gift and thus as potentially having a particular meaning, even if that meaning were not easy to ascertain or would have to be worked out through one's life. Certainly it would be less easy—and surely more problematic—to throw it away. Suicide would have to be understood as a manifestation of ingratitude. Maybe a dissolute, aimless, or intentionally destructive life would have to be understood as a violation of the gift, as a fundamentally immoral stance toward existence?

One might also wonder what difference it would make to respond to one's existence in gratitude. Would it make one's existence manifest as happier, healthier, or better adjusted? Would one conduct one's life with a different posture if one were to live it with gratitude? Would difficulties, pain, or suffering that come our way be experienced as less cruel, as containing some sort of meaning? Would it affect one's overall emotional or psychological make-up to feel or even cultivate this particular emotion or stance? Could it become a fundamental *Befindlichkeit*—a way of "finding" oneself in the world that would ground and shape one's moods and attitudes? Would one respond differently to others because of this attitude or posture? Would it impose an obligation, render the person more passive than would otherwise be the case, turn one's life into a kind of response rather than an active taking charge—and would that be more or less desirable (positive? fundamental?) than a more assertive attitude to life that tries to own or possess it in more controlling fashion? One might wonder whether gratitude could be one of the primordial postures toward existence besides the angst Heidegger identifies. Would gratitude make us feel more at home in the world, if angst is what renders the world uncanny (*unheimlich*), not "at home"? Would this lead to a complacency that immerses us in the crowd and does not allow us to live our own lives or would it rather make possible a more robust being-with-others than the one Heidegger describes? Would such a stance mean that life cannot be owned or possessed but must always be lived more precariously, in a receptive rather than grasping posture? These are the directions in which a phenomenological analysis might point and that would have to be examined in detail for a fuller grasp of the phenomenon.

Notes

1 Hedwig Conrad-Martius explicitly criticizes Heidegger on this point, claiming that such a restriction makes humans tantamount to the divine, inasmuch as their "essence" becomes defined by their existence, and that existence (*Dasein*) ought to be used more widely for all living beings, including animals and plants. See Conrad-Martius (1957) and her essay "Phenomenology and Speculation" (1965: 370–84).
2 For finding ourselves in an "environment" (*Umwelt*), see *Sein und Zeit*, §15–16, for "thrownness" see §29 and §38, for not being at home (*Unzuhause* and *Unheimlichkeit*), see §40. Heidegger (1993).
3 See the sixth chapter of the first part (for angst) and the first chapter of the second part (for death) of *Being and Time*.

4 See the second chapter of the second part of *Being and Time*.
5 This is greatly exacerbated by the misleading English translation of "authenticity" and "inauthenticity" (for *Eigentlichkeit* und *Uneigentlichkeit*, respectively), in which it is almost impossible not to hear normative connotations or at least a censure of inauthenticity. The German *eigentlich* just means "really," "truly," "in fact" and contains the word for "own" (*eigen*), which is what Heidegger emphasizes. To live *eigentlich* is to own oneself, and grasping one's death is the ownmost (*eigenste*) possibility for doing so. But Heidegger's dismissive way of depicting our losing ourselves in the crowd (§27), drifting along with it in self-forgetting (§35, §51–2), becoming wrapped up in curiosity for the newest thing (§36), and being otherwise merely "fallen" into existence (§38) rather than grasping it decisively and owning it with determination (§53) surely gives the impression that the latter is to be far preferred over the former. One should also note that *Erschlossenheit* has connotations of conquering in the sense of "opening up" a new territory, and *Entschlossenheit* certainly connotes decisiveness and implies a sense of taking control. It was Lévinas who accused Heidegger of a "virile" conception of death, although for Lévinas existence is a burden we cannot escape even far more so than for Heidegger, precisely because the fundamental question for Lévinas is not my own death but the death of the other—and thus my continued existence in face of the other's death (especially survival after the Shoah). This is already suggested in his early essay "On Escape" (Lévinas 2003) and much more fully explored in *Existence and Existents* and *Time and the Other* (Lévinas 2001, 1987).
6 See Heidegger (2007).
7 See especially his "Memorial Address" for the composer Conradin Kreutzer, but also many other texts from the same time period. (English translation in Heidegger 1969.) Anthony Steinbock thinks that Heidegger's thinking about givenness has "disastrous consequences," especially because he misses the interpersonal relation and does not think the uniqueness of the human person (Steinbock 2018: 23, 46). The argument is worked out fully in chapter two of the book, which also reviews Heidegger's thinking about the *es gibt* and the *Ereignis*.
8 Here also Lévinas disagrees vigorously and denies all the "positive" connotations of gratitude with which Heidegger seeks to endow the term. French uses yet another auxiliary verb for the same expression, namely *avoir* ("to have"). The *il y a*, which Lévinas employs to translate *es gibt* (i.e., also "there is" but without either "being" or "giving"), is a scary, haunting, unsettling, even terrorizing, echoing absence in the dead of night when plagued by insomnia, no generous giving. See Lévinas (2001: 51–60; 1987: 44–51).
9 Mauss (1990).
10 For a quite different discussion by an anthropologist and sociologist, see Hénaff (2010, 2020). The latter text includes a chapter on Derrida (chapter 1), one on Lévinas (chapter 3), and one on Marion (chapter 5).

11 Derrida (1992).
12 Steinbock describes this as follows: "This is not to say that 'there is' no gift; rather, if there is a gift, it must be the experience of the impossible. Accordingly, the gift 'as such' is impossible; it is not merely an impossible experience, but the experience of the impossible." (Steinbock, 2018: 104).
13 See Derrida and Dufourmantelle (2000, also Derrida, 2000: 3–18).
14 Derrida (1995).
15 See, for example, Derrida (2001a).
16 On Greek, Roman, and Christian notions of grace and their relation to the gift, see chapter 7 of Hénaff (2010: 241–94).
17 Ricœur (2004: 479–86). See also Hénaff's discussion of Ricœur in chapter 6 of Hénaff (2020).
18 For Jankélévitch (2005), it is the gift of an abundant or excessive love that "outweighs" in some form the abundant or excessive evil that calls for punishment or retribution. Both the evil—in his case, especially that of the Shoah—and the notion of love exceed any measurable boundaries.
19 Aside from Derrida (2001a), see also Derrida (2001b: 21–51; 2004: 111–56; 2019, 2020).
20 Ricœur (2004: 489–93).
21 He already spoke of giving and loving as superior to being (and more appropriate language for the divine) in Marion (1991), especially "The Present and the Gift" (161–82) and Marion (2002b), especially "The Gift of a Presence" (124–52). The original French publications (1982 and 1986, respectively) precede the publication of Derrida's *Donner le temps* (1991; *Donner la mort* was published in 1999). Derrida did, however, lecture on the topic of the gift at the École Normale roughly at the same time as Marion's writing, so Marion would certainly have been aware of this, although he was teaching in Poitiers at the time. For a comparison of Marion and Derrida on the gift, see Alvis (2016).
22 Marion, "Sketch of a Phenomenological Concept of the Gift," originally published 1994 and retranslated in *The Visible and the Revealed* (2008: 80–100). See also Marion (2002a, especially Part II, 71–118) and (2015, especially chapters III and IV, 51–154). (Both chapters are revisions of earlier pieces that have also appeared separately.) I have traced the progression of Marion's thinking about the gift more fully in chapter 5 of my *Degrees of Givenness* (Gschwandtner, 2014: 124–45).
23 He responds to this objection in several places. In the first chapter of *In Excess*, for example, he insists that "the givenness evoked here only belongs to phenomenology and thus depends on the reduction in its very certitude, that is to say, it puts in parentheses all transcendence, including that of God." The translation of Husserl's *Gegebenheit* is not "illicit" because "givenness does not indicate so much here the origin of the given as its phenomenological status. . . . givenness characterizes the given as without cause, origin, and identifiable antecedent, far from assigning them

to it.... givenness does not submit the given to a transcendent condition, but rather frees it from that condition." Marion (2002c: 23–4, 25). See also Marion (2002a: 66–8).

24 See especially Marion (2002a: 7–70; 2002c: 1–29).

25 Marion does, in fact, often stress this "self" of the phenomenon. For example: "Let me suggest that the phenomenality of givenness lets us detect the 'self' of the phenomenon.... Such a 'self' consists in the gap that distinguishes and connects the arising (givenness) to its given. What rises into appearing does so under the pressure of givenness and laden with this move. The appearing of the phenomenon is not imposed in reality because it already has the rank of object or being; rather, it holds these (or other) ranks because its appearing comes forward beneath the authority of a givenness that pulsates and posits in it. To show oneself by oneself demands a 'self.' It comes only from the givenness that operates the given and that tinges it with a phenomenological mark, the very arising toward visibility. The phenomenon can and must show *itself*, but solely because it gives *itself.*" Marion (2002a: 70).

26 This is worked out most fully in Marion (2002a: Part III, 119–78).

27 A conclusion drawn most fully at the end of Part IV of Marion (2002a: 245–7; see also 117–18), after introducing the saturated phenomenon, but a claim that pervades Marion's subsequent writing.

28 This is first developed in the "Sketch" and worked out most fully in Part II of Marion (2002a: 71–118).

29 Marion (2002a: 113). He concludes that a truly phenomenological account escapes the "natural attitude," which he identifies with the situation of economic exchange, in which he thinks Mauss and Derrida remain confined. Marion (2002a: 114).

30 "The visible arrives to the I as a gift and, reciprocally, because the phenomenon arises, offers itself, rises toward itself—and takes form in it" (Marion 2002a: 117). "The gift in its three moments, then, can be reduced to givenness in it. It is bestowed all the better when it lacks one of the terms of reciprocity and is freed from what the economy claimed to downgrade it to in each instance: the quid pro quo relation of exchange" (Marion 2015: 97).

31 Marion (2015: 93–103).

32 Marion (2015: 106–14).

33 Marion (2015: chapter IV, 115–54).

34 Marion (2015: 131–2).

35 Marion (2015: 140–7).

36 Marion (2015: 147–54). For the earlier analysis that stresses the undoing of "being" in the parable, see Marion (1991: 95–102). Heidegger also comments a couple of times on the Greek connotation of *ousia* as property (reproduced to some extent in German by the term *Anwesen*, which can refer to a large farm or other property).

37 Marion (2015: 153–4).

38 Especially Marion (2002a: Part I, 248–319). L'adonné is translated in *Being Given*, somewhat unhappily, as "the gifted," but means something like "devoted," "given over to," even "addicted." Marion seeks to overcome the metaphysical subject by conceiving a self that would no longer be in control, not impose parameters on the phenomenon, not even constitute it in intentionality, but instead serve as the "screen" of its manifestation, as the mere recipient of its self-giving. Thus the self becomes abandoned to the abundant gift. See also Marion (2002c: 44–9), which tries to negotiate the balance between pure passivity and a kind of active receptivity.

39 Marion (2007), especially 174–5, 184–95, 206–22. Marion insists here, as he had already done in *God without Being*, that loving "does not belong to the horizon of being" (Marion 1991: 193). See also Marion (2002b: 71–101, 153–69; 2017: 116–22).

40 Marion (2002c: 49–53), for example: "the painter renders visible as a phenomenon what no one had ever seen before, because he or she manages, being the first to do that every time, to resist the given enough to get it to show *itself*" (51). See also "What Gives," chapter II in: Marion (2004: 24–45) (the first version of the French was published in 1986).

41 To give with *l'abandon* means to give with abundance, with abandon, and with abandonment; Marion often exploits this dual meaning of the term, thus the phenomenon is given "abundantly" precisely by being fully "abandoned" to whatever the recipient may do with it, including the possibility of ignoring or squashing it or, in either case, failing to phenomenalize it fully. Thus what is given for Marion is always characterized by an essential generosity.

42 Marion (2017: 111–15). See also Marion (2008: 62).

43 Marion (2017: 132).

44 Marion (2017: 134).

45 Marion (2016).

46 Marion (1981/1991/2009).

47 Marion (2008: 49–65).

48 This extends to our receptivity: "The Trinity becomes the place of the uncovering as much as its stake: we can see that which shows itself only by receiving it as it gives itself, that is, only be receiving ourselves from the one who gives himself, and who gives . . . everything, including our seeing it" (Marion 2016: 88).

49 Marion (2016: 112–13). He also stresses, yet again, the characteristic of abandonment that is essential to the phenomenality of the gift: "What is proper to the gift consists in the fact that the more it is perfectly accomplished, and thus the more it delivers with perfect abandonment and without return what it gives—the gift datum irreversibly placed at the recipient's disposition—the more the giver and with him the process of the gift must themselves withdraw from presence, disappear from the ontic (or even objective) evidence of the gift given, fade away from the scene of the gift, bereft now of the very given gift that opened it" (Marion 2016: 114).

50 Marion (1991: 132–5).
51 Marion (1991: 138).
52 Marion (2017: 3–13, 66–75).
53 Marion (2015: 15–26).
54 Marion (2015: 31, 17) (with a reference to Heidegger's *Vorhandenheit* in the footnote). He suggests that this ontological reductionism becomes especially visible in the treatment of undocumented persons (2015: 33–5).
55 "I recognize myself only by recognizing myself *as* a 'God,' just as one recognizes a Cézanne as a 'Cézanne'" (Marion 2015: 41).
56 Marion (2015: 50).
57 Marion (2012: 230–7). For an attempt to read creation as "gift" (for ecological purposes), see Manolopoulos (2009).
58 Marion (2012: 236). See also the analysis of nothingness on 245–7.
59 Marion (2012: 243–52). He summarizes this as follows: "So, the creature's place is not found in itself but always in God, such that the place for the *confessio* of God is determined by and in God, to such an extent that creation consists only in the opening of the place of *confessio*. It is hence a universal rule" (2012: 252). He also stresses here again the essential invisibility and indefinability of the human as likeness of the divine (Marion 2012: 252–60).
60 He contrasts "being" and "loving" here again by saying: "Not only does the question never consist in to be or not to be, for it only concerns loving, but the question of love never consists in loving or not loving since as ultimately possibility, it demands of me, with neither break nor vacation, that I love no matter what" (Marion 2012: 272). This alludes also to the quip in his preface to the English translation of *God without Being*: "But with respect to Being, does God have to behave like Hamlet?" (Marion 1991: xx).
61 Marion (2012: 286, 287).
62 Marion (2012: 288).
63 Steinbock (2018: 22).
64 Chapters 2 and 3 of Steinbock (2018), respectively. Chapter 4 is on the "poor phenomenon" in Marion and the first part of chapter 5 articulates the critique of Derrida and Marion on the gift.
65 See, for example, Henry (2003). Henry does not, however, explicitly address either the topic of the gift or of gratitude.
66 Steinbock (2018: 118–19).
67 Steinbock (2018: 123).
68 Steinbock (2014).
69 Steinbock (2014: 278).
70 Steinbock (2014: 232–3). See also 7–11.
71 Steinbock (2014: 237).
72 Steinbock (2018: x). The first chapter is on surprise and humility, 1–23.

73 Steinbock (2018: 15–18). He argues that via surprise I turn affectively toward the experience; I am not merely passive but respond in some fashion (2018: 11–12). Its valence can be both positive and negative (2018: 13–14); presumably in the case of a gift the positive valence would be more likely. Surprise is at work in the gift, but surprise itself is not a moral emotion, because it is not essentially interpersonal (2018: 14–15).
74 Steinbock (2018: 19).
75 Steinbock (2014: 238).
76 Steinbock (2014: 240, 246).
77 Steinbock (2018: 18).
78 Steinbock (2014: 250). Steinbock argues that "humility has a rich temporality peculiar to it and is irreducible to a presentation, retention, and expectation. I qualify these temporal modes of givenness as presence-at which is expressed as a being thankful for, as ante-memorial reception, and as accepting ahead, reflected in devotion" (2014: 257–8). This seems to suggest that gratitude would be included in humility in some form, at least in regard to temporality.
79 On this latter idea, see Marion's analysis of paternity as an example of gift-giving: Marion (2002a: 300–2; 2015: 93–103).
80 It is worth remembering here Lévinas' account of existence as a burden and the descriptions of Camus and Sartre that often imply that existence is cruel and meaningless. (Already Hobbes spoke of life as "cruel, nasty, brutish, and short." Perhaps the experience of one's existence is in some measure correlated to whether life is conceived or experienced in terms of scarcity or abundance.)

References

Alvis, Jason. (2016). *Marion and Derrida on the Gift and Desire: Debating the Generosity of Things*. Dordrecht: Springer.

Conrad-Martius, Hedwig. (1957). *Das Sein*. Munich: Kösel Verlag.

Conrad-Martius, Hedwig. (1965). *Schriften zur Philosophy*. Vol. 3. Munich: Kösel Verlag.

Derrida, Jacques. (1992). *Given Time I: Counterfeit Money*, trans. Peggy Kamuf. Chicago, IL: University of Chicago Press.

Derrida, Jacques. (1995). *The Gift of Death*, trans. David Willis. Chicago, IL: University of Chicago Press.

Derrida, Jacques. (2000). "Hospitality." *Angelaki: Journal of the Theoretical Humanities*, 5 (3): 3–18.

Derrida, Jacques. (2001a). *On Cosmopolitanism and Forgiveness*. London: Routledge.

Derrida, Jacques. (2001b). "To Forgive: The Unforgiveable and the Imprescriptible." In John D. Caputo, Mark Dooley, and Michael J. Scanlon (eds.), *Questioning God*, 21–51. Bloomington, IN: Indiana University Press.

Derrida, Jacques. (2004). "*Versöhnung, Ubuntu,* Pardon: Quel Genre?" *Le Genre humain*, 43: 111–56.
Derrida, Jacques. (2019). *Le parjure et le pardon, vol. 1: Séminaire (1997–1998)*. Paris: Seuil.
Derrida, Jacques. (2020). *Le parjure et le pardon, vol. 2: Séminaire (1998–1999)*. Paris: Seuil.
Derrida, Jacques, and Anne Dufourmantelle. (2000). *Of Hospitality*. Stanford: Stanford University Press.
Gschwandtner, Christina M. (2014). *Degrees of Givenness: On Saturation in Jean-Luc Marion*. Bloomington, IN: Indiana University Press.
Heidegger, Martin. (1993). *Sein und Zeit* (Tübingen: Max Niemeyer, originally 1927), translated by John Macquarrie and Edward Robinson as *Being and Time*. New York: Harper & Row, 1962.
Heidegger, Martin. (1969). *Discourse in Thinking*, trans. John M. Anderson. New York: Harper & Row.
Heidegger, Martin. (2007). *Zur Sache des Denkens*. In vol. 14 of the *Gesamtausgabe*, ed. Friedrich-Wilhelm von Hermann. Frankfurt/M: Vittorio Klostermann.
Hénaff, Marcel. (2010). *The Price of Truth: Gift, Money, and Philosophy*, trans. Jean-Louis Morhange. Stanford: Stanford University Press.
Hénaff, Marcel. (2020). *The Philosophers' Gift: Reexamining Reciprocity*, trans. Jean-Louis Morange. New York: Fordham University Press.
Henry, Michel. (2003). *I am the Truth: Toward a Philosophy of Christianity*, trans. Susan Emanuel. Stanford: Stanford University Press.
Jankélévitch, Vladimir. (2005). *Forgiveness*, trans. Andrew Kelley. Chicago, IL: University of Chicago Press.
Lévinas, Emmanuel. (2003). *On Escape*, trans. Bettina Bergo. Stanford, CA: Stanford University Press
Lévinas, Emmanuel. (2001). *Existence and Existents*, trans. Alphonso Lingis. Pittsburgh, PA: Duquesne University Press.
Lévinas, Emmanuel. (1987). *Time and the Other*, trans. Richard A. Cohen. Pittsburgh: Duquesne University Press.
Manolopoulos, Mark. (2009). *If Creation is a Gift*. Albany, NY: State University of New York Press.
Marion, Jean-Luc. (1981/1991/2009). *Sur la théologie blanche de Descartes: Analogie, création des vérités éternelles, fondement*. Paris: Presses Universitaires de France.
Marion, Jean-Luc. (1991). *God without Being*, trans. Thomas A. Carlson. Chicago, IL: University of Chicago Press.
Marion, Jean-Luc. (2002a). *Being Given: Toward a Phenomenology of Givenness*, trans. Jeffrey L. Kosky. Stanford, CA: Stanford University Press.
Marion, Jean-Luc. (2002b). *Prolegomena to Charity*, trans. Stephen E. Lewis. New York: Fordham University Press.

Marion, Jean-Luc. (2002c). *In Excess: Studies of Saturated Phenomena*, trans. Robyn Horner and Vincent Carraud. New York: Fordham University Press.

Marion, Jean-Luc. (2016). *Givenness and Revelation*, trans. Stephen E. Lewis. Oxford: Oxford University Press.

Marion, Jean-Luc. (2004). *The Crossing of the Visible*, trans. James K. A. Smith. Stanford, CA: Stanford University Press.

Marion, Jean-Luc. (2007). *The Erotic Phenomenon*, trans. Stephen E. Lewis. Chicago, IL: University of Chicago Press.

Marion, Jean-Luc. (2008). *The Visible and the Revealed*. New York: Fordham University Press.

Marion, Jean-Luc. (2012). *In the Self's Place: The Approach of Saint Augustine*, trans. Jeffrey L. Kosky. Stanford, CA: Stanford University Press.

Marion, Jean-Luc. (2015). *Negative Certainties*, trans. Stephen E. Lewis. Chicago, IL: University of Chicago Press.

Marion, Jean-Luc. (2017). *Believing in Order to See*. New York: Fordham University Press.

Mauss, Marcel. (1990). *The Gift: The Form and Reason for Exchange in Archaic Societies*, trans. W. D. Halls. New York: W. W. Norton.

Ricœur, Paul. (2004). *Memory, History, Forgetting*, trans. Kathleen Blamey and David Pellauer. Chicago, IL: University of Chicago Press.

Steinbock, Anthony. (2014). *Moral Emotions: Reclaiming the Evidence of the Heart*. Evanston, IL: Northwestern University Press.

Steinbock, Anthony. (2018). *It's Not About the Gift: From Givenness to Loving*. London: Rowman & Littlefield.

5

Gratitude for Life-force in African Philosophy

Thaddeus Metz

1 Introducing African Philosophy of Religion

For all we can tell, every long-standing culture has had philosophy of religion, at least if "religion" is taken broadly enough and does not require postulation of a deity as per Buddhism and Confucianism. However, in the case of the African tradition, it is only recently that such thought has been put down in writing. Until the twentieth century, a very large majority of indigenous sub-Saharan peoples had used oral means of communication to the exclusion of the written word. Although Europeans and Arabs had brought writing hundreds of years ago to some of the continent, it was not often used to recount, interpret, or develop African cultures, instead usually deployed to impart Christianity, Islam, and other exogenous worldviews. However, beginning in earnest in the 1960s, colonialism began to wane, Africans started to attend universities, and literacy spread. Consider that it was only in 1969 that the locus classicus of African philosophy of religion appeared, namely, the first edition of John S. Mbiti's *African Religions and Philosophy*, which largely expounds the salient religious and philosophical ideas Mbiti encountered upon engaging with some 300 sub-Saharan peoples about their worldviews.

In the absence of a large written corpus, probably combined with ignorance and disinterest (if not arrogance) on the part of other philosophers around the world, African philosophy of religion lacks a real presence in international books and journals. That is unfortunate since we can expect any culture that has existed for many centuries to have some insight into the human condition. In the case of Traditional African Religion, as it is often labeled by expositors and adherents, it turns out to be well understood as a form of monotheism different from what one encounters in the Abrahamic faiths of Judaism, Christianity, and Islam. How many philosophers beyond the continent are aware that the African tradition characteristically posits the existence of a God who is self-aware, lives in an imperceptible realm, created the perceptible universe, and sustains the lives of everyone in it?

Although there are these broad similarities between the African God[1] and the Abrahamic God, there are also substantial differences between them in respect of God's nature, human nature, and the sort of afterlife for which to hope,[2] and hence, in effect, regarding what it is to be the highest being, what our less than highest essence is, and what the highest state of existence is that we beings could obtain. Cross-cultural comparisons and, more than that, debates are warranted.[3]

However, in this chapter I spend more time addressing elements of African philosophy of religion in their own right, specifically considering the intellectual resources it offers in support of the judgment common among indigenous sub-Saharans that life is a gift from God. "The cock drinking water raises its head to God in thankfulness" is an influential proverb of the Akan people in Ghana.[4] It is the epigraph on the very first page of a book about African religion by Laurenti Magesa,[5] a Tanzanian theologian who is one of the most important philosophers of religion in the post-Mbiti era. In the following, I draw on works by Mbiti, Magesa, and other literate African thinkers to construct a formal argument for the conclusion that we have reason to be thankful to God, not merely for the availability of water and other resources needed for life, but also, and in the first instance, for life itself. The following quotations are not unusual to encounter in works addressing African religio-philosophical ideas:

> In African societies, emphasis is put on vitality. Life is regarded as the most precious gift of God.[6]
>
> (I)t is believed in African Traditional Religions that a person is created by God.... It is equally believed that life is the highest gift of God to humanity.[7]
>
> Africans see God as being the Creator. The vital force manifested by the world in the generation of new life to whom everybody relates is God Himself.... Life is a gift from the Creator, the greatest of all gifts.[8]
>
> At the centre of traditional African morality is human life. Africans have a sacred reverence for life, for it is believed to be the greatest of God's gifts to humans.[9]

These quotations are descriptive reports of characteristically African beliefs, whereas in this chapter I am particularly keen to address what merits belief. Supposing God exists, should we regard life as God's most precious, highest, or greatest gift to us? If so, should we be thankful to God for it? In the following I present and evaluate an argument that draws on characteristically African ideas in support of the conclusion that we should be thankful to God for having given us the gift of intense and sophisticated life-force, roughly an imperceptible, divine energy that constitutes our selves and bestows a dignity on us that is lacking in the rest of the perceptible world on earth.

One way of assessing the argument would be to test its metaphysical claims, for example, that God as understood in the African tradition exists, that God created us, that our selves are constituted by life-force, and so on. However, I instead focus on the argument's axiological claims, so as to enrich our understanding of what a salient part of the African tradition's approach to value is and how philosophically attractive it might be. Specifically, I defend the argument from several ways of objecting to the idea that being given a dignity can provide reason to be thankful.

In the following, I begin by reconstructing an African religio-philosophical argument for thinking that we should express gratitude to God for our dignity-conferring life-force (Section 2), after which I critically discuss some value-theoretic components of the argument (Section 3). For example, I respond to the objections that having an inherent dignity is not a benefit of a sort warranting gratitude and that those with bad lives have no reason to be grateful. I conclude roughly that while those with unavoidably bad lives indeed have some reason to be disappointed about the quality of their life, that is compatible with there also being some reason for them to express gratitude for their dignified life-force. I conclude the chapter by considering the prospects for secularizing the African position (Section 4), so that there might be reasons to be thankful for one's dignity in respect of merely perceptible conditions, supposing we doubt the contested metaphysical claims that God and life-force exist.

2 Life-force as God's Gift to Us

In this section I expound an argument for the conclusion that we have reason to be grateful and act gratefully toward God for our existence. The broad form of the argument is simple: God has given us a life-force that constitutes our selves and our dignity; if God has given us a life-force that constitutes our selves and our dignity, then we have reason to express gratitude to God for our existence; therefore, we have reason to express gratitude to God for our existence. I here provide some prima facie motivation for the argument's key axiological claims but leave consideration of objections to them for the following section.

Consider the premise that God has given us a life-force that constitutes our selves and our dignity, focusing, first, on the nature of God and God's creation.

Earlier I noted that the characteristically African conception of God shares several features with the Abrahamic view of God. In particular, for both, God is understood to be a person living in an imperceptible realm who is responsible for the form of the perceptible realm and hence the existence of life within it. Now, there are philosophically important differences between these monotheistic traditions in the way God is conceived, with just two being the fact that, for many African peoples, God exists in a location and did not create matter out of nothing.[10] However, these differences do not seem to bear on the present rationale for expressing gratitude to God, and so I set them aside. I instead address other differences between the two traditions that do affect our understanding of why we might have reason to express thanks to our creator.

One difference is that African philosophers and religionists often conceive of God as the ultimate source of life-force and think of every concrete object that exists as composed of (or at least imbued with) life-force. This metaphysical worldview involves a force rather than object ontology.[11] That is, instead of the ultimate nature of reality being held to consist of different substances, which might persist independently of each other (particularly in respect of dualist worldviews), in the African tradition it is much more common to encounter the view that what exists is at bottom a web of interdependent energies. We are to think of stars, trees, cats, and humans ultimately not as things but, rather, as forces, ones that constantly interact not only with other perceptible forces but also with imperceptible ones such as God, lesser divinities, and ancestors.

Furthermore, all forces are commonly thought to be (or at least be imbued with) vitality, an offshoot of God conceived essentially as *bios* (life), not so much *logos* (reason). From this perspective, even apparently inanimate things such as rocks have divine energies in them, albeit ones that are low in terms of might and complexity.[12] "Life-force varies quantitatively (in terms of growth and strength) and qualitatively (in terms of intelligence and will)."[13] It is frequently suggested that there is a hierarchy or great chain of being in the world,[14] such that rocks are at the bottom for having the least quantity or poorest quality of life-force. Plants are thought to have a greater life-force than rocks, say, for being capable of reproduction and movement. Animals have a greater one than plants, for example, for being capable of self-motion and some pattern-making (consider a bird's nest or beaver's dam). Finally, "(o)ver all visible beings, in terms of intensity of vital force, stands humanity,"[15] particularly for having self-awareness and genuine creativity.[16]

With regard to humans, the usual thought among indigenous Africans is not that we have a soul, that is, an immortal, spiritual substance that has come from

God, but instead a long-lasting, imperceptible life-force that has come from God. The person or self is (or at least is constituted by) an intense and complex divine energy that is for a time embodied but that will survive the death of its body and continue to reside on Earth as an invisible "living-dead," at least for a time. More specifically, it is commonly thought that one's disembodied self, metaphysically dependent on other forces, will persist for about four or five generations, which is about as long as descendants engage with one. Upon the sixth generation or so, a family typically no longer remembers its living-dead relatives and so no longer provides them sustaining energy, causing their selves to disintegrate and die.[17]

In respect of those African thinkers who maintain that there is a hierarchical order of beings in terms of life-force, most hold that final value tracks the hierarchy. That is, the stronger or more sophisticated the life-force something has, the more goodness for its own sake it has because of that.

> Life implies the existence and interaction of mystical powers in the universe. Conversely, the continuous blending of mystical powers in the universe makes life possible. Thus, "reality is seen and judged especially from its dynamic aspects closely related to life. The farther a being is from these elements, the more unreal and valueless it is conceived to be."[18]

This approach grounds an environmentalism according to which even landscapes and rivers have a moral status, that is, have a value such as to be capable of being wronged in themselves.[19] Although so-called inanimate objects do morally matter from this perspective for having vital force in them, biologically living beings matter much more. Indeed, human beings matter the most (of the class of perceptible forces). Even if every perceptible force has some noninstrumental value, "all life forces, that is, all creation, are intended to serve and enhance the life force of the human person and society."[20] As Placide Tempels, a Belgian missionary often credited with being the first European to use the word "philosophy" to characterize African thought, remarks of the views of Bantu-speaking peoples:

> Life belongs to God. It is he who summons it into being, strengthens and preserves it. His great and holy gift to men is the gift of life. Other creatures which, according to Bantu ideas, are lower or higher vital forces, exist in the divine plan only to maintain and cherish the vital gift made to man.[21]

Implicit in this passage is the idea that ancestors, who have a higher vital force than us, are nonetheless morally obligated to help human beings, insofar as the ancestors once themselves took a human form and have been, and continue to be, part of a family.

African thinkers frequently maintain that, because of the divine spark in us, that is, the vital energy that has come from God and is stronger or more complex than any other life-force in the visible realm, we have a dignity, a superlative noninstrumental value inhering in our nature. Here is one clear statement of this view, held by the Akan people in Ghana:

> (A) person is the result of the union of three elements.... The first, the *okra*... is supposed to be an actual speck of God that he gives out of himself as a gift of life along with a specific destiny. By virtue of possessing an *okra*, a divine element, every person has an intrinsic value, the same in each.... Associated with this value is a concept of human dignity, which implies that every human being is entitled in an equal measure to a certain basic respect.[22]

Here is yet another mention of life being a gift from God--or more carefully *of* God. For the African tradition, human life is not merely a biological process but also a divine force that constitutes our identity, is greater than what one encounters in the animal, vegetable, and mineral kingdoms, and is what confers on us a dignity. While African peoples commonly think that God has given us what we need to sustain our lives and to flourish,[23] in the first instance and most importantly it is life itself, that is, our existence as persons, that is God's precious, highest, greatest, or holy gift to us.

The second major premise of the argument is that if God has given us a life-force that constitutes our dignity, then we have reason to express gratitude to God for our existence. The quintessential case in which gratitude is apt is when an agent intentionally and voluntarily bestows a good on someone that the latter was not entitled to receive from the former and does not do so merely in the expectation of long-term gain. There is substantial debate about not only how far to extend the concept of gratitude, for example, whether it is possible to be thankful without reference to any beneficiary,[24] but also when gratitude is appropriate, for example, whether it is appropriate to be thankful to an agent who did not intentionally bestow a benefit on the one benefited.[25] However, the African conception of human life-force as a gift from God that merits thanks appears to lie squarely within both the conceptual and normative cores of gratitude: God is an agent who aimed to create us and freely did so; our creation is a high final good, specifically a matter of having the greatest life-force in the perceptible realm, which is dignity-conferring; we were not entitled to have been created by God (indeed could not have been entitled to that, given our prior nonexistence); and then presumably God did not create us merely so that, say, God could demand a favor from us down the road.

When I say that "gratitude is appropriate" or that "we have reason to be thankful" or the like, I mean two things. On the one hand, it is morally *right* that we *act* in certain ways. For instance, we should do things such as accept God's gift of life (i.e., not commit suicide), treat our gift well, communicate thanks to God, and be willing to do God's bidding. We owe God a debt of gratitude for our existence as human persons, and it would be wrong not to pay one's debt in these behavioral ways. On the other hand, it is also *virtuous* to *be* grateful, that is, to judge that one has received a benefit from God *qua* agent and to feel positive emotions such as goodwill toward one's benefactor and gladness about having been God's beneficiary.

So defined, one could act in grateful ways without being grateful, and one could also be grateful without acting in grateful ways. Given the prominence in Traditional African Religion of not only prayers but also offerings and sacrifices,[26] it is natural to suggest that, according to it, both acting gratefully and being grateful are expected. Indeed, the ideal is surely to act gratefully in an outward manner toward God to *express* the inner gratitude one has for having been created with a dignified nature.

I note that it is not clear that a requirement to be grateful and to act gratefully follows from the sort of vitalist *morality* that is in the African tradition standardly paired with the vitalist account of *final value* articulated earlier. Those who hold that we have a dignity by virtue of our intense and sophisticated life-force usually hold the moral principle that what is right is what produces life-force and what is wrong reduces it. Consider, for instance, these remarks from African theologians whom I have already quoted in this chapter:[27]

> I want to address more specifically the question of the general moral/ethical consciousness that the African view of the world engenders. . . . (I)n no way is any thought, word or act understood except in terms of good and bad, in the sense that such an attitude or behavior either enhances or diminishes life.[28]

> In African societies life-force is the meaning of being and the ultimate goal of anyone is to acquire life and live happily. . . . A person is good in so far as he or she promotes, supports or protects his or her life force and the life-force of his or her neighbours. Alternatively, a person is bad or evil in as much as he or she undermines or destroys this life-force.[29]

The problem is that expressing gratitude does not seem to serve the function of promoting life-force in others, at least not reliably, and so does not seem to be morally prescribed when it is intuitively apt. For one, *being* grateful, for example, feeling certain ways, is not likely to foster life-force in a benefactor more than merely *acting* gratefully toward him. For another, when it comes to a divine benefactor, God would already have the maximum quantity and highest quality of life-force; we could not improve it.

In reply, some would argue that expressing gratitude to God and any lesser divinities for past acts would make it more likely that these agents would do all the more to support *one's own* life-force down the road, where they would know if one did not actually exhibit the virtue.[30] Yet even if that were true, that function is an implausible explanation of why gratitude is morally appropriate. Intuitively one has ethical reason both to be grateful and to act gratefully simply because one has already been a beneficiary, not merely because one hopes to be a beneficiary again in the future. Even if one's motive for expressing gratitude were not to obtain more life-force, it is still philosophically dubious to suppose that expressing gratitude is morally appropriate if and only if doing so would serve that function.

Here is another way to put the point: God would be disinclined to promote one's life-force in the future because God would judge one's ingratitude to be wrong. That is the converse of the claim that one's ingratitude would be wrong because it would fail to get God to promote one's life-force.

It might be that a shift away from a teleological orientation of promoting life-force and toward a deontological one of honoring it would fill the gap. Is one appropriately honoring the dignity of great life-force, both God's and one's own, when one is grateful to God for having created one's life-force? An affirmative answer is plausible.

However, if the answer to that question is "No," it is ultimately open to the proponent of the argument I have constructed in this section to hold a vitalist account of final value and to deny that moral rightness or virtue is at bottom a function of vitality. For instance, he could coherently draw on another strain of African moral thought, one that is fundamentally relational and prescribes communal or harmonious interaction of a sort that would bring gratitude in its wake.[31]

Recall that I am downplaying metaphysical issues in this chapter. In the following, when evaluating the earlier argument for thinking that we should express gratitude to God for our existence, I do not question claims such as that God exists, God created us, and what we are (or at least have) is an intense and sophisticated life-force. I also grant a broadly vitalist picture of what has final value, and in particular that we have the highest (of perceptible beings) on earth. Instead, I address reasons for doubting that having been created with a dignity is the sort of thing that would make gratitude toward God appropriate.

3 Does Dignity Merit Gratitude?

In this section I address three reasons for denying that life is a gift of a sort prescribing gratitude to God for our existence. All three objections to the argument from the previous section grant that God has created us with a life-force that confers a dignity on us but deny that this fact is enough to make gratitude on our part appropriate.

3.1 Benefit as the Proper Object of Gratitude

First, consider the fact that having a dignity on the face of it differs from receiving a benefit, where it is the latter that normally merits gratitude. For instance, one bare-bones analysis of the concept of gratitude, from the *Stanford Encyclopedia of Philosophy*, is that it is "the proper or called-for response in a beneficiary to benefits or beneficence from a benefactor."[32] Similarly, a critical overview of recent work on gratitude notes that a "common assumption in philosophical analyses of gratitude is that it constitutes a triadic concept where the three variables involved are the beneficiary, the benefit, and . . . the benefactor to whom the beneficiary is grateful."[33]

Now, a benefit is straightforwardly understood as a welfarist good, that is, as something that makes one's life go prudentially better or improves one's well-being. Standard philosophical views of welfare include subjectivism, the idea that it is identical to pleasant experiences, satisfied desires, or positive emotions, and objectivism, that it is a matter of states and relationships such as knowledge, autonomy, love, and creativity. Welfare is a high quality of life, but dignity involves life itself having a superlative worth. Welfare is a personal value, while dignity is the noninstrumental value of a person. Welfare is a matter of self-interest being advanced, whereas dignity is a matter of the self being inherently good. Since dignity seems not to be a benefit, it is not a proper occasion for gratitude, so goes the first objection.

One tempting way to reply to this objection would be to point to non-welfarist goods apart from dignity that are plausibly the occasion for gratitude. For instance, consider the perfectionist good of having developed human nature, say, by having exercised rationality in an exemplary fashion[34] or engaging in the ways that members of Homo sapiens characteristically bond and procreate.[35] For another example, consider the good of meaningfulness, where one's life merits pride or admiration for, for example, having made sacrifices (of one's own welfare) in order to advance a worthy cause or having received positive recognition for an aesthetic or intellectual accomplishment.[36] Perfection and meaning are standardly contrasted with welfare, and if others were to promote one's perfection or meaning, one would have reason to express thanks to them. Hence, gratitude can sensibly be occasioned by more than receiving benefits in the narrow sense of welfare.

Now, I believe the reply plausibly shows that receiving goods beyond welfare can merit gratitude. However, I am not sure that dignity is analogous to the non-welfarist counterexamples of perfection and meaning. Even if the latter goods are distinct from well-being, they are ones that are *in* a life, whereas dignity is above taken to inhere in life(-force) itself. The critic can plausibly maintain that the best way to construe talk of "benefits" is in terms of what helps make a life go well for a person, which differs from what makes a person valuable. Arguably gratitude is rightly a response to what we have in the course of a life, not to what we essentially are. It makes no sense to be grateful for not being a cat or a tree, since one could not have been one of those things.

Consider, therefore, a second way to reply to the objection, namely, a thought experiment. Suppose that someone prevented you from losing your strong and complex life-force. Perhaps that individual rescued you from a calamity in which you would have suffered severe brain damage, say, by pulling you out of the path of an oncoming bus. Intuitively, you should be grateful and, indeed, the natural thing to say would be, "Thanks for having saved my life." Insofar as part of the gratitude is for avoiding a condition in which your self would have died or your personhood would have been impaired, it can be appropriate to express gratitude for what we essentially are, not merely for benefits construed in terms of what improve the course of a life. Although it probably does not make sense to be grateful for not being a cat or a tree, it does make sense to be grateful for being a live self as opposed to dead.

The critic will respond that "Thanks for having saved my life" is short for "Thanks for having saved my life so that I can have the opportunity to live well." That is, she will maintain that the only reason to be grateful for one's life having been saved is the desirable quality of life that is expected, not the dignity of the life itself.

However, I doubt that fully captures the reaction you would have if your life were saved—part of it would include being glad, appreciative, and indeed grateful that *you* continue to survive. David Benatar and Frances Kamm have both argued that what makes death bad is not reducible to being deprived of benefits such as welfare, perfection, and meaning but also includes the loss of the self.

> Each individual, speaking in the first person, can say: "My death obliterates me. Not only am I deprived of future goods but *I* am also destroyed. This person, about whom I care so much, will cease to exist. My memories, values, beliefs, perspectives, hopes—my very self—will come to an end, and for all eternity."[37]

In the way it would be bad for its own sake if a great work of art were destroyed, so it would be bad for its own sake if a self perished or personhood were seriously harmed.[38] It does seem to make sense to express gratitude for the good (if not "benefit") of avoiding such a bad condition. By analogy, it makes sense to express gratitude for having been made a self or person in the first place, not merely for goods such as the fulfillment of self-interest or those coming in the course of a person's life.

3.2 Improvement as the Proper Object of Gratitude

A second reason to doubt that the dignity of life-force is sufficient to merit gratitude is consistent with the idea that receiving the good of being prevented from having one's self or personhood destroyed is an appropriate ground for being thankful. However, according to the second objection, that is true only once one's self or personhood exists. After a human life-force is real, it would be an improvement for it to be sustained relative to it disintegrating. However, so the present objection goes, there is no improvement when a human life-force is created in the first place, making gratitude inappropriate for the "gift of life."

There are two ways this objection might be plausibly advanced. First off, consider the principle that for a person to be benefited in a way that merits gratitude, the benefactor must "make him better off than he was before."[39] When a person is created in the first place, he is never made better off than he was before, since he did not exist before. Therefore, gratitude for having been created is never merited. This argument has been advanced as a reason for thinking that children never owe their parents a debt of gratitude for having brought them into existence,[40] and it applies with comparable force to the argument that we owe God a debt of gratitude for having created us with a divine speck.

However, the principle that, for gratitude to be warranted, a benefactor must make a person better off than he was before admits of many counterexamples.

For a first one, consider the bus case earlier. If someone pulls you from the path of an oncoming bus and your life is saved, you are not better off than you were before. You are quite possibly in the same position as you had been. You should be grateful nonetheless, specifically for not being any worse off than you were.

Second, consider a variant of the bus case, where, in order to get you out of the way of the bus, you have to be shoved hard, and you end up with some cuts and bruises. Now you are worse off than you were before the shove. Even so, you should be grateful, since you would have been even worse off than that in the absence of the shove.

To avoid these kinds of cases, consider a second version of the objection, according to which, for a person to be benefited in a way that merits gratitude, the benefactor must make him better off than he would have been. This principle avoids and also explains the two bus cases. Had you not been shoved out of the way of the bus, you would have been injured or killed, whereas, upon being shoved, you avoid such conditions and at worst end up with some cuts and bruises, entailing that gratitude is appropriate. And it likewise follows from the present principle that a person never has reason to be grateful for having been created; he is never made better off than he would have been, since he did not exist before.

However, there are also strong counterexamples to this principle. Suppose that if Agent 1 had not shoved you out of the path of the bus, Agent 2 would have done so. In that case, Agent 1 does not make you better off than you would have been had she not shoved you, since Agent 2 would then have shoved you. By the present principle, no gratitude is owed to Agent 1, but that is surely counterintuitive.[41]

For another sort of counterexample, consider the point that merely trying to confer a benefit on someone is sufficient to make gratitude appropriate. If one aims to make another person better off than he would have been and takes steps reasonably expected to do so, then gratitude can be owed even if "the world gets in the way" and the person is not in fact made better off. A nice example is a colleague taking the time to nominate you for an award that you do not end up winning.[42]

Perhaps there is a way of reformulating the sense in which there must be "improvement" to a person's life in order for her to count as a beneficiary who has reason to be grateful and act gratefully. However, the above two formulations parallel distinctions in other debates, for example, about when the conferral of benefits on others makes one's life meaningful,[43] which suggests they are, if not exhaustive, then at least central.

3.3 A Good Life as the Proper Object of Gratitude

The third objection is distinct from the first two; its proponent can accept that the creation of a dignified being, as opposed to the conferral of benefits on the course of a life or sustaining a life that already exists, is in principle the sort of good that pro tanto merits gratitude. However, it might be that life itself is something to be grateful for only when the quality of life is also something for which to be grateful. Maybe the good *of* life merits thanks only when one has much good *within* the life. Many anti-natalists would suggest that few of us in fact have a good life, or at least that the *good of* life has come at the objectionable cost of much *bad within* the life,[44] making gratitude to God for having been created inappropriate.

Consider a dignified person who is living a crummy life. If a person's life is filled with pain, dissatisfaction, regret, ignorance, oppression, enmity, and ugliness, it is natural to say that it would be reasonable for this person not to be grateful to be alive (or to have been created). If a bad life means that no gratitude is warranted, then the life-force (or selfhood or personhood) as such is not sufficient to make gratitude warranted.

A number of different explanations are prima facie plausible for thinking that, despite the dignity of life, gratitude is unwarranted in the face of a crummy life. One explanation of why gratitude is not warranted is that, although life as such is something of a gift and *contributes* to the conditions for which one should be grateful to God, it is not *sufficient* on its own to be grateful, which requires a good quality of life. Another is that, upon having reason to be grateful and to act gratefully for a good quality of life, one also has reason to in respect of what is necessary for that,[45] that is, life itself. For any one of these or other reasons, one might think that "Thanks, but no thanks" is apt when the quality of life is bad. Indeed, "Thanks for nothing" might seem to be the right response when one's life is particularly crummy.

In reply, one might be inclined to change the initial argument somewhat, to make it a claim not about our actual lives as having been created by God but, rather, about possible lives having been so created. That is, instead of holding that God exists, one might view the argument as a claim about what would follow if God existed, namely, that we would have a life-force of a certain intensity and sophistication that would constitute our selves and have a dignity. If one went this conditional route, then one could also suggest that if God existed, then God would not allow any lives to be so badly off as to make gratitude inappropriate. By this reasoning, the presence of crummy lives means the absence of God, where the presence of God would be sufficient for both a dignified life-force and a good quality of life, and hence the aptness of gratitude on our part.

However, I do not think that this reply targets the heart of the objection. The objection is not so much that gratitude for being alive *is* unwarranted because some lives *are* crummy or otherwise face serious harms, but rather that it *would be* unwarranted if some lives *were* crummy or faced them. The latter point suggests that the mere fact of a dignified existence (in the form of great life-force or selfhood or personhood) is not sufficient to be grateful for having been created. Life in itself is not a gift that calls for gratitude.

A stronger reply, I think, is to say that it is coherent to be grateful about some facets of life and not grateful about others. Throughout this section I have routinely been drawing a distinction between the dignity inhering in having a life-force, instantiating a self, or being a person, on the one hand, and the benefits that come in the course of a life or a good quality of life, on the other. If one has a crummy life or suffers real harm, then, with the anti-natalists, it would be sensible not to be thankful for the course or quality of one's life, but (probably *contra* most anti-natalists) it could still be sensible to be thankful for existing in the form of a superlatively finally valuable life-force.[46] There are simply two different objects under evaluation, where talk of "being alive" or mere "existence" is ambiguous and glosses over the difference. In sum, supposing one had been created by God and one's nature has a dignity, one would have reason to be grateful and to act gratefully toward God for having done so, even if one would indeed also have reason to be disappointed about one's quality of life being poor. A mixed blessing would call for mixed reactions.

4 Conclusion: Secularizing the Argument

In this chapter I have drawn on sources from the African philosophy of religion to construct and evaluate the argument that we have reason to express gratitude to God for our existence since God has given us an intense and complex life-force that constitutes our selves and our dignity. As I have pointed out, I have set metaphysical issues aside, so as to focus squarely on the contributions that the African tradition might make to axiological matters, particularly about when and why gratitude is appropriate. In that respect, I have defended the argument by rebutting reasons for doubting that having been created with a dignified nature provides reason to be grateful to God.

Suppose, though, that debates about the metaphysics did not go in favor of Traditional African Religion. That is, suppose there is no God, no ancestors, and also no life-force. Would there still be reason to be grateful for existing with a certain essence?

One might doubt that the existence of dignity and other evaluative and normative categories are compatible with a scientific understanding of the world. However, as an adherent to value realism of a kind that parallels scientific realism,[47] I myself am not troubled by the suggestion. Even if the value of dignity and moral reasons to be grateful could exist in a purely physical world, it might seem that being thankful for existing with a dignity (say, in virtue of one's being a self or a person) would be out of place in a world without God, for then there would be no one to thank for having been given a gift of life. Is that more of a problem?

Now, there have been suggestions in the literature that it is coherent and even appropriate to be thankful for benefits without reference to any source of them or thankful to a source of benefits that is impersonal, for example, to nature.[48] However, it is plausible to suppose that these cases are better understood in terms of gladness or appreciation, not gratitude in a suitably narrow sense. Working, then, with a notion of gratitude according to which it is coherent and appropriate only ever to be grateful and act gratefully toward a personal benefactor, there is, I submit, a clear sense in which it would be fitting in a world in which God does not exist, namely, as directed toward one's parents. Indeed, even if God does exist, the logic of the argument for expressing gratitude to God applies with comparable force to doing so in respect of one's parents, who put in the lion's share of the labor.[49]

Notes

1 When I call something "African" or otherwise employ a geographical label, I mean to connote what is *salient* in that part of the world. I am mentioning what is recurrent or prominent there in a way that it tends not to be elsewhere around the globe. Hence, to call something "African" does not necessarily mean that it is true of literally all African people, and nor does it imply that it is true of only them. For more on this approach to geographical labels, see Metz (2022: 7–12).
2 Emphasized by Wiredu (1990, 1998, 2011); P'Bitek (2011).
3 For an initial stab at the latter, see Metz and Molefe (2021).
4 Okrah (2003: 18–9).
5 Magesa (2013: 3).

6 Kasenene (1994: 140).
7 Pato (1997: 55).
8 Nkemnkia (2004: 684, 700).
9 Onah (2012). For additional mention of life as a gift in the context of indigenous African religio-philosophy, see the quotations below from Tempels and Wiredu, as well as passages in Mulago (1991: 123), Bujo (2006: 19), Molefe (2018: 24).
10 See, for example, Wiredu (2011).
11 See Imafidon (2014), Ijiomah (2016: 85, 101), Lajul (2017: 27-9).
12 Given the existence of thousands of ethnic groups in Africa, there are naturally some who do not hold the views articulated here, including the Akan in Ghana in respect of the claim that everything is composed of vital force (Wiredu 2011: xxiv-xxv).
13 Anyanwu (1984: 90).
14 For example, Magesa (1997: 39-51), Imafidon (2014: 40-2), Molefe (2018: 23-4).
15 Magesa (1997: 51).
16 Note that ancestors, residing in an imperceptible realm on earth for an unusually long time, are deemed to have an even greater life-force than humans.
17 Menkiti (1984: 174), Mbiti (1990: 25).
18 Magesa (1997: 51), quoting from Charles Nyamiti's *The Scope of African Theology*.
19 For example, Etieyibo (2017).
20 Magesa (1997: 51).
21 Tempels (1959: 56).
22 Wiredu (1990: 244).
23 For example, Mbiti (1975: 44-6; 1990: 41-3), Mulago (1991: 126, 130), Magesa (1997: 39).
24 Discussed in Gulliford, Morgan, and Kristjánsson (2013: 297-301).
25 Discussed in Manela (2019), section 2.
26 Mbiti (1975: 54-62).
27 See also Anyanwu (1984), Bujo (2006), Molefe (2018).
28 Magesa (1997: 57-8).
29 Kasenene (1998: 25).
30 Cf. Bewaji (2004: 398-9), and Wiredu (2011: xxvii-xxviii), on the largely pragmatic function of religious practices among African peoples.
31 Paris (1995), Tutu (1999: 34-5), Murove (2016), Metz (2022).
32 Manela (2019).
33 Gulliford, Morgan, and Kristjánsson (2013: 297).
34 E.g. Sumner (1992); Hurka (1993).
35 Kass (1972).
36 Metz (2013).
37 Benatar (2017: 104). See also Kamm (1993: 43-53).
38 Benatar (2017: 106-7).

39 Mentioned in Manela (2019) section 2.
40 McConnell (1993).
41 Notice that it will not do to suggest reformulating the principle so that for a person to be benefited in a way that merits gratitude, the benefactor must make him better off than he would have been, setting aside the interventions of other agents. Just imagine that if Agent 1 had not shoved you out of the way of the bus, a gust of wind would have done so. Even though you are not better off than you would have been without Agent 1's intervention, you should be grateful to Agent 1.
42 McConnell (1993: 44).
43 On which see Metz (2017: 15–7).
44 Cf. Shiffrin (1999).
45 Cf. Adams (2019).
46 The question of whether we have reason to be grateful for having been created differs from that of whether we would be wronged by having been created, where the latter is the normal anti-natalist focus (of, for example, Shiffrin 1999). It seems to me that it can be apt to express gratitude to someone who has wronged us, if, say, she meant well and succeeded in doing us good.
47 See, for example, Brink (1989), Miller (1992).
48 See discussion in Gulliford, Morgan, and Kristjánsson (2013: 297–301).
49 For comments on a prior draft, I am grateful to Kirk Lougheed and an anonymous referee for Bloomsbury.

References

Adams, Robert Merrihew. (2019). "Love and the Problem of Evil." In P. Tabensky (ed.), *The Positive Function of Evil*, 1–13. New York: Palgrave Macmillan.

Anyanwu, K. Chukwulozie. (1984). "The Meaning of Ultimate Reality in Igbo Cultural Experience." *Ultimate Reality and Meaning*, 7: 84–101.

Benatar, David. (2017). *The Human Predicament*. New York: Oxford University Press.

Bewaji, J. A. I. (2004). "Ethics and Morality in Yoruba Culture." In K. Wiredu (ed.), *A Companion to African Philosophy*, 396–403. Malden, MA: Blackwell Publishing.

Brink, David O. (1989). *Moral Realism and the Foundations of Ethics*. New York: Cambridge University Press.

Bujo, Benezet. (2006). *African Theology in Its Social Context*, trans. J. O'Donohue, reprinted ed. Eugene, OR: Wipf and Stock Publishers.

Etieyibo, Edwin. (2017). "Anthropocentricism, African Metaphysical Worldview, and Animal Practices." *Journal of Animal Ethics*, 7: 145–62.

Gulliford, Liz, Blaire Morgan, and Kristján Kristjánsson. (2013). "Recent Work on the Concept of Gratitude in Philosophy and Psychology." *Journal of Value Inquiry*, 47: 285–317.

Hurka, Thomas. (1993). *Perfectionism*. New York: Oxford University Press.
Ijiomah, Chris. (2016). *Harmonious Monism: A Philosophical Logic of Explanation for Ontological Issues in Supernaturalism in African Thought*. Bloomington, IN: Xlibris.
Imafidon, Elvis. (2014). "On the Ontological Foundation of a Social Ethics in African Tradition." In E. Imafidon and J. A. I. Bewaji (eds.), *Ontologized Ethics: New Essays in African Meta-Ethics*, 37–54. Lanham, MD: Lexington Books.
Kamm, F. M. (1993). *Morality, Mortality, Volume 1: Death and Whom to Save from It*. Oxford: Oxford University Press.
Kasenene, Peter. (1994). "Ethics in African Theology." In J. de Gruchy and C. Villa-Vicencio (eds.), *Doing Ethics in Context: South African Perspectives*, 138–47. Cape Town: David Philip.
Kasenene, Peter. (1998). *Religious Ethics in Africa*. Kampala: Fountain Publishers.
Kass, Leon R. (1972). "Making Babies—The New Biology and the 'Old' Morality." *The Public Interest*, 26: 18–56.
Lajul, Wilfred. (2017). "African Metaphysics: Traditional and Modern Discussions." In I. Ukpokolo (ed.), *Themes, Issues and Problems in African Philosophy*, 19–48. Cham: Springer.
Magesa, Laurenti. (1997). *African Religion: The Moral Traditions of Abundant Life*. Maryknoll, NY: Orbis Books.
Magesa, Laurenti. (2013). *What Is Not Sacred? African Spirituality*. Maryknoll, NY: Orbis Books.
Manela, Tony. (2019). "Gratitude." In E. Zalta (ed.), *Stanford Encyclopedia of Philosophy*. https://plato.stanford.edu/entries/gratitude/.
Mbiti, John S. (1975). *Introduction to African Religion*. New York: Praeger.
Mbiti, John S. (1990). *African Religions and Philosophy*, 2nd ed. Oxford: Heinemann.
McConnell, Terrance C. (1993). *Gratitude*. Philadelphia, PA: Temple University Press.
Menkiti, Ifeanyi A. (1984). "Person and Community in African Traditional Thought." In R. Wright (ed.), *African Philosophy: An Introduction*, 3rd ed, 171–81. Lanham, MD: University Press of America.
Metz, Thaddeus. (2013). *Meaning in Life*. Oxford: Oxford University Press.
Metz, Thaddeus. (2017). "Neutrality, Partiality, and Meaning in Life." *De Ethica*, 4: 7–25.
Metz, Thaddeus. (2022). *A Relational Moral Theory: African Ethics in and Beyond the Continent*. Oxford: Oxford University Press.
Metz, Thaddeus and Motsamai Molefe. (2021). "Traditional African Religion as a Neglected Form of Monotheism." *The Monist*, 104: 393–409.
Miller, Richard W. (1992). *Moral Differences*. Princeton, NJ: Princeton University Press.
Molefe, Motsamai. (2018). "African Metaphysics and Religious Ethics." *Filosofia Theoretica*, 7: 19–37.
Mulago, Vincent. (1991). "Traditional African Religion and Christianity." In J. K. Olupona (ed.), *African Traditional Religions in Contemporary Society*, 119–34. New York: Paragon House.

Murove, Munyaradzi F. (2016). *African Moral Consciousness*. London: Austin Macauley Publishers Ltd.

Nkemnkia, Martin N. (2004). "The World as an Eternal Entity and Vitalogical Living Reality." *Analecta Husserliana*, 79: 683–704.

Okrah, Kwadwo A. (2003). *Nyansapo (The Wisdom Knot): Toward an African Philosophy of Education*. New York: Routledge.

Onah, G. (2012). "The Meaning of Peace in African Traditional Religion and Culture." http://beeshadireed.blogspot.com/2012/08/the-meaning-of-peace-in-african.html.

Paris, Peter J. (1995). *The Spirituality of African Peoples: The Search for a Common Moral Discourse*. Minneapolis, MN: Fortress Press.

Pato, Luke Lungile. (1997). "Being Fully Human: From the Perspective of African Culture and Spirituality." *Journal of Theology for Southern Africa*, 97: 53–61.

P'Bitek, Okot. (2011). *Decolonizing African Religions*, rev. ed. New York: Diasporic Africa Press.

Shiffrin, Seana. (1999). "Wrongful Life, Procreative Responsibility, and the Significance of Harm." *Legal Theory*, 5: 117–48.

Sumner, L. W. (1992). "Two Theories of the Good." *Social Philosophy and Policy*, 9: 1–14.

Tempels, Placide. (1959). *Bantu Philosophy*, 2nd ed., trans. C. King. Paris: Présence Africaine. Digitized (online) in 2006. https://pdf4pro.com/amp/view/bantu-philosophy-placide-tempels-1be879.html.

Tutu, Desmond. (1999). *No Future Without Forgiveness*. New York: Random House.

Wiredu, Kwasi. (1990). "An Akan Perspective on Human Rights." In A. A. An-naim and F. M. Deng (eds.), *Human Rights in Africa: Cross-Cultural Perspectives*, 243–60. Washington, DC: Brookings Institution Press.

Wiredu, Kwasi. (1998). "Toward Decolonizing African Philosophy and Religion." *African Studies Quarterly*, 1: 17–46.

Wiredu, Kwasi. (2011). "Introduction: Decolonizing African Philosophy and Religion." In O. P'Bitek, *Decolonizing African Religions*, rev. ed, xi–xxxvii. New York: Diasporic Africa Press.

6

On the Contingent Necessity of the World

Michael Almeida

1 Introduction

The most widely accepted metaphysics of creation is theistic actualism. Theistic actualism is committed to the view that everything that exists, in the most unrestricted sense, is included in the actual world. According to the metaphysics of theistic actualism, there is a unique, absolutely actual world. And God's creative activity explains why the actual world obtains and why actual beings exist. Since we are the undeserving recipients of our own existence, and our existence is a great good, gratitude to God is both appropriate and morally required. I discuss the account of creation in theistic actualism in Section 2.

In Section 3 I consider the most serious problem for the actualist account of divine creation. According to Peter van Inwagen's modal collapse argument, ultimate explanation entails that gratitude for one's existence is totally inappropriate. Ultimately, the actual world, and everything in it, is self-explanatory and not a consequence of divine creation. So, the argument goes, there are just two options. Either the world is ultimately inexplicable and so a brute fact or the world is ultimately explicable and so necessarily obtains. In either case gratitude for one's existence is an entirely inappropriate attitude. So much for the requirement of gratitude.

In Section 4 I argue that van Inwagen's argument is unsound. It is consistent with an ultimate explanation of the world and an actualist account of creation that the actual world is *contingently necessary*.[1] If God actualizes the world as a matter of necessity—specifically, contingent necessity—then it might be true both that the world has a complete explanation and that gratitude to God for one's existence is perfectly appropriate. On this account it is true that we exist as a matter of necessity, but that necessary existence is itself just a contingent fact. There are possible worlds in which we fail to exist altogether.

In Section 5 I offer a broader defense of weakening the background logic in philosophical theology to at least $K_{p\sigma}$ (B) from S5 to make possible inter alia such alternative accounts of creation. I offer some concluding remarks in Section 6.

2 Creation in Theistic Actualism

According to theistic actualism the totality of creation—everything that exists, obtains, or occurs—is contained in the actual world. There are other possible worlds, other ways things might have been, but even those worlds are contained in the actual world. If there exist impossible worlds—worlds where everything is possible and nothing is necessary—then those too exist in the actual world. There are in any case impossible *world-like* items existing in the actual world. So all possible and impossible worlds, insofar as those worlds exist, are actual objects.

But possible, non-actual, objects—non-actual possibilia— do not exist in the actual world and so do not exist simpliciter. It is true that Wittgenstein might have had a daughter, as the familiar example goes, but there is no actual object that is Wittgenstein's possible daughter. So Wittgenstein's possible daughter does not exist. It is an odd feature of theistic actualism that merely possible objects *exist in* possible worlds and possible worlds *exist in* the actual world, but merely possible objects do not *exist in* the actual world. "Exist in" is oddly non-transitive on theistic actualism.[2]

The object of divine creation is in fact the actual universe or the actual multiverse. It is of course possible on theistic actualism that a world contains no spatiotemporal regions at all and so contains no universe(s) at all. There are worlds with no universes, and worlds with empty universes. A universe is the largest spatiotemporally connected region in a possible world and includes every spatiotemporally located concrete object in a world. Tigers, humans, water, aluminum, clouds, impure sets, talking donkeys, waves, thoughts, and pains are concrete objects existing in a universe. But there are also objects with force but no mass, photons are candidates, and there are objects located but unextended, point-sized objects, for instance, and objects that are unextended in both space and time such as temporal parts. These are all candidates for concrete objects existing in a universe. Not all of them exist in our universe. Pure sets, numbers, geometrical objects, meanings, propositions, properties, and God are all examples of objects not existing in any universe.

According to the metaphysics of creation in theistic actualism, God creates every contingently existing concrete object in the universe. The creation of contingent objects is specifically the instantiation of proxy objects or sets of properties comprising the individual essences of objects. In order to create Smith, for instance, and not merely an indiscernible counterpart or duplicate of Smith, God must instantiate a set of properties that belong to Smith uniquely. These are Smith's haecceities, the properties that Smith alone exemplifies in every world in which she exists and no other object exemplifies in any possible world. But what then about objects like Mt McKinley? Presumably, if Mt. McKinley is a genuine object, then God creates Mt. McKinley just if God instantiates the individual essence of Mt. McKinley, and so on. In general, creation is instantiation on this view.

The creation of contingent objects in the universe entails the actualization of contingent state of affairs in the actual world. Creation is not identical to actualization but entails actualization. In creating Smith atop Mt. McKinley, for instance, God actualizes the state of affairs of Smith's being on top of Mt. McKinley. Apart from the creation of contingent, spatiotemporal objects, everything that God thinks and does also brings about states of affairs in the actual world. God brings about the state of affairs of God's being impressed by a certain set of reasons for creating by being impressed by those reasons. God brings about God's believing that creation is good by believing that it is good and God brings about God's being moved to create the Gobi desert by being moved to create the Gobi.

Possible worlds on this account are not collections of spatiotemporal connected objects. Possible worlds are maximally consistent abstract states of affairs. The largest or most inclusive object requiring explanation is the actual world—the actual world in its totality. The actual world in its totality is the one and only maximal state of affairs that in fact obtains. Every state of affairs S or its negation ~S is included in the actual world, and it could not consistently include even one more state of affairs. In divine creation, God brings about or actualizes the largest consistent collection of states of affairs. God could not actualize one more state of affairs without actualizing an impossible world—that is, without making a contradiction true. There are no states of affairs that obtain, but that are not included in the actual world.

Divine creation, according to theistic actualism, involves God choosing one possible world to actualize from infinitely many possible worlds. Since these worlds—all infinitely many of them—are all possible, God might have actualized any one of them. And since worlds are maximally inclusive, God's actualization of a possible world is the actualization of absolutely everything that contingently obtains. And since God's creative activity *contingently* actualizes the world, according to theistic actualism, God might have actualized some other possible world, indeed, *any other* possible world.

In Section 3 I consider van Inwagen's well-known argument against actualist accounts of divine creation. According to van Inwagen, divine creation provides the ultimate explanation of the world only if there are necessarily no contingent states of affairs. If van Inwagen is right, then actualist accounts of divine creation make it completely inappropriate to offer gratitude for our existence. Actualist accounts of creation entail that we exist as a matter of metaphysical necessity or as a matter of chance.

3 Van Inwagen on Ultimate Explanation

According to Peter van Inwagen, Jonathan Bennett, William Rowe, and several other philosophers, there *could be no* absolute explanation for the actual world.[3] Absolute explanations are in fact the best sorts of explanations—explanations on which, according to Richard Swinburne, "everything really is explained." The problem with absolute explanations, according to van Inwagen, is that they are incompatible with the contingency of the actual world. If there is an absolute explanation for the actual world, then there are no contingent objects, events, or states of affairs. Here is Swinburne's account of absolute explanation:

> An absolute explanation of E is an ultimate explanation of E in which the existence and operation of each of the factors cited are either self-explanatory or logically necessary. Other explanations cite brute facts that form the starting points of explanations; there are no brute facts in absolute explanations—here everything really is explained.[4]

But Swinburne also denies that there could be an absolute explanation for the actual world:

> I do not believe that there can be any absolute explanations of logically contingent phenomena.... You cannot deduce anything logically contingent from anything logically necessary.... These are among the many reasons why it must be held that God is a logically contingent being, although maybe one necessary in other ways.[5]

Absolute explanations are in fact the only explanations that satisfy the principle of sufficient reason.[6] The unfortunate consequence of the absolute explanation of the actual world, according to van Inwagen, is complete modal collapse.

> For every state of affairs that obtains, there is a sufficient reason for its obtaining. ... [The principle of sufficient reason] PSR must be rejected, for it has an absurd consequence: the collapse of all modal distinctions. ... In order to see this we must take a brief look at the concept of a sufficient reason. ... First, if x is a sufficient reason for y, then x must entail y. That is, it must be impossible for x to obtain without y's obtaining. For if it were *possible* for x to obtain and y to fail to obtain, how could the obtaining of x be a *sufficient* reason for the obtaining of y? Second, no *contingent* state of affairs may be its own sufficient reason. ... We may now show that PSR leads to the collapse of all modal distinctions. Let P be the conjunction of all contingently true propositions into a single proposition. ... It is evident that P itself is a contingent proposition, for a necessary proposition may not have a single contingent conjunct. Now, according to PSR, there exists a state of affairs S that is a sufficient reason for P. S must be contingent or necessary. But it cannot be either. It cannot be necessary, for, if it were necessary then P (which, by our first principle, is entailed by S) would be necessary. It cannot be contingent, for if it were contingent it would be a conjunct of P; and if it were a conjunct of P [then a contingent proposition would explain itself]. ... Since S cannot be either necessary or contingent, it cannot exist and PSR is false. ... Hence if PSR is true, there are no truths but necessary truths: there is no distinction to be made between truth and necessity.[7]

Let the conjunction of all contingent truths be $w_@$. According to van Inwagen's argument against contingent creation, (i) a contingent state of affairs S cannot explain the actual world $w_@$ since every contingent state of affairs is included in the conjunction $w_@$ and (ii) no contingent state of affairs is self-explanatory.

Van Inwagen does not note that the argument against God's contingent creation of the actual world—and against the contingent explanation of a world generally—is valid only if we assume a logic at least as strong as S5. According to S5, every necessary state of affairs is *necessarily* necessary and every contingent state of affairs is necessarily contingent. Since S5 precludes the possibility of contingently necessary states of affairs, it is impossible—logically impossible, we are to believe—that a contingently necessary state of affairs S explains why $w_@$ obtains or is actual. And since it is impossible that a contingently necessary state of affairs S explains $w_@$, it is impossible that there are any *contingently self-explanatory* states of affairs. Assuming S5, then, it is true that no contingent state of affairs could provide an absolute explanation for $w_@$.

It should be noted that van Inwagen's argument against God's necessary creation of the actual world—and against a necessary explanation of a world generally—is invalid even if we assume a logic as strong as S5. According to van Inwagen's argument against necessary creation, a necessary state of affairs

S cannot explain $w_@$ since (iii) $w_@$ is a maximally consistent, contingent state of affairs and (iv) every necessary explanation S for a contingent state of affairs $w_@$ entails that $w_@$ is necessary.

Van Inwagen fails to observe that there cannot be a necessary explanation S for the state of affairs $w_@$ quite independently of the contingency $w_@$ or the necessity of $w_@$. It is in general false that S provides any explanation of $w_@$ even on the assumption that $\Box S$ and $\Box(S \longrightarrow w_@)$. It is in general true that $w_@$ is self-explanatory on the assumption that $\Box S$ and $\Box(S \longrightarrow w_@)$.[8] And in S5 a state of affairs $w_@$ is self-explanatory only if $w_@$ is necessarily self-explanatory. So it is impossible that God necessarily creates or necessarily explains $w_@$. $w_@$ can only explain itself.

So under the assumption of S5 it is impossible that God's creative activity is the absolute explanation for the actual world. Ultimately, if there is an explanation for $w_@$, then $w_@$ exists necessarily and so is self-explanatory.[9] And since the fact that $w_@$ obtains is not explained by God's creative activity, gratitude to God for one's existence is simply inappropriate.

If van Inwagen is right, then gratitude for one's existence is inconsistent with the most widely accepted metaphysics of creation. Theistic actualism entails that the world is either self-explanatory or a brute fact. In either case it is inappropriate to express gratitude to God for one's existence.

4 On Contingently Necessary Creation

According to van Inwagen's modal argument against contingent creation, no contingent state of affairs S can explain the actual world $w_@$, since every contingent state of affairs is included in $w_@$ and no contingent state of affairs can explain itself. But van Inwagen's argument depends entirely on the assumption that the logic of modality is at least as strong as S5. And that assumption is almost certainly false.

In the weakened logic $K_{\rho\sigma}$ (or B) for instance, it is false that no contingent state of affairs are self-explanatory.[10] There are in fact *contingently necessary* states of affairs, and contingently necessary states of affairs are themselves contingently self-explanatory. Contingently self-explanatory states of affairs are self-explanatory in the way that all necessary states of affairs are self-explanatory. But since they are contingently necessary, there are some possible worlds in which they are self-explanatory and some possible worlds in which they're not.

Contingently necessary states of affairs can provide contingently *absolute* explanations for possible worlds. God might have actualized a possible world as a matter of contingent necessity, for instance. If the explanation for why a possible world obtains is contingently necessary, then the world itself obtains as a matter of necessity but might not have obtained as a matter of necessity. There are other possible worlds that could have been necessarily actualized and could have necessarily obtained. The concept of a contingently necessary state of affairs *sounds* peculiar, no doubt, but that is because S5 is almost always the implicit—and largely undefended—background logic.

If we let P be a maximal conjunction of propositions true at the actual world $w_@$, then we can describe a simple model permitting contingently necessary worlds. In fact there are any number of more or less complex models permitting contingently necessary worlds in $K_{\rho\sigma}$. In the following model, for instance, $w_@$ necessarily obtains and so the principle of sufficient reason is satisfied at $w_@$. But $w_@$ is contingently necessary, so there are worlds at which P is false and worlds at which □P is false. Arrows indicate the accessibility relations among worlds; we assume that every world has access to itself.

$w_@$:   P & □P

   ↕

w_1:   P & ~□P ↔w_2: P' & ~□P' ↔w_3: □P'

The model shows where the van Inwagen argument goes wrong. It is true at $w_@$ that □P—the maximal conjunction P necessarily obtains—but also true that ◊~□P— the maximal conjunction P might not have necessarily obtained. Every state of affairs in $w_@$ is either *necessarily* necessary or *contingently* necessary. Since it is true that □P, every state of affairs in $w_@$ has an absolute explanation—everything is fully explained—but since it is also true in that ◊~□P, there are possible worlds in which at least some of the conjuncts of P are false. The truth of ◊~□P ensures contingency in $w_@$ despite the fact that □P is true there. Since it is contingently necessary that God actualized $w_@$, another possible world might have been actual.

It is true in some models for $K_{\rho\sigma}$ that not every possible world has direct access to every other possible world. In the abovementioned small model, for instance, every world has either direct or indirect access to every other world. w_1 is possible relative to $w_@$, and w_2 is possibly possible, and so on. But there are some models for S5, too, in which each world has access to itself alone, or to a small isolated cluster of worlds. S5 validates all of the theorems of $K_{\rho\sigma}$, and that's good, but S5 also validates a number of equivalences that conflate important distinctions in philosophical theology.

In the simple model it is true that the only world directly accessible to and from $w_@$ is w_1, but this feature is not essential. There might be infinitely many possible worlds accessible to and from $w_@$. There might be as many possible worlds accessible to and from $w_@$ as there are in the entire pluriverse. It is perfectly possible to have vast regions of the pluriverse satisfy S4 or S5 theorems, if you like, or propositions that approximate those theorems.[11] But the theorems of S4 and S5 will be only contingently necessary in those regions.

$$
\begin{array}{c}
w_@: \quad P \,\&\, \Box P \\
\updownarrow \quad \searrow \\
w_1: \quad P \,\&\, \Box P \leftrightarrow w_2: \; P \,\&\, \Box P \\
\searrow \quad\quad \updownarrow \\
w_3: \; P \,\&\, \sim\!\Box P \\
\updownarrow \\
w_4: P' \,\&\, \sim\!\Box P'
\end{array}
$$

In this simple model, P is again contingently necessary at $w_@$, and God's creative activity provides an absolute explanation for every state of affairs in $w_@$. PSR is again satisfied. In w_3 and w_4 P is not necessary at all. Note that in $w_@$ and w_1 all of the S5 theorems are true, including $\Box P \rightarrow \Box\Box P$, $\Diamond\Box P \rightarrow \Box P$, $\Diamond P \rightarrow \Box\Diamond P$, and so on. Those theorems are in fact contingently necessary in $w_@$ and w_1 and regionally govern necessity and possibility in $w_@$ and w_1. For anyone who has doubts about rejecting the S5 theorems, $K_{\rho\sigma}$ does not preclude S5 from governing necessity and possibility in your part of the pluriverse. But that would be a matter of contingent fact—contingently necessary fact. $K_{\rho\sigma}$ ensures that those theorems are false in other regions of metaphysical space.

God might have actualized w_2 or w_3 instead of $w_@$, as the theistic actualist says, simply by instantiating the objects existing in those worlds with the properties those objects exemplify in those worlds. God might have actualized a world, for instance, in which none of us exist or only some of us do. So, though it is true that we necessarily exist, it is a contingent fact that we necessarily exist. It is true that $w_@$ is necessarily actual, but that too is just a contingent fact about $w_@$. It is also true that $w_@$ is possibly not necessarily actual. $w_@$ is in fact a *contingently necessary world*.

The small model also shows that God might have necessarily actualized w_2 instead of $w_@$. Had God actualized w_2, then it would have been true that the principle of sufficient reason was fully satisfied. God's creative activity would have provided an absolute explanation for w_2 and everything in w_2 would have been fully explained. The model shows that it's false that no contingent state of affairs is self-explanatory, since □P is both contingent and self-explanatory. The model also shows that it's false that there are no contingent explanations for necessary maximal states of affairs. $w_@$ is a necessary maximal state of affairs and $w_@$ has a contingent explanation.

5 Theism and $K_{ρσ}$

Van Inwagen's argument against contingent and necessary explanation implicitly assumes the logic of S5—as do the similar arguments from Bennett, Rowe, Geirsson, Ross, and others. It is the S5 theorems that guarantee that there are no contingently necessary states of affairs, no contingently necessary explanations, and no contingently self-explanatory states of affairs.[12] But it is the possibility of contingently necessary states of affairs that makes it possible to provide an absolute explanation for a possible world without modal collapse.

S5 generates a number of other problems for philosophical theology. Since S5 is such a strong logic, it conflates a number of philosophically important distinctions. For instance, given the logic of S5, we are unable to distinguish between strongly negative states of affairs and weakly negative states of affairs.[13] We are unable to distinguish between states of affairs that provide *some evidence* against the existence of God and states of affairs that provide *conclusive evidence* against the existence of God.[14] We are also unable to distinguish between weakly positive and strongly positive states of affairs. That is, we cannot distinguish between states of affairs that provide some evidence in favor of the existence of God and states of affairs that provide conclusive evidence in favor of the existence of God. In S5, every weakly negative state of affairs is logically equivalent to a strongly negative state of affairs. This is just to say that any state of affairs that provides the slightest evidence against the existence of God also provides conclusive evidence against the existence of God. Weakly positive states of affairs suffer from a perfectly analogous problem.

S5 entails the incredible metaphysical position that either we inhabit a miserable pluriverse or we inhabit an impeccable pluriverse.[15] There are no other alternatives. If we inhabit an impeccable pluriverse, then every possible state of affairs provides conclusive evidence in favor of God's existence. In the impeccable pluriverse every weakly negative or neutral state of affairs is impossible. If we do not inhabit an impeccable pluriverse, then we inhabit a miserable pluriverse. In a miserable pluriverse, every possible state of affairs provides conclusive evidence against God's existence. In a miserable pluriverse all weakly positive and neutral states of affairs are impossible.

S5 does not permit us to distinguish between exemplifying essential properties necessarily and exemplifying essential properties contingently.[16] It is impossible for God or anything else to acquire an essential property it does not already exemplify or to lose an essential property it does exemplify. It is impossible, for instance, that God might acquire a human nature—as so many theists believe both possible and actual. And it is impossible to lose the essence of humanity, if God does exemplify it. It is impossible, to consider another familiar example, that anything that is essentially water should become essentially wine. It cannot happen as a matter of the logic of essential properties. S5 rules out the possibility of such changes on logical grounds.

On the other hand, $K_{p\sigma}$ is consistent with traditional theism and avoids the unwelcome consequences listed earlier. In $K_{p\sigma}$ weakly negative states of affairs do not entail that the traditional God does not exist. Weakly positive states of affairs do not entail that the traditional God does exist. So, the weakly negative fact that Jones endures a serious harm is consistent with the existence of God. And the weakly positive facts that Jones leads a fulfilling life or Smith is reasonably virtuous are consistent with the nonexistence of God. And there are simple countermodels in $K_{p\sigma}$ to the thesis that we inhabit either a miserable pluriverse or an impeccable pluriverse.

$K_{p\sigma}$ allows us to model some features of metaphysical space that are inconsistent in S5. It is possible that the traditional God exists, and it is also possible that there obtains widespread intrinsically evil states of affairs. Further, it is possible that the traditional God does not exist and also possible that some worlds are naturally and morally perfect. In the simple four-world model here, the traditional God exists in w_0, but the traditional God does not exist in world w_3. The arrows again indicate accessibility; every world is assumed to have access to itself. Let $\Box F_G$ represent the proposition that God is essentially omniscient, omnipotent, and morally perfect.

w_0: $\Box F_G$ (God is essentially Fx)
       $\updownarrow$ $\searrow$

w_1: $\Box F_G$ $\leftrightarrow$ w_2: F_G (God is Fx) $\leftrightarrow w_3$: $\sim F_G$ (God is not Fx)

It is true at w_0 that, in every possible world, God exemplifies omnipotence, omniscience, and moral perfection. Since it is a matter of philosophical dispute whether the S5 principle $\Box F_G \rightarrow \Box\Box F_G$ is true, $K_{p\sigma}$ allows us to model various positions on this issue. The question of whether $\Box F_G \rightarrow \Box\Box F_G$ is true of the essential properties of God depends on how the theological dispute is settled. Different positions are representable in $K_{p\sigma}$.

The worlds that are possible at w_0 are w_1 and w_2, but of course there are likely infinitely many worlds—as many worlds as there are in all of metaphysical space—possible at w_0. These are enough worlds to represent every possibility. But there are also absolutely possible worlds—w_3 for instance—in which the traditional God does not exist, and there obtains widespread intrinsic evil. Whether there are infinitely many absolutely possible worlds in which there is intrinsic evil is a metaphysical issue, and $K_{\rho\sigma}$ can represent a variety of views on the matter. It is possible to model the position according to which the essential properties of God are contingently noncontingent, and virtually any other plausible view. That issue in $K_{\rho\sigma}$ is philosophical and not logical. It's crucial that $K_{\rho\sigma}$ does not rule out on logical grounds positions that have at least some philosophical merit.

In the simple four-world model, the dispute between traditional theists and traditional atheists is whether the actual world is w_0 or w_3. The dispute does not involve either the traditional atheist or the traditional theist holding an absolutely impossible position. Each of the positions is absolutely possible. As we should expect, there is more or less significant evidence for and against theism and atheism throughout the pluriverse. The pluriverse is not a collection of exclusively positive states of affairs or a collection of exclusively negative states of affairs.

6 Concluding Remarks

Given $K_{\rho\sigma}$, it is consistent with theistic actualist accounts of creation that God necessarily actualizes the world $w_@$, every state of affairs in $w_@$ necessarily obtains, every object in $w_@$ necessarily exists, and it is *perfectly appropriate to express gratitude* to God for one's existence. That is the result we were after. It is consistent in $K_{\rho\sigma}$ that $w_@$ has an absolute explanation—God's necessary creation of $w_@$ absolutely explains $w_@$—and that God freely created the world. Since it is possible in $K_{\rho\sigma}$ that the world is contingently necessary, it is true both that $w_@$ obtains as a matter of necessity and that $w_@$ might not have obtained as a matter of necessity. Indeed, there are parts of metaphysical space where $w_@$ does not obtain at all. So God's creation of the world is necessary, but contingently so.

The logic of necessity in $K_{\rho\sigma}$ invalidates van Inwagen's argument that divine creation ultimately explains the world only if there are no contingent states of affairs. Divine creation ultimately explains $w_@$, the states of affairs in $w_@$ necessarily obtain, but the fact that the states of affairs in $w_@$ necessarily obtain is a contingent fact. Things might have been different—things might have been entirely different. We might all have failed to exist, despite the fact that we necessarily exist. So gratitude is perfectly appropriate.

Finally $K_{\rho\sigma}$ has all of the advantages described in Section 5. The logic provides the basis for making important distinctions in philosophical theology that we cannot make in S5. $K_{\rho\sigma}$ allows us to maintain the principles of various stronger or weaker logics in various regions of the pluriverse, for instance, if there are reasons to believe that those principles are contingently necessary. So it is not as though the S5 and S4 principles are entirely incompatible with the truth of $K_{\rho\sigma}$.

Notes

1 It is a distinctive feature of S4-S5 that A is necessarily true only if A is necessarily necessary. In S5, the same goes for contingent truths: if A is contingently true, then it is necessarily contingent. Among the untenable consequences of these strong logics is that we cannot represent the agnostic position—the agnostic position is a logical impossibility. Further, there cannot be evidence S for theism and evidence S' against theism without generating a contradiction, but obviously there is evidence both for and against theism. These consequences are unacceptable. In the weaker logic $K_{\rho\sigma}$ it is possible that propositions are necessary, but only contingently so. Such propositions are in fact necessary but might not have been necessary. The system $K_{\rho\sigma}$ is equivalent to the Brouwer system B. More on this later.
2 This is a crucial fact for actualists who insist that objects included in other possible worlds do not exist, so they welcome the fact that "exist in" is not transitive.
3 van Inwagen (1983: 202–4); see also his (2009: 150 ff), Bennett (1984: 115), Rowe (1998: 94 ff).
4 See Swinburne (2004: 79ff).
5 Swinburne (2004: 79ff).
6 I have in mind the stronger, genuine versions of PSR. All weaker versions of PSR permit at least some brute facts. But genuine versions of PSR are not consistent with the existence of any brute facts.
7 van Inwagen (1983: 202–4).
8 If $\Box S$ and $\Box(S \longrightarrow w_@)$, then $\Box w_@$. But if $\Box w_@$, then $w_@$ is self-explanatory. So, $\Box S$ necessarily explains $w_@$ only if it doesn't. That is, only if $w_@$ explains itself.
9 There are accounts of divine creation that do not aspire to absolute explanations for $w_@$. In the most developed account of contingent creation, God actualizes our world $w_@$ because God just happens to act on the set of reasons he possesses to actualize $w_@$. In other possible worlds, God just happens to act on the best set of reasons he possesses to actualize those worlds. There is no explanation at all why God chooses to act on the reasons to actualize $w_@$ rather than to act on the reasons to actualize

some other world w. It cannot be the case, even, that there is a slightly better set of reasons to actualize $w_@$ rather than some other world. It cannot be the case in general that there is a slightly better set of reasons to actualize one world rather than another. If there were a slightly better reason to actualize $w_@$ than to actualize any other, then God could not actualize any other world. There are equally good reasons to actualize each possible world in the pluriverse. So, it is just chance that God chooses to act on reasons to actualize $w_@$. Compare Pruss (2007: chapter 2, 24–100).

10 The logic $K_{\rho\sigma}$ or B is reflexive and symmetrical but not transitive. $K_{\rho\sigma}$ is weaker than both $K_{\rho\tau}$ (S4) and $K_{\rho\sigma\tau}$ (S5).
11 In this simple model, $w_@$, w_1, and w_2 differ only with respect to their haecceities. The state of affairs of the world = $w_@$ obtains in $w_@$ but in no other world, for instance.
12 In particular the S5 theorems $\forall x(\Diamond\Box Fx \longrightarrow \Box Fx)$ and $\forall x(\Box Fx \longrightarrow \Box\Box Fx)$.
13 It is an S5 theorem that $\forall S \sim\Box(S \longrightarrow \Box F_G) \longleftrightarrow \Box(S \longrightarrow \sim\Box F_G)$, where S ranges over possible states of affairs. The theorem states that, for all states of affairs S, S is weakly negative just if S is strongly negative.
14 It is true in S5 that, for all states of affairs S, if S is weakly negative, then $\Diamond S \longrightarrow P(\Box F_G|S) = 0$.
15 It is a theorem of S5 that every state of affairs in every possible world is strongly positive or every state of affairs in every possible world is strongly negative, $\forall S\Box(S \longrightarrow \sim\Box F_G) \lor \forall S\Box(S \longrightarrow \Box F_G)$.
16 For instance, we cannot distinguish between not exemplifying Fx essentially and not exemplifying Fx contingently, since it is an S5 theorem that $\Diamond\sim\Box F_G \longleftrightarrow \Diamond\sim F_G$. It ought to be possible to fail to exemplify Fx essentially without it being possible to fail to exemplify Fx contingently.

References

Bennett, Johnathan. (1984). *A Study of Spinoza's Ethics*. Indianapolis, IN: Hackett.
Pruss, Alexander. (2007). "The Leibnizian Cosmological Argument." In J. P. Moreland and W. L. Craig (eds.), *The Blackwell Companion to Natural Theology*, 24–100. Oxford: Wiley-Blackwell Publishers.
Rowe, William. (1998). *The Cosmological Argument*. New York: Fordham University Press.
Swinburne, Richard. (2004). *The Existence of God*. Oxford: Oxford University Press.
van Inwagen, Peter. (1983). *An Essay on Free Will*. Oxford: Clarendon Press.
van Inwagen, Peter. (2009). *Metaphysics*. 3rd ed. Boulder, CO: Westview.

7

Existential Gratitude in Avicenna's *Metaphysics of the Healing*

Catherine Peters

Ibn Sīnā, or Avicenna as he was known in the Latin west, was one of the most significant figures of the Islamic Golden Age of the eighth–fourteenth century. Born near Bukhārā (present-day Uzbekistan) AD *c.* 980, he lived an eventful and sometimes tumultuous life as a renowned polymath, whose influence was extensive and persisted after his death in AD 1037 in Hamadhān (present-day Iran).[1] The corpus of work left behind is impressive, both in terms of quantity and variety. It includes multiple philosophical *summae* and a medical encyclopedia, *The Canon of Medicine*, which remained authoritative for centuries. In his works, Avicenna masterfully drew on Hellenic and Islamic sources to produce his own innovative system. Consequently, he evades any simple ascription to a single school of thought. *The Book of Healing (Kitâb al-Shifâ')* was his philosophical magnum opus, a multivolume canon of philosophical science which displays Avicenna's excellence as a synthesizer.[2] Though a renowned physician, his purpose in *The Healing* was not to cure the body but rather the soul by systematically dispelling ignorance. This goal is reached by guiding the reader through the natural sciences to the philosophical sciences before finally arriving at "the best knowledge of the best thing known" in metaphysics.[3]

The Metaphysics of the Healing is composed of ten books. In book I, Avicenna establishes the subject of metaphysics (the existent, inasmuch as it exists) and the principles of metaphysics (which I will discuss shortly), before turning in books II–V to consider what pertains to the existent: in book II, substantiality; in book III, the categories; in book IV, priority and posteriority, potency and act, completeness and incompleteness; in book V, generality and specificity and how these enter into definitions. In book VI he then presents an account of the "causes," fundamental explanatory factors which, once grasped, yield knowledge of whatever is under consideration. In book VII Avicenna then considers metaphysical unity before turning, in book VIII, to offer an argument for the ultimate source of existence: God (in Avicenna's preferred terminology, "The Necessary Existent") and the nature of such a being. In book IX he treats how existence passes from the Necessary Existent to created beings before concluding this work, in book X, with a relatively brief treatment of religion and politics.

A persistent theme running throughout this work is the difference between "possible" and "necessary," in particular how things that are possible in themselves are brought into and remain in existence. Avicenna strongly—and perhaps shockingly—claims that all things that exist, insofar as they exist, are "necessary." Given that something (say my cup of coffee) exists, it is no longer merely *possible* (such as it was before it was brewed) and so, in Avicenna's view, it is necessary. In order to safeguard a difference between the necessary existence of God and the necessary existence of creatures (i.e., all other beings besides God), Avicenna clarifies that creatures are causally dependent for their necessity while the Necessary Existent is uncaused and necessary in Himself. Thus, while holding that all existence is "necessary," Avicenna safeguards the uniqueness of God by arguing that this being alone is necessary in Himself and not through a cause.

Avicenna's view of existence as "necessary" prompts a question: Are we *grateful* that necessary things are necessary? The claim that creatures are "necessary" seems, at first, to make gratitude for their existence uncalled for or superfluous. Am I *grateful*, for example, that $2 + 2 = 4$? I suppose that we *could* be grateful for this, but it seems much more natural and likely that we are grateful for what *need* not be but still *is*: that I have a home, that my dog is well, or that someone came up with a process to produce coffee. Moving beyond these somewhat mundane occasions of gratitude, reflecting on one's own existence can lead to the realization that, although one *does* exist, one *could not* exist. Such realization seems, often, to inspire existential gratitude. But casting metaphysics into the mold of necessity raises certain problems insofar as gratitude seems to be inspired more by realized possibilities than by matters of necessity. In the present study, I intend to argue that Avicenna's view of existence as "necessity" does *not* preclude existential gratitude. To the contrary, properly understood, his view of "possibility" and "necessity" offers strong warrant for us to be grateful, most especially for our very existence.

I must make, however, an immediate qualification: namely, the distinction between the *rendering* and *reception* of gratitude. While I maintain that there is strong support for creatures to *render* gratitude for their existence, Avicenna expresses strong hesitation about the *reception* of gratitude by the Necessary Existent. In the present study, I propose that, while he might perhaps deny the *reception* of gratitude by the Necessary Existent, this denial does not forbid the *rendering* of gratitude by creatures.

My study is divided into two parts. In the first, I present an overview of the *Metaphysics of the Healing*. I begin with an explanation of "possible" and "necessary" and then turn to the important distinction Avicenna draws between the necessity of God (the Necessary Existent, who is necessary in Himself) and the necessity of creatures (which are necessary only through another). To conclude this first part, I then present Avicenna's view of the caused necessity of creatures or, in other words, the dependence of all things other than God on an existential cause. The second part then reflects on existential gratitude. I begin by composing two arguments against existential gratitude gleaned from Avicenna's texts. I then propose an argument in favor of existential gratitude which, while not provided by Avicenna himself, I argue is reconcilable with his metaphysical view of the existential dependence of creatures.

1 Avicenna on Existential Dependence

Avicenna presents in the *Metaphysics of the Healing* the final stage of his philosophical "healing." Metaphysics occupies the highest and final place of his philosophical system and is the stage at which one can come to true wisdom, "the best knowledge of the best thing known" (I, 2, 18). The culmination of this work is the argument for God, the Necessary Existent, the ultimate source of all existence. This philosophical masterpiece is expansive in its scope, but two themes that course through Avicenna's metaphysics are, first, the distinction between possibility and necessity and, second, the distinction between essence (*what* something is) and existence (*that* something is). These distinctions are closely related to each other: essence is associated with possibility while existence is defined in terms of necessity.

The association of "existence" with "necessity" is a central tenet of Avicenna's thought but might strike his readers as perplexing, if not outright mistaken. Certainly, the coffee I am drinking at the moment *exists*, and there is a sense in which I might colloquially say that it is "necessary" (for my productivity, increased endorphins, etc.), but is the coffee *itself* "necessary"? Or am *I*, someone who came into existence at some point in the past but will cease to exist (at least in *this* life), a "necessary" being? Is my dog, presently lying at my feet, *necessary*? While I am happy that he is there, surely he could *not* be there. Reason and experience both seem to counter any claims that these things are necessary. Avicenna understands "possibility" and "necessity" in a different way. For him, a being that is "possible" does not actually exist. "Possibility" refers to the potential of a thing to exist, unlike the "impossible" which is a being that does not and cannot ever exist (e.g., immaterial coffee). "Necessity," by contrast, is a being that actually does exist. A being that actually exists (such as my dog) is no longer merely possible, then, but "necessary." So, for Avicenna, there is a distinction between my possible daughter (who does not exist but could at some point in the future) and my actual dog (who does exist). Given the association of possibility with nonexistence—a nonexistence that does not preclude existence at some point, unlike the "impossible"—and existence with necessity, Avicenna consistently argues that all beings, insofar as they exist, are "necessary." In other words, to claim that whatever exists is "necessary" is to maintain that, insofar as something exists *it does exist*, and so its simultaneous *nonexistence* is impossible. Thus, there is a conceptual distinction between existence and necessity for Avicenna, but not a real one: both refer to the existent.

Yet, maintaining that coffee, canine, or human creatures are *necessary* seems to verge on the blasphemous, something that any monotheist should soundly reject. This seems, at first, to be equating to the existence of God and the existence of creatures. Cognizant of this concern, Avicenna draws a further distinction: a thing is either necessary *in itself* or it is necessary *through another*. The difference between these two kinds of necessity is traced back to causality. God is the Necessary Existent that is necessary in itself and uncaused. Creatures are necessary through another and are always dependent on a cause for their existence.

To unpack the meanings of these terms and the relation between them, one must consider Avicenna's own presentation of them. He begins the *Metaphysics of the Healing* by identifying its subject as "the existent inasmuch as it is an existent" (I, 2, 12). This means that metaphysics is concerned with something that exists not inasmuch as it is a particular *kind* of thing but, rather, insofar as it is *at all*. Other philosophical sciences (physics or ethics, for example) are concerned with particular aspects of existents (that they are mobile or the "rightness" or "wrongness" of an action or the "goodness" or "badness" of a being or thing), but metaphysics considers *anything* that exists *insofar* as it exists. In establishing the subject matter of metaphysics, Avicenna considers and rejects both causality (even the ultimate causes) and the existence of God as being the subject. While metaphysics does not treat the causes as its subject, they are examined insofar as they relate to the existent. The existence of God is likewise not the subject matter of metaphysics—though other philosophers had proposed this—but it is instead the end or culmination of it.[4] In order to understand how and why Avicenna regards "existence" as "necessary" and the caused necessity of creatures, let us consider his treatment of each in turn.

1.1 The Necessary, the Possible, the Impossible

Having established the subject matter as the "existent," Avicenna then presents certain key terms that explicate this subject, beginning with a delineation of the "possible," the "necessary," and the "impossible." Presenting these three terms jointly, he explains that

> The impossible is that whose existence is not possible, or that whose nonexistence is necessary; the necessary is that whose nonexistence is not allowable and is impossible, or that for which it is not possible not to be; the possible is that for which it is not impossible to be or not to be, or that for which it is not necessary to be or not to be. All this, as you see, is clearly circular. (I, 5, 23)

Each of these terms refers to existents in some way, not just propositions. In other words, these are metaphysical and not logical notions. "Necessary" refers to actually existing beings while both "possible" and "impossible" refer to beings which do not actually exist (although, in the case of the "possible," it *could*, while an "impossible" cannot). While both "possible" and "impossible" are alike insofar as neither exists, Avicenna insists on a critical difference between them: while the possible could exist, the impossible does not, cannot, and will never be able to exist. Despite the circularity in trying to define each of these terms, there is nonetheless a hierarchy of importance and meaning among them. To see this order, one must grasp the meaning of each.

"Impossible" does not play a significant role in Avicenna's metaphysics apart from elucidating the meanings of "possible" and "necessary." The reason for this is clear from Avicenna's description of "impossible" as "that for which is it not possible to exist" (I, 5, 22). Rather than the existent insofar as it exists, the "impossible" concerns the nonexistent, considered as unable to exist. The "impossible," however, has some explanatory value insofar as it contrasts with the "possible" and "necessary." "Possible" considered in itself means the lack of existence, but a lack that does not exclude existence (so, for example, my coffee does not exist, but it is not *impossible* for it to exist).[5] Although Avicenna will expound on possibility later, here he establishes its basic meaning as "that for which it is not impossible to be or not to be, or that for which it is not necessary to be or not to be" (I, 5, 23). In this way, "possible" is distinguished from "impossible" because, while the latter can never come to exist, the former could, though it does not.[6] In a similarly succinct explanation, Avicenna presents "necessary" as that which is opposed to "impossible" and "that whose nonexistence is not allowable and is impossible, or that for which it is not possible not to be" (I, 5, 23).

So, for example, immaterial coffee is *impossible*, because immaterial coffee does not and cannot exist. Unless I brew the cup of coffee, though, my coffee remains merely *possible*, because it does not *actually* exist but it *could* exist. The coffee sitting on my desk now, by contrast, is no longer *merely* possible because it *actually* exists and, so, it is *necessary* insofar as it exists. Similarly, while I do, in fact, have a dog (and thus my dog is certainly not *impossible* and no longer merely *possible*), my sister does not. So, my sister's dog is *possible* because it does not *actually* exist but it *could* exist. My dog, because it *actually* exists, is no longer merely *possible* but rather, in Avicenna's terminology, *necessary*.

Though these three terms involve circularity, they do not have equal existential importance. The hierarchy Avicenna establishes is grounded in the relation between these notions and existence, with priority granted to the "necessary." As he explains,

> of these three, the one with the highest claim to be first conceived is the necessary. This is because the necessary points to the first assuredness of existence, existence being better known than nonexistence. [This is] because existence is known in itself, whereas nonexistence is, in some respect or another, known through existence. (I, 5, 24)

In this way, Avicenna slowly reveals a foundational tenet of his metaphysics: namely, the identification of existence with necessity. Here he echoes the Aristotelian priority of act over potency: necessity has priority over possibility because it is only the necessary that actually exists. Avicenna will expound on this point later, but for the moment he limits himself to showing why "necessary" is prior in conception to "impossible" and "possible." One cannot discuss beings possible in themselves (following the example earlier, my sister or her dog) without reference to the fact that the former actually exists (although she need not) and that the latter does not actually exist (but could in the future). In the same way, it is impossible to discuss impossible beings (e.g., a square circle) without reference to existing squares and circles whose shapes are incompatible with each other. The notion "necessary" is given preference above the merely "possible" and, a fortiori, the "impossible" because only the "necessary" actually exists. So, my coffee, insofar as it exists, is *necessary* and not merely *possible*. Existence ("necessary") is ontologically prior and superior to nonexistence (both "possible" and "impossible") because nonexistence depends on existence even for intelligibility. Thus, any attempt to clarify "possible" and "impossible" relies on the "necessary." At first glance, this equating of "existence" with "necessity" would seem to preclude distinguishing God from other existents (be they a celestial sphere, a man, a dog, or even a rock) because they would all exist necessarily. While not denying that, insofar as something exists, it exists necessarily, Avicenna draws a distinction between how a thing exists which allows him to maintain a difference between creatures and God.

1.2 Necessary in Itself and Necessary through Another

While holding that all existence is necessary, Avicenna recognizes that a distinction must be made if the uniqueness of God from creatures is to be maintained. As he begins chapter six of book I, Avicenna presents a twofold division among existents, consisting of

> that which, when considered in itself, its existence would not be necessary. It is [moreover] clear that its existence would also not be impossible, since otherwise it would not enter existence. This is within the bound of possibility. There will also be among them that which, when considered in itself, its existence would be necessary. (I, 6, 1)

This passage is not aimed at showing why existence is necessary but, rather, the difference between what is in itself necessary (the Necessary Existent) and what in itself is merely possible. God, the Necessary Existent, is necessary by reason of Himself; creatures are necessary by reason of something else. Because creatures are necessary only by reason of something else, this "something" must cause their existence. God, as necessary in Himself, is therefore uncaused. Later in chapter six Avicenna goes on to show why he regards existence—even of things possible in themselves—as necessary, albeit necessary through another.

> We thus say: [The possible in itself] must become necessary through a cause and with respect to it. For, if it were not necessary, then with the existence of the cause and with respect to it, it would [still] be possible . . . whatever is possible in its existence does not exist unless rendered necessary with respect to its cause. (I, 6, 6)

A possible existent, in Avicenna's metaphysical terminology, is a contradiction. Insofar as a thing exists, it exists necessarily. Were it merely possible, it would not actually exist. This does not mean that anything possible in itself (e.g., my coffee) must exist. Rather what is meant is that, insofar as a possible being actually exists now, it can no longer be merely possible. So, for example, the necessity that I or my coffee have is not the same as the necessity of God, because I and my coffee are dependent on a cause that renders us necessary; considered in ourselves, we remain always possible. We are not now, however, merely possible, because I and my coffee do actually exist.[7]

The distinction between the "necessary in itself" and "possible in itself, necessary through another" is traced to the distinction between essence and existence in creatures and the unity of essence and existence in the Necessary Existent, God.[8] That which is necessary in itself has no composition of essence and existence. That which is possible in itself, even when rendered necessary through another, is always composed of essence and existence. In light of this distinction between essence and existence, then, Avicenna must account for how things possible in themselves can cross the ontological chasm between nonbeing and being or, in other words, how possibles become necessary. Avicenna explains the distinction between "necessary in itself" and "necessary through another" by means of causality. "That which in itself is a necessary existent has no cause, while that which in itself is a possible existent has a cause" (I, 6, 2). That which is merely possible, then, in order to become necessary and existing, relies on an external cause.

Although the question of the real distinction is threaded throughout the metaphysics, Avicenna presents explicit arguments for it in select books. For the purpose of this chapter, I focus on his argument in book I, chapter 6. There he argues that the essence of a being either is sufficient or is not sufficient for its existence. If an essence is not sufficient for existence, then its existence must be due to something other than the essence. The essence of a possible being is not sufficient for its existence.[9] The possible in itself, therefore, "must become necessary through a cause and with respect to it" (I, 6, 6). Here Avicenna insists on identifying existence with necessity. He does this because he views possibility as essentially nonexistent. Insofar as something possible in itself actually exists, he holds, it exists necessarily, albeit through another. Existence must be necessary, for

> if it were not necessary, then with the existence of the cause and with respect to it, it would [still] be possible. It would then be possible for it to exist or not to exist,

being specified with neither of the two states. . . . As such, its existence would not have been realized. . . . Hence it has been shown to be true that whatever is possible in its existence does not exist unless rendered necessary with respect to its cause. (I, 6, 6)

The point Avicenna makes here is that existence cannot be merely possible. Given that something exists, it exists necessarily. Returning to the examples earlier, insofar as I exist here and now, I am necessary. My essence, however, is not sufficient to explain my existence. Hence, I am made necessary by another and thus exist. Any dog of my sister, on the other hand, is merely possible and does not actually exist because he or she has not been rendered necessary.[10] God and I both exist necessarily, according to Avicenna, but God is necessary in Himself, while I—and all other creatures—exist not through myself but rather through a cause (and for that matter, if my sister's dog were ever to become actual, he or she would be necessary through a cause).

1.3 The Caused Necessity of Creatures

If all possible beings come to exist necessarily through a cause, the next question is *how* beings that are possible in themselves are brought into existence. Avicenna turns to this question in book VI when presenting the four causes. He opens by stating that

> We have discoursed on the matter of substances and accidents, on considering the priority and posteriority pertaining to them, and on knowing the correspondence between definitions and the universal and particular things defined. It behooves us now to discuss cause and effect, because these two are also among the things that attach to the existent inasmuch as it is an existent. (VI, 1, 1)

Avicenna then immediately turns to the traditional fourfold division of causes into the formal cause, the material cause, the efficient cause, and the final cause. Although natural philosophy also considered the four causes, metaphysics' concern with causes, not surprisingly, is how these they contribute to or explain the existence of something. The formal cause is that cause which allows a particular being to subsist (i.e., exist as a whole) and to exist as a certain kind of thing (as a human instead of as coffee, for example). Conjoined with the formal cause is the material cause of a thing, the "stuff" out of which something is composed. The material cause also explains the ability of an existing thing to change (so, for example, the water and beans that are the matter of coffee and which, before they were brewed, could become coffee). Moving away from the two causes that directly compose a given thing, the agent or efficient cause is the cause which identifies the bringing into existence of something (someone who brews the coffee, for example). The final cause, termed "purpose," identifies the goal or end to be achieved by the efficient cause (such as boiling water to make coffee, or making coffee to stay awake).

Having presented and defined each of the four causes, Avicenna turns to consider which of these might serve as a cause of existence. One might expect him to identify form, or perhaps matter, as the cause of existence because a given existing thing is constituted by these conjoined causes. But the material cause refers to the potential that a thing possesses, not its actuality, and the formal cause is that cause "in terms of which the thing is what it is in actuality" (VI, 1, 2). Though it is a principle of actuality, the formal cause refers to the essence of the thing or, in other words, the *proper* existence of a thing. Neither matter nor form is sufficient to bring themselves into existence nor even to maintain themselves in existence once rendered necessary, because the essence of a thing remains always possible considered in itself.

Having considered but rejected the material and formal cause, then, Avicenna settles on the efficient cause as that cause which makes possible things actually necessary by bestowing "an existence that is other than itself" (VI, 1, 2). To show that the efficient cause is also the cause that maintains a being in existence (i.e., causes sustained existence, not just origination), Avicenna distinguishes between natural and ontological causality. The latter is more important, but the former is what is often meant by efficient causality. As he explains,

> The metaphysical philosophers do not mean by "agent" only the principle of motion, as the naturalists mean, but the principle and giver of existence, as in the case of God with respect to the world. As for the natural efficient cause, it does not bestow any existence other than motion in one of the forms of motion. Thus, in the natural sciences, that which bestows existence is a principle of motion. (VI, 1, 2)

This passage should not be taken to mean, of course, that these two aspects of the efficient cause split it into two separate causes. The natural and metaphysical efficient causes are related to each other in that the natural can function as a preparatory efficient cause for the ontological.[11] Clearly, though, the ontological efficient cause is of greater importance to Avicenna while explaining the caused necessity of possibles. Although he maintains that all existence is necessary, things merely possible in themselves never become necessary in themselves.

Avicenna, in other words, rejects the idea that the efficient cause is needed only to bring a being into existence. Rather, he maintains that the existence of possible beings depends on a cause so long as they exist:

> Hence, if it is clear that the existence of the quiddity is connected with what is other inasmuch as it is an existence for that quiddity, not inasmuch as it is [something that comes to be] after not having been, then that existence in this respect is caused—so long as it exists. Likewise, it is an effect connected with what is other. Thus, it becomes evident that the effect needs that which bestows existence on it by essence—[conferring only] existence itself—but [it becomes evident also] that origination and other things are matters that occur to it accidentally and that the effect needs that which bestows existence on it always, permanently, as long as [the effect] exists. (VI, 1, 17)

The possible in itself, even when rendered necessarily existing through another, remains of itself essentially possible. In this passage, Avicenna shows that all beings other than the Necessary Existent are merely possible in themselves and, thus, always dependent on an ontological cause for their existence. In this way, even if the world is eternal (as he maintains),[12] it is nonetheless always dependent on a cause because it is, in itself, merely possible. As one commentator strikingly expresses it, "all beings other than God are inherently infected with contingency."[13] Even when something comes to exist, it remains possible in itself. The contingency of creatures forms one of the cornerstones of Avicenna's argument for the existence of God in *Metaphysics of the Healing* VIII, 1-3.[14] The Necessary Existent must exist, for him, because otherwise possible beings would never be able to come into existence. The Necessary Existent is the uncaused cause that brings possible beings from nonbeing into necessary existence.[15] It is beyond the scope of this chapter to examine Avicenna's presentation of origination, creation, and emanation.[16] It is nonetheless important to recognize that, no matter how a possible is rendered necessary and existing, it depends on a cause for its existence so long as it exists.

To summarize, an overarching goal of Avicenna's metaphysics is to explain how beings that are possible (i.e., nonexistent) considered in themselves become necessary (i.e., existent). All beings other than God, the Necessary Existent, are merely possible when considered in themselves. All creatures, then, depend on a cause for their existence, not only to come into but to remain in existence. Avicenna is thus able to offer an account of *why* the necessity of God and the necessity of creatures differ. Given the identification of essence and existence in God, He exists necessarily in Himself. In the case of creatures, however, there is a distinction between their essence and existence such that they exist necessarily only insofar as they are caused. Given this view of the essential and continuing possibility of creatures considered in themselves, there seems strong warrant to affirm the appropriateness of existential gratitude. Given that I am only possible in myself and I always remain possible in myself, there is existential reason to be grateful for every moment of my existence. At this point, we are able to return to the question that began this study: Is existential gratitude necessary?

2 The Necessity of Gratitude

Avicenna raises the issue of gratitude in *Metaphysics of the Healing* VI, 5 and defines it as "praise in which [a benefactor] exults," that is, a kind of recompense (VI, 5, 40). He thus emphasizes the *reception* of gratitude by the benefactor instead of the *rendering* of gratitude by the benefacted. With this definition in mind, he rejects the suggestion that the Necessary Existent might receive or seek gratitude. In order to understand his reasoning for this position, it is important to grasp the meanings of gratitude and munificence. While gratitude is conceived almost transactionally as the giving of a good (praise) in response to receiving another good from a benefactor, munificence negates this exchange insofar as the benefactor receives nothing in return. As Avicenna explains, "munificence" is the "bestowal upon another of a perfection in his substance or states without there being recompense for it in any manner whatsoever" (VI, 5, 42). So, munificence excludes gratitude insofar as praise is a kind of recompense: praise given *for* the bestowal of some perfection. Indeed, Avicenna maintains that "every agent who enacts a deed for a purpose that leads to something like recompense is not munificent" (VI, 5, 42).

Existence is the perfection par excellence because existence makes all other perfections actual and necessary (my dog, for example, cannot be a *good* dog if he does not even exist), so surely the Necessary Existent is munificent insofar as He bestows existence.[17] But, if God caused a creature to exist in order to receive gratitude as a recompense, then He would no longer be "munificent." Avicenna insists that God *is* munificent and "does not seek an objective for himself" (VIII, 7, 13). Therefore, it seems as if God does not *receive* gratitude because to do so would belie munificence. Existence, that which makes something merely possible to exist and which in turn makes all other things possible, is a perfection. The Necessary Existent, as the bestower of existence, is a benefactor—arguably the greatest one—but, given Avicenna's understanding of munificence, seems unreceptive to gratitude. Answering the question of whether creatures owe gratitude to God, then, is surprisingly complex. Let us now consider this in greater detail.

2.1 Avicenna's Arguments against Receiving Existential Gratitude

Employing the definitions and treatments of these issues in the *Metaphysics of the Healing*, one can formulate two different but related arguments against existential gratitude. The first depends on the meaning of "gratitude" and "recompense" and the characterization of the Necessary Existent as "munificent." An argument can be formulated as follows:

1. Gratitude is praise in which a benefactor exults.
2. That in which one exults is a kind of recompense.
3. No munificent being seeks recompense.
4. The Necessary Existent is munificent.
5. Therefore, the Necessary Existent does not receive gratitude.

We have already seen the meaning of the terms used in this argument. Given Avicenna's conception of gratitude and his affirmation of the Necessary Existent as munificent, God does not *receive* gratitude.

A second, related, argument rests on Avicenna's conception of the Necessary Existent as ontologically perfect and the connection between end-directed actions and ontological perfection. This argument can be formulated as follows:

1. Receiving gratitude is an end achieved through acts of beneficence.
2. Seeking an end implies a deficiency in the essence of the agent.
3. The Necessary Existent has no deficiency in His essence.
4. Therefore, the Necessary Existent does not receive gratitude.

These arguments are related insofar as both of them ultimately depend on Avicenna's conception of the Necessary Existent. They differ slightly, however, in that the first depends on the definition of "gratitude" as a kind of recompense while the second assumes an existential deficiency of some sort in end-directed actions. Let us now examine the premises of this second argument in greater detail.

Recall that the definition of gratitude, for Avicenna, centers on the *receiver* of gratitude. Gratitude is thus defined in relational terms, but with an emphasis on the *recipient*, not the *renderer*. But for a benefactor to act for the sake of praise implies a deficiency on the part of the benefactor. Simply put, acting for an end is only possible when the end is not yet possessed by the being seeking it. There is, in other words, a deficiency on the part of the acting agent.[18] Were the Necessary Existent to act for praise (i.e., gratitude), then this would imply a deficiency on His part. As Avicenna explains,

> A purpose and [something] needed in what is intended befalls only someone whose essence is deficient. This is because the purpose is either in terms of himself in his essence, or in terms of the interests of his essence, or in terms of some other thing in his essence, or in terms of the interests [of this other thing], [or in terms of some other thing]. It is known that, if it is in terms of his essence or some other matter relating to his interest-in general, in terms of something that, in some manner, reverts to himself-then his essence is deficient in its existence or in its perfections. (VI, 5, 43)

The Necessary Existent is necessary in Himself and fully actual, the perfect uncaused cause of all other existents. Imperfect beings (like me) can act for an end because they lack something, but the Necessary Existent does not. As Avicenna insists, the Necessary Existent "desires and seeks nothing. This, then, is His will which is devoid of [any] deficiency brought about by desire and [any] disturbance in the quest of some objective" (VIII, 7, 3). Therefore, the Necessary Existent does not act for an end, even praise for bestowing existence.

Within the context of munificence Avicenna does briefly treat its relational aspect, but he again emphasizes that a munificent being does *not* receive recompense. That which is *received* through munificence is a good "regardless of whether or not it is accompanied by recompense" (VI, 5, 48). The being who *renders* munificence, however, cannot receive recompense in any way. The perfection that the Necessary Existent bestows (existence) on beings that are merely possible considered in themselves, then, is a good in relation to creatures and, on their side, can be accompanied by recompense or not. But the Necessary Existent does not receive recompense for bestowing existence because to do so would render His act no longer munificent. The heart of Avicenna's discussion of gratitude, then, is his conception of the ontological perfection of the Necessary Existent.

At this point, one might object that Avicenna's definition focuses on the *reception* of gratitude, not the *rendering* of it. But gratitude, in order to be grasped adequately, must be seen in its totality: a relational act from the *recipient* of a good to the *agent* of the act. Though not discussing "gratitude" in relational terms, Avicenna's insistence on the essential possibility of creatures seems to offer strong warrant to maintain that they owe gratitude to God, their existential cause. Yet Avicenna insists that the Necessary Existent as a munificent being does *not* receive gratitude. Gratitude, as defined by Avicenna, would seem to be of complete disinterest to the munificent Necessary Existent. Having outlined arguments *against* existential gratitude (i.e., against divine *reception* of praise), let us consider a possible argument in support of *rendering* gratitude.

2.2 Proposed Defense of Rendering Existential Gratitude

While the Necessary Existent would not *receive* gratitude according to Avicenna, I argue that this does not mean that creatures would not or should not *render* gratitude. Indeed, there is a strong metaphysical reason for them *to be* grateful. If gratitude is the giving of praise to a benefactor, what greater benefactor could there be than the giver of existence? Reflection on the essential possibility of all other things besides God—not just my coffee, my dog, or me, but *everything*—and their radical dependence on the Necessary Existent for existence can and should inspire praise for the being who maintains them in existence. Instances of gratitude are common in lived experience. Returning to my abovementioned examples, I am *grateful* to the person who makes me coffee and, perhaps, even more generally grateful that such a thing as coffee exists at all. Similarly, I am *grateful* that I am able to have a dog, or grateful to the people who reared him as a puppy. If I am grateful to those people and for those things which make certain aspects of my existence possible, there is an even stronger warrant to be grateful for the cause of my existence *itself*, that which is needed for any other possible aspect or part of my existence to be necessary.

I suggest that an argument in favor of existential gratitude, also derived from Avicenna's texts, could be formulated as follows:

1. Creatures depend on an existential cause.
2. Existential causes are benefactors.
3. Beneficiaries owe praise to their benefactor.
4. The Necessary Existent is an existential cause.
5. Therefore, creatures owe the Necessary Existent praise.

The starting point of this argument is the existential dependence of creatures. While it does conclude with what is owed to the Necessary Existent, the focus of the argument is on what creatures *qua* beneficiaries owe to their cause. In other words, it focuses on the *rendering* of gratitude, not the *receiving* of it. The approach of considering gratitude from the aspect of a beneficiary praising their benefactors is not adopted by Avicenna, but reframing the question of existential gratitude in this way seems reconcilable with his account of gratitude in the *Metaphysics of the Healing*.

One might, at this point, object that the Necessary Existent may not be able to intend *anything*. This is, apparently, Avicenna's position. Immediately after arguing in favor of the First Cause, the Necessary Existent, in *Metaphysics of the Healing* VIII, Avicenna turns to an extensive discussion of the emanation of existence from the Necessary Existent in book IX. Intricate, nuanced, and technical though this discussion may be, Avicenna is clear that existence is *not* immediate (i.e., the Necessary Existent does not directly cause his material creatures: neither me, nor my dog, nor my coffee) but rather mediated through a series of causal spheres.[19] The existential causality of these intermediate existential causes, though efficient in bringing new beings into existence, derives their efficacy from the First through a kind of final causality or desire. Contemplating the existence of their cause, these intermediate causes imitate the First, but their subsequent effects are not directly connected to the First. As Avicenna states:

> The very desire to imitate the First, inasmuch as He is in act, [renders] the movement of the celestial sphere proceeding from Him in the manner in which a thing proceeds from the conception that necessitates it, even though this is not intended in itself by the first intention. (IX, 2, 19)

The existence of creatures is not directly intended by the Necessary Existent because, again, Avicenna's conception of intention as necessarily entailing deficiency is incompatible with divine perfection. But, as a response to the perfection of the Necessary Existence, other beings are causally effective and perfected by their causality.

In maintaining that God does not intend other beings, Avicenna does not mean that God is unaware of His effects. Rather, the Necessary Existent has full and perfect knowledge of Himself and, because he is the only being that is necessary in itself, perfect knowledge of Himself as the source of existence.[20] Nonetheless, Avicenna insists that the Necessary Existent does not have any intention beyond Himself:

> It is impossible that there should, in any manner whatsoever, be for Him a principle and a cause-neither [the cause] from which [something] comes to be, [nor the cause] either in which or by which [something] comes to be, nor [the cause] for [the purpose] for which [a thing] is, whereby He would be for the sake of something. For this reason it is impossible for the existence of all things [proceeding] from Him to be by way of intention—like our intention—

for forming the whole and for the existence of the whole, so that He would be intending for the sake of something other than Himself. . . . We have endowed [the argument] with the special characteristic of showing the impossibility of His intending the existence of the whole [that proceeds] from Him, in that this would lead to a multiplicity in His essence. (IX, 4, 2)[21]

Intending an object entails a multiplicity insofar as the intending agent is aware of something outside the agent's essence. Given the simplicity of the Necessary Existent, then, Avicenna seems to deny divine intentionality of external objects.[22] Nonetheless, while denying that the Necessary Existent receives gratitude, Avicenna allows some kind of response from a caused being to its cause. As he explains, intermediate causes bring existence and motion about out of a desire for the perfection and actuality of their cause (i.e., the Necessary Existent). This motion, he explains, is "a kind of worship, angelic or pertaining to the celestial sphere" (IX, 2, 21).[23]

3 Conclusion

Avicenna's notions of possibility and necessity offer a clear and powerful view of the existential dependence of caused beings on God. Because creatures, considered in themselves, are merely possible, they remain always dependent on a cause for their existence. Given the dependence of creatures on the Necessary Existent, then, one might naturally wonder about what response or acknowledgment creatures might render to their cause. As Avicenna's treatments of existence, causality, gratitude, and munificence make clear, the question of existential gratitude is hardly a modern one. Yet, perhaps surprisingly, he largely denies existential gratitude. Avicenna's denial of gratitude as an end for the Necessary Existent emphasizes the radical and total perfection of God. Intending an end of receiving praise implies, for Avicenna, a deficiency. To conceive of the Necessary Existent as anything less than perfect is unacceptable, given Avicenna's metaphysical convictions about the Necessary Existent as first and uncaused cause. Avicenna's definition of gratitude focuses on the *reception* of gratitude by God and his conception of the Necessary Existent. Nonetheless, I have shown that there are resources within Avicenna's metaphysical thought that allows an argument in favor of the *rendering* of existential gratitude. While there might be other, intermediate, causes of our existence—certainly, for example, of our coming into existence—there must be an ultimate source and first cause of existence. While Avicenna denies, given his conception of the Necessary Existent, that God *receives* gratitude, I have argued that there is strong reason for creatures to *render* gratitude. Creatures essentially and always dependent on God for their existence. For what would we be more grateful?

Notes

1. For some treatments on the life and works of Avicenna, see chapter I of Jon McGinnis (2010). See also chapter II in Afnan (1958). Olga Lizzini provides an annotated chronology of Avicenna's life and works at the end of her monograph *Avicenna* (Lizzini 2012), especially 303–6.
2. One should note regarding the title of this work that "the Healing" is sometimes translated as "the Cure." Both "cure" and "healing" refer to the same term: *shifa*. I tend to use "healing" but other authors will use "cure."
3. Avicenna, *Metaphysics of the Healing* I, 2, 18; Avicenna (2005). Quotations are hereafter cited in-text; all other citations are referred to as *Metaphysics of the Healing*. My thanks to Theresa G. Peters for her translation consultations.
4. See Avicenna (2005: I, 1, 11-12). "The existence of God—exalted be His greatness—cannot be admitted as the subject matter of this science; rather, it is [something] sought in it" (I, 1, 11).
5. Avicenna (2005: I, 5, 22). "Thus, for example, if they define the possible, they would at one time say that it is that which is not necessary, or [at another] that it is the presently nonexistence whose existence at any supposed moment in the future is not impossible."
6. For example, my sister has no dog now but might someday. For this reason, her dog is neither impossible nor necessary, but rather possible.
7. For the purpose of the present study, the difference between the *kinds* of existence that I (a natural substance) and my coffee (an artifact) possess is irrelevant. The existential distinction of importance is between creatures and the Necessary Existent. Consequently, my examples of creatures encompass various kinds (natural substances both rational and irrational, artificial beings, etc.).
8. See Avicenna (2005: I, 7, 14).
9. So, for example, there is nothing about coffee itself that can account for its existence. Similarly, the essence of dog, considered in itself, does not entail the existence of dog.
10. To reiterate, this does not mean that the necessity of God and the necessity of creatures is the same. As Caterina Belo explains, in one sense all that exists is necessary and to be understood generally as "certainty or affirmation of existence. In another, more restricted sense, if one introduces causality, only God is necessary

in Himself, all other beings are necessary through another, i.e., through their causes." Belo (2009: 403–26, 416).
11 For an elaboration of this point, see McGinnis (2010: 192–3).
12 See Avicenna (2005: IX, 1, 2).
13 Rahman (1981: 12).
14 Although Avicenna will also show the finitude of the material, formal, and final causes, the efficient cause is again granted priority both because of its role of bestowing existence and its uniqueness. See Avicenna (2005: VIII, 3, 5).
15 See Avicenna (2005: IV, 1, 11).
16 Avicenna discusses these points in particular in books VI and IX of *Metaphysics of the Healing*. Some relevant passages on origination and creation are found in VI, 1, 7-15, VI, 2, 9-14, and VIII, 3, 6-8. For emanation, see IX, 3 and 4.
17 See, for example, Avicenna (2005: VIII, 6), esp. 3.
18 An example might help: Say that I go into my kitchen and brew coffee. I go into the kitchen intending to make coffee and—unless something happened to hinder me—I do so. Would I intend to brew coffee if I already had coffee? Probably not. I could, of course, perhaps to have even more or to make some for another person, but if I were to brew coffee while holding a full cup, one might reasonably question my action. If I already have something, why would I intend it? I *intend* to brew coffee because I *lack* something.
19 See especially Avicenna (2005: IX, 2).
20 See Avicenna (2005: IX, 4, 3).
21 See also Avicenna (2005: VIII, 7, 12).
22 This is a fraught issue within Avicennian scholarship, but, because it lies outside the direct focus of my present study, I will not elaborate on it at present. For some treatment, see Lim (2009: 75–98), especially 76–83.
23 Avicenna does not dwell on the existential motivation for worship, though, and largely restricts his consideration of this concept to the acts of worship proscribed by religion in Avicenna (2005: X, 3). He returns to religious proscription of worship at X, 5, 4 & 9 and X, 5, 11.

References

Afnan, Soheil. (1958). *Avicenna: His Life and Works*. London: George Allen & Unwin Ltd.
Avicenna. (2005). *The Metaphysics of Healing*, trans. Michael Marmura. Provo, UT: Brigham Young University Press.
Belo, Catarina. (2009). "Essence and Existence in Avicenna and Averroes." *Al-qantara*, 30: 403–26.

Lim, Kevjn. (2009). "God's Knowledge of Particulars: Avicenna, Maimonides, and Gersonides." *Journal of Islamic Philosophy*, 5: 75–98.

Lizzini, Olga. (2012). *Avicenna*. Rome: Carocci.

McGinnis, Jon. (2010). *Avicenna (Great Medieval Thinkers)*. Oxford: Oxford University Press.

Rahman, Fazlur. (1981). "Essence and Existence in Ibn Sina: The Myth and the Reality." *Hamdard Islamicus*, 4: 3–14.

8

Lessons from Anti-natalism on God and Gratitude for Our Existence

Kirk Lougheed

1 Introduction

A common claim within Judeo-Christian theism is that everything that exists is good, at least insofar as it exists. Simply existing necessarily entails having a positive value, at least to some degree. In other words, to be real is to be essentially valuable. In light of this, each person owes God a debt of gratitude for their existence.[1]

This chapter explores challenges to this idea from a recent debate in ethics about the moral permissibility of procreation. I outline five unique arguments for anti-natalism, which is the view that it is (almost) always impermissible to bring other humans into existence. These are the Asymmetry Argument, the Deluded Gladness Argument, the Hypothetical Consent Argument, the No Victim Argument, and the Exploitation Argument. I do not argue that any of these arguments are in fact sound. Instead, I aim to show that *if* any of them are sound, they imply that humans should not be grateful to anyone for their existence, let alone grateful to God. I conclude by explaining that not only does anti-natalism challenge a core tenet of classical theism, but I suggest that there is a simple route from anti-natalism to atheism. For if anti-natalism is true, then God could not be morally justified in creating humans in our particular world. I then explore whether this problem reduces to other long-standing challenges to theism in the form of the Problem of Evil or the Problem of No Best World. While I don't claim to demonstrate the truth of anti-natalism in this chapter, I do show that theists need to start taking the arguments for anti-natalism seriously.

2 Existence and Gratitude in Classical Theism

In this section, I briefly outline the basic reasons classical theists have for thinking existence is good and hence why we ought to be grateful for it. I'm going to focus on what Aquinas says about this topic while relying on Brian Davies's book, *Thomas Aquinas on God and Evil*, for interpretation (2011). Of course, there are numerous competing interpretations of Aquinas on many different topics. But it's not my concern to wade into these disputes as this isn't a project on Aquinas or the history of philosophical theology. There is, I think, enough agreement among classical theists about what I say in this section to suit my particular purposes here.

Aquinas "thinks of an essence as what something (a substance) has to have in order to exist as the kind of thing it is [... And an e]ssence, he says, is that which is signified by the definition of a thing" (Davies 2011: 20). If something has an essence, then it necessarily exists. Nonexistent essences are impossible such that Aquinas would eschew many contemporary understandings and usages of possible worlds (Davies 2011: 21). So, for Aquinas all essences necessarily exist and hence are actual.

According to Aquinas, "to call something good is first and foremost to say that it is desirable" (Davies 2011: 30). However, what makes one thing desirable might be different from what makes some other thing desirable such that desirability in a sense is always qualified (Davies 2011: 31). There is one exception, though, in that "Aquinas thinks that there is such a thing as unqualified goodness, goodness that is not that of a good such-and-such. His word for this is 'God'" (Davies 2011: 32). Davies explains:

> For him [Aquinas], therefore, goodness is objective but also relative: objective in the sense that to call something good is to say something true or false about it; relative in the sense that to understand what "X is good" involves an understanding of what X is. And here I need to emphasize the word "is," for Aquinas strongly connects goodness and being. In his view, to be good is *to be* somehow, meaning that a good X positively or actually has certain desirable attributes. (Davies 2011: 32)

Aquinas says that "[g]oodness and being are really the same. They differ only conceptually. . . . Something is obviously good inasmuch as it is a being" (ST Ia.5.I quoted from Davies 2011: 32). This is quite different from contemporary views which take it as obvious that something can exist without necessarily being good (Davies 2011: 32).

To sum up, consider the following question: What needs to be the case for there to be a human being? For Aquinas the answer is simple: there needs to be a human being. In other words:

> There has to be what can be truly thought of as something that is human. So there has to be what *succeeds* in being human for there *to be* a human being in the first place. In other words, the notion of existing is bound up with the notion of achievement or success, which is what Aquinas thinks. His line is that, insofar as something actually is such-and-such, then it must have what is needed to be a such-and-such and is, therefore, good. (Davies 2011: 32)[2]

And finally:

> His meaning is that something is good insofar as it possesses what is desirable for it is considered as what it is by nature. And with this thought in mind, he concludes that being and goodness are seriously equivalent. He does not think that the terms "being" and "goodness" are synonymous. He does, however, hold that for something to exist at all is for that thing to possess features that make for goodness in it—a conclusion that he takes to be perfectly compatible with many existing things being defective or thwarted in various ways. (Davies 2011: 32–3)

I won't focus on the Thomistic understanding of badness, but it's worth considering briefly by way of contrast with goodness. According to Aquinas badness doesn't exist in the sense that it lacks an essence. Rather, "it consists in the absence of anything actually existing (formally or accidentally)" (Davies 2011: 33). So, badness is really a lack of existence or being (i.e., a lack of what ought to be there). It's important to note this doesn't mean Aquinas denies the reality of evil. Rather, consider the following examples: for Aquinas blindness is only understood by virtue of sight. Blindness is a lack of being able to see. The same goes for sickness which is only understood in terms of good health. Sickness is a lack of good health (Davies 2011: 34). To sum up:

> [Aquinas] would not be happy with them if construed as asserting that there are any such substances as blindness or sickness. He would say that neither blindness nor sickness are substances. He would also say that their reality consists in the absence of something and not the presence of any actually existing accidental form. His view is that to call something blind or sick is simply to draw attention to what it lacks, to what does not actually exist. And this is what he thinks when it comes to all instances of badness or evil. (Davies 2011: 35)

While this is a rather terse summary of Aquinas on the goodness of existence, it should be sufficient for my purposes. I'm going to assume that the abovementioned description is broadly representative of the classical theistic tradition. Inasmuch as different interpretations of Aquinas and the classical tradition more generally are consistent with what I've said here, then the arguments I offer later apply to them as well. Inasmuch as they are not consistent, then what follows may not be applicable to differing accounts. For the reader who is concerned about this, they can simply read the rest of this as a conditional: *If* the above mentioned description of classical theism is true, *then* it follows that existence is a good.

In light of the earlier discussion, here's a standardized version of the argument that we should be grateful to God for our existence:

The Gratitude Argument

(1) Existence is a good.
(2) God gives people their existence.
(3) People should be grateful to whoever gives them good things.
   Therefore,
(4) People owe gratitude to God for their existence.

3 Lessons from Anti-natalism

Arguments for anti-natalism typically fall into two different groups. Philanthropic arguments focus on the harm done to individuals who are brought into existence. They tend to conclude that procreation is *always* all things considered impermissible. Misanthropic arguments, on the other hand, appeal to the harm that individuals brought into existence will cause others (e.g., Benatar 2015). They often conclude that given our current circumstances it is impermissible to bring other humans into existence. However, if the harm that humans typically cause could be greatly reduced or eliminated, then it might be permissible to procreate. My focus is on philanthropic arguments, and in this section, I will outline five different philanthropic arguments. I am *not* arguing that any of the arguments in question are in fact sound. Instead, I aim to highlight the consequences of such arguments for theism and gratitude for existence *if* they turn out to be sound. After explicating each argument, I will outline its consequences for theism and point to avenues for future research.[3]

3.1 The Asymmetry Argument

The first two arguments in this section are from the well-known pessimist philosopher David Benatar. Though he has published widely on anti-natalism, his views have in general not changed since his book *Better Never to Have Been: The Harm of Coming into Existence* (2006). I will thus mostly refer to this work in what follows.

In what has come to be known as the *Asymmetry Argument*, Benatar defends the claim that coming into existence in *our world* is always a harm. In this sense, Benatar defends a contingent truth, not a necessary truth. Coming into existence wouldn't be a harm in really good worlds where no one ever suffers. The claim also isn't that to not exist is somehow better than to exist. This is because there is no referent to "non-existent being." Benatar's idea is simply that "existence is always bad for those who come into existence" (Benatar 2006: 4).

Suppose that genetic makeup is essential to personal identity such that if a person's genetic makeup changes, they cease to exist. Some have argued that in light of this fact it's not wrong to bring people into existence who have genetic impairments since they could not be brought into existence without them (Benatar 2006: 19). Since such people couldn't exist without the genetic impairments in question, bringing them into existence cannot constitute a harm.[4] According to Benatar, the problem with this line of reasoning is that it fails to distinguish between a life worth *continuing* and a life worth *starting*. Whether life is worth continuing can only be asked by someone who already exists. But whether a life is worth starting is a question about a nonexistent being (Benatar 2006: 22). It's therefore problematic when people conflate the former question with the latter.

Benatar explains that "[t]hose lives not worth living are those that would not be worth continuing. But the problem is that these notions are then applied to future-life cases. In this way, we are led to make judgments about future-life cases by the standards of present-life cases" (Benatar 2006: 23). For it could be worth continuing a life even if it is wrong to start such a life in the first place. This is because "there is a crucial difference between harms (such as pains) and benefits (such as pleasures) which entails that existence has no advantage over, but does have disadvantages relative to, non-existence" (Benatar 2006: 30). Here's a key distinction Benatar needs to establish his thesis: the absence of pain is good even if no one experiences that good while the absence of pleasure is not bad unless someone is deprived of it. Thus, the absence of pain is good even if the best or perhaps the only way to achieve it is by the very absence of the person who would otherwise experience it. This asymmetry between harm and pleasure explains why it is wrong to have a child because they will benefit from that existence, while "it is not strange to cite a potential child's interests as a basis for avoiding bringing a child into existence" (Benatar 2006: 34).[5]

Some people may well regret not having had children, but this regret isn't about potential beings who were not brought into existence. Rather, it's about failing to have had the experience of parenthood. To see this, realize that "nobody really mourns for those who do not exist on Mars, feeling sorry for potential such beings that they cannot enjoy life" (Benatar 2006: 35).

A key reason for affirming the asymmetry between pleasure and pain is that it offers the best explanation for a number of intuitions about procreation. The first is the asymmetry between the claim that we have a strong duty not to intentionally bring someone into existence who will suffer, but we do not have a corresponding duty to bring happy persons into existence (Benatar 2006: 32). The second asymmetry is between the strangeness of citing the benefit to a potential child as the reason for bringing them into existence and the coherence of citing the harms to a potential child as the reason for not bringing them into existence (Benatar 2006: 34). The third asymmetry involves our retrospective judgments. While we can regret both bringing an individual into existence and not bringing an individual into existence, it is only possible to regret bringing an individual into existence for the sake of that individual. If that individual hadn't been brought into existence, they would not exist and hence nothing could be regretted for their sake (Benatar 2006: 34). The fourth asymmetry is between our judgments about distant suffering and uninhabited regions. We should rightly be sad and regret the former, but we should not be sad or regret that some faraway planet (or island in our own world) is uninhabited (Benatar 2006: 35).

With this asymmetry established, Benatar concludes that coming into existence in our world is always a harm. This is due to the fact that the absence of pain is better than the presence of pain while the presence of pleasure is not better than its absence (Benatar 2006: 38). In sum, "[t]he fact that one enjoys one's life does not make one's existence better than non-existence, because if one had not come into existence there would have been nobody to have missed the joy of leading that life and thus the absence of joy would not be bad" (Benatar 2006: 58).[6]

3.1.1 Lesson

If the Asymmetry Argument for anti-natalism is sound, then humans do not owe God gratitude for their existence. Every person in this world experiences at least some harm in their life. Benatar only has human procreation in mind. So one relevant question is whether there is a relevant difference between a prospective couple procreating a child they know will inevitably experience harm and

God creating a world knowing that all sentient beings (who ultimately exist only because of God's creative work) will experience harm. Is there a relevant difference that could justify creation in the latter case but not in the former? Are there unique ways that theists might reject the asymmetry?

3.2 The Deluded Gladness Argument

Benatar also offers a second argument in support of his anti-natalist conclusion, what I will call the Deluded Gladness Argument. The main thrust of this argument is to show that while typical life assessments are often quite positive, they are almost always mistaken. This serves as a standalone argument for the claim that we should refrain from procreating since all (or almost all) lives are quite bad. It also offers support for the Asymmetry Argument which says that if an individual's life will contain even the slightest harm, it is impermissible to bring them into existence. This argument aims to show that in the vast majority of cases, the harms contained in human lives are far from slight. Benatar argues that "even the best lives are very bad, and therefore that being brought into existence is always a considerable harm" (2006: 61).

Most people's self-assessments of their lives are positive. In other words, most people are glad to have been brought into existence and don't think they were seriously harmed by being brought into existence. What I'm labeling the "Deluded Gladness Argument" is Benatar's reasons for thinking that such self-assessments are almost always the result of delusion. Benatar explains that "[t]here are a number of well-known features of human psychology that can account for the favorable assessment people usually make of their own life's quality. It is these psychological phenomena rather than the actual quality of a life that explain (the extent of) the positive assessment" (2006: 64). The most important psychological factor is the Pollyanna Principle, which says that people are strongly inclined toward optimism in their judgments. People recall positive experiences with greater frequency and reliability than negative experiences. This means that when people look back on the past, they tend to inflate the positive aspects of it while minimizing the negative features. This also affects how people view the future, with a bias toward overestimating how well things will go. Subjective assessments about overall well-being are also consistently overstated with respect to positive well-being (Benatar 2006: 64–5). Just consider that "most people believe that they are better off than most others or than the average person" (Benatar 2006: 66). People's own assessments of their health do not correlate with objective assessments of it. The self-assessments of happiness of the poor are (almost) always equivalent to those offered by the rich. Educational and occupational differences tend to make insignificant differences to the quality of life assessments too (Benatar 2006: 66–7).

Benatar claims that some of this Pollyannaism can be explained by "adaptation, accommodation, or habituation" (2006: 67). If there is a significant downturn in a person's life, their well-being will suffer. However, they often readjust their expectations to their worse situation, and so eventually their self-assessments do not remain low; they move back toward their original level of well-being (Benatar 66–7). Subjective well-being report changes more accurately than actual levels of well-being. People often also assess their own well-being by making relative comparisons to others. This means that self-assessments are more often comparisons of well-being, instead of assessments of actual well-being (Benatar 2006: 68). Benatar further argues that on three main theories of how well a life is going in hedonistic theories, desire-fulfillment theories, and objective list theories, assessments of how well one's life is going are almost always too positive. He consistently points out there is a distinction between the well-being that an individual ascribes to their own life and the actual well-being of that individual's life. Benatar's point is that these things do not often align. Once we have a more accurate picture of how bad our lives really are, we should ask whether we would inflict the harms that occur in any ordinary life on a person who already exists. The answer, according to Benatar, is clearly "no" (Benatar 2006: 87–8). While it's possible to have a life that avoids most harms, we aren't in a good epistemic position to identify whether this will apply to our own offspring. Given that the odds of avoidance are slim, to begin with, procreation is akin to a rather nasty game of Russian roulette.[7]

3.2.1 Lesson

If the Deluded Gladness Argument is sound, then humans do not owe gratitude to God for their existence.[8] This is because God should reasonably believe that most of the humans she creates will have bad lives. The conflict here is clear. If existence itself is a good, then every life is in some sense good and likely worthy of being brought into existence.[9] Benatar doesn't just deny that most lives are overall good but asserts the stronger claim that *most* lives are on balance bad. Theists have yet to really engage with the empirical work Benatar cites to support his claims.

3.3 The Hypothetical Consent Argument

After Benatar's work, the Hypothetical Consent Argument is probably the most discussed argument for anti-natalism in the literature. The basic idea of the argument is that procreation imposes unjustified harm on an individual to which they did not consent (Shiffrin 1999; Singh 2012; Harrison 2012). But what makes procreation an unjustified harm? For there are clearly certain cases where harming an unconsenting individual is justified. Consider the following oft-discussed case:

> Rescue. A man is trapped in a mangled car that apparently will explode within minutes. You alone can help. It appears that the only way of getting him out of the car will break his arm, but there is no time to discuss the matter. You pull him free, breaking his arm, and get him to safety before the car explodes. (DeGrazia 2012: 151)

It is permissible in this case to harm the man in a nontrivial way without his consent because doing so clearly prevents the greater harm of his death. We can say that in such a case you have the man's *hypothetical* consent because he would (or rationally ought to) consent to the harm if he could. But now consider a different case that is also frequently discussed:

> Gold manna. An eccentric millionaire who lives on an island wants to give some money to inhabitants of a nearby island who are comfortably off but not rich. For various reasons, he cannot communicate with these islanders and has only one way of giving them money: by flying in his jet and dropping heavy gold cubes, each worth $1 million, near passers-by. He knows that doing so imposes a risk of injuring one or more of the islanders, a harm he would prefer to avoid. But the only place where he can drop the cubes is very crowded, making significant (but nonlethal and impermanent) injury highly likely. Figuring that anyone who is injured is nevertheless better off for having gained $1 million, he proceeds. An inhabitant of the island suffers a broken arm in receiving her gold manna. (DeGrazia 2012: 151–2)

What makes this eccentric millionaire's actions impermissible in this case is that the benefit imposed does not involve avoiding greater harm. This is what ethicists refer to as a *pure benefit*. So, the idea is that it is impermissible to confer a pure benefit on someone who hasn't consented to it, while it is permissible to confer a benefit on someone to prevent nontrivial harm to them. In the Rescue case, there is hypothetical consent to the harm, whereas in the Gold manna case there is no such consent.

The anti-natalist urges that procreation is analogous to the Gold manna case, not the Rescue case. Procreation imposes nontrivial and unconsented harm on the individual who is created for the purposes of bestowing a *pure benefit*. Those who would procreate, then, do not have the hypothetical consent of the individuals they procreate. Why is this the case? Well, if an individual doesn't exist, she cannot be harmed nor benefited. Language is misleading here because when procreation doesn't occur there is no "individual" who doesn't exist. There is simply nothing. There is no person in a burning car, no people on the island, and no free-floating soul waiting to be created. So, procreation always involves bestowing a pure benefit, something this argument says is impermissible.

3.3.1 Lesson

If the Hypothetical Consent Argument is sound, then humans do not owe gratitude to God for their existence. Of course, God did not have anyone's consent when she created. Furthermore, each person is clearly exposed to nontrivial harm when brought into existence. Now, the theist might respond that while prospective parents cannot have hypothetical consent, that given certain conceptions of divine foreknowledge (i.e., if Molinism is true), that God can have hypothetical consent with respect to creation. This response might not require the strong claim that every life is good, but only the weaker claim that every life is worth continuing. However, some lives appear to be so miserable, so full of suffering, and so lacking in reasonable hope of a better future that they are not worth continuing. In other words, for this potential response to the Hypothetical Consent Argument to even get off the ground, the theist needs to establish that every single life is worth continuing (if not that every single life is good). Otherwise, there will remain lives where God did not have hypothetical consent to create them.

3.4 The No Victim Argument

Gerald Harrison argues that to coherently posit the existence of moral duties means there must be a possible victim (that can be hurt by the breaking of a duty). In light of this, he suggests that "we have a duty not to create the suffering contained in any prospective life, but we do not have a duty to create the pleasures contained in any prospective life" (2012: 94). It's intuitive to think that we have the following two duties: (1) There is a duty to prevent suffering; and (2) There is a duty to promote pleasure (Harrison 2012: 96). Since there would be no victim if one failed to create happy people, this nicely explains why we don't have a duty to procreate even if we are sure our offspring will have very happy lives. However, this also explains why we have a duty not to create suffering people since if we do so there are clearly victims (i.e., the suffering people who were created). Since all lives contain suffering, there is a duty to never procreate. For in procreating, we always fail to do our duty to prevent suffering because there is an actual victim of suffering. That an individual has an on-balance or overall happy life cannot outweigh the duty to not procreate because in failing to procreate there is no victim (Harrison 2012: 97–9).

3.4.1 Lesson

If the No Victim Argument is sound, then humans do not owe gratitude to God for their existence. It's controversial to ascribe moral duties to God.[10] But supposing God can be said to have such duties, then her act of creation does indeed create victims. No one would have been harmed by not coming into existence. This also explains why God would not be obligated to create a world she could ensure would be a utopia. The best way out for the theist may be to show why God does not have moral duties to humans, without also entailing that humans do not have moral duties to each other. If this strategy were to succeed, it would show a relevant difference between God's act of creation and human procreation.

3.5 The Exploitation Argument

The Exploitation Argument for anti-natalism, offered by Christopher Belshaw, involves the idea that procreation fundamentally involves exploitation (Belshaw 2012). Consider that we have the intuition that we should end the lives of animals who are suffering even if there is some chance that they could be happy in the future (Belshaw 2012: 120). Suppose that there are categorical desires, which involve reasons to ensure our future existence. Further suppose that there are also conditional desires, which, assuming a future, offer reason to think that one state of affairs will obtain over some other one (Belshaw 2012: 121). Belshaw continues to suggest that while a baby is a human animal, it is necessarily *not* a person in a more robust sense. This is because babies are not psychologically knit together, nor do they have categorical or conditional desires (Belshaw 2012: 124). Likewise, there is no continuity between a baby and the adult it becomes; it's implausible to think these are the same person. For a baby:

> [H]as no developed notion of itself, or of time, no desire to live on into the future, no ability to think about the pain and decide to endure it. Further, if we think seriously about a baby's life we'll probably agree it experiences pain in more than trivial amounts. Even perfectly healthy babies come into the world

screaming, cry a lot, suffer colic and teething pains, keep people awake at night. None of us can remember anything about it. (Belshaw 2012: 124)

An important claim of the Exploitation Argument is that such a life is not worth living. Even if only through a baby can a person be brought into existence, this doesn't compensate the baby for the harm it experiences (Belshaw 2012: 124). This means that we must exploit babies in order for them to be humans. I might be glad that there was a baby who was exploited in order for me to come to exist, but it would still be better for that baby had it never been born. In procreating "we are inevitably free-riding on the several misfortunes of small, helpless and short-lived creatures" (Belshaw 2012: 126).

3.5.1 Lesson

If the Exploitation Argument is sound, then humans do not owe gratitude to God for their existence. The truth of theism does not change the fact that every human has to be a baby in order to become an adult. If God desires fully adult humans, and such adults are closer to divine image bearers than babies, then humans are exploited by God's creation. There's also another interesting connection to versions of theism that posit the existence of an afterlife. Some argue that the reward of a good heaven justifies all of one's earthly sufferings. But notice that if this Exploitation Argument is sound, it is problematic to appeal to heaven in order to justify our suffering on earth. If heaven is the "final product" where we have perfect union with God and no longer suffer, we have been exploited inasmuch as we had to go through our earthly lives and suffer a great deal during them in order to get to heaven. Of course, showing that we suffer so much in our earthly lives as adults that this constitutes exploitation involves appealing to considerations discussed in the other arguments.

4 A New Argument for Atheism?

The philanthropic arguments for anti-natalism described earlier, if sound, demonstrate that the Gratitude Argument is unsound. They show that premise (1) of that argument is false. Existence is not a good. It's logically possible that in certain worlds humans do in fact have good existences, but in the actual world, existence is not intrinsically good. Or at least this is an entailment of the earlier arguments. So, one lesson here is that the truth of anti-natalism entails that it is false that people should be grateful to God for their existence. This shows that an important tenet of classical theism, which is sometimes even taken as a truism, is false if anti-natalism is true. This might appear like a rather obvious conclusion, but until now no one had really done the work to reveal how anti-natalism conflicts with theistic attitudes of gratitude. With this lesson in the background, I now turn to examine ways in which anti-natalism (if true) can be leveraged into a new argument for atheism. After all, if anti-natalism challenges an important tenet of classical theism, it's intuitive to ask whether it challenges theism itself. I further examine ways in which this new argument may or may not reduce to two existing arguments for atheism in the Problem of Evil and the Problem of No Best World.

4.1 The Argument for Atheism from Anti-natalism

Suppose that one, some, or all five of the arguments for anti-natalism discussed earlier are sound. This would mean that premise (1) of the Gratitude Argument is false. Namely, it is false that existence is a good. Not only it is false, but we have seen a number of reasons to think:

(1)* Existence is bad (i.e., serious harm).

Clearly, the Gratitude Argument does not succeed on (1)*. Instead, we begin to see a new route to atheism.

The Existence Argument

(5) If existence is bad, then the fact that we exist constitutes evidence against God's existence.

So,

(6) God does not exist (or it is less likely that God exists).

If the philanthropic arguments explained earlier are sound, then (1)* is true. If (1)* is true, then (5) is true because God would not be morally justified in creating the world. For God would be creating a world where *every human* experiences some pain, no matter how small (the Asymmetry Argument), where humans typically overrate their happiness (the Undeluded Gladness Argument), where she does not have the consent of humans to create them (the Hypothetical Consent Argument), where creating humans inevitably makes them victims (the No Victim Argument), and where babies are exploited in order to create adults (the Exploitation Argument).[11] The problem is that God's actions must be morally justifiable, and they can't be if anti-natalism is true. So, the fact that the world exists turns out to be evidence for the nonexistence of God if anti-natalism is true. The route to atheism from anti-natalism appears to be straightforward.

4.2 Isn't this just the Problem of Evil?

Much of the force of the philanthropic arguments for anti-natalism is derived from observations about the suffering, pain, and harm that people inevitably experience throughout the course of their lives. So an important question is whether the Existence Argument simply reduces to the Problem of Evil. The logical Problem of Evil states that God's existence is *logically incompatible* with evil (e.g., Mackie 1982; Plantinga 1989). A world containing *any* evil cannot be one where God exists. The Asymmetry Argument implies that procreation is only permissible in worlds where humans experience no harm at all. The Exploitation and Hypothetical Consent Arguments also suggest that procreation is permissible only in worlds very different from our own. When applied to theism, why not take this to be a restatement of the logical Problem of Evil? On the other hand, *probabilistic* arguments for evil purport to show that while God's existence is logically compatible with certain quantities and qualities of evil, the types of evil that (probably) exist in our world make God's existence less likely than God's existence (e.g., Rowe 1979). Why not think the Undeluded Gladness Argument is just a restatement of such probabilistic arguments from evil? Isn't all of this really just a different way of stating the Problem of Evil?

These are fair questions, though I don't think they do anything to defeat the force of the Existence Argument. For even if it does reduce to the Problem of Evil, discussions of anti-natalism focus on all of our little sufferings, instead of just the major ones usually focused on in the Problem of Evil literature (e.g., child abuse and sexual assault). This discussion might therefore *expand* the scope of evil typically under consideration. Restatement of problems can help us to see them in a different light. Discovering that the Existence Argument reduces to the Problem of Evil is still a discovery worth making. However, a lot more work needs to be done in order to make the connection between the Existence Argument and the Problem of Evil. The first step is to carefully show the arguments for anti-natalism, when applied to theism, reduce to the Problem of Evil. I have really only gestured at ways that this might be done here. Perhaps most interesting, it needs to be investigated whether the standard solutions to the Problem of Evil can be used to respond to the arguments from anti-natalism (e.g., Adams 2000; Wykstra 2012). Can they be used to justify God's act of creation? If yes, can they also be used to justify human procreation? To my knowledge, so far no one working on anti-natalism (proponents or detractors) has made any explicit connections to the Problem of Evil literature. I submit that this is fertile ground for future philosophical investigations.

4.3 Isn't this just the Problem of No Best World?

Another question is whether these considerations reduce to a different argument for atheism, namely, the Problem of No Best World. This problem says that as a morally unsurpassable being, God's creation must be morally unsurpassable. But anti-natalism tells us that God's creative work is indeed morally surpassable. Not only is it quite easy to imagine worlds better than ours, but for any world, God could create there could always be a better world. If this is right, then God is not morally justified in creating any world at all. Thus, the very existence of our world is evidence God doesn't exist since God could not have been justified in creating it (Lougheed 2014; Rowe 2004). Applied to the dialectical context here, maybe the objection is something like this: if any world God could create is morally surpassable, then it's impossible for God to have created a world where we aren't harmed (or victims or exploited). So God is never justified in creating.

There is now a vast contemporary literature on this problem. As with the Problem of Evil, it is important to both explore whether this really reduces to the problem in question and if yes, then whether responses to it apply here too. Many theists have tried to show that God is morally permitted to create in a "less than best" scenario where there is no best world God can create (Howard-Snyder and Howard-Snyder 1994; Kraay 2011). It would be interesting to know if these responses could rebut the Existence Argument and also whether they could be applied to cases of human procreation.

5 Conclusion and Future Directions

That existence is intrinsically good is a truism of classical theism. Each person owes God gratitude for their existence. But if philanthropic arguments for anti-natalism are sound, then existence is not a good. This means that people would not in fact owe God gratitude for their existence. The truth of anti-natalism challenges a core tenet of classical theism. Further exploration is needed to discover whether there are relevant differences between divine creation and human procreation such that this challenge can be avoided. If relevant differences cannot be established, the implications for theism need to be examined. For it appears to be a small step from the truth of anti-natalism to atheism. This is because if the philanthropic arguments for anti-natalism are sound, then God was not morally justified in creating. Anti-natalism has not frequently been cited as a challenge to theism. I hope to have shown that it is, and as such philosophers who are concerned to defend the rationality of theism ought to start engaging with the various arguments on offer for anti-natalism.[12] If theists want to insist that challenges to theism from anti-natalism reduce to preexisting arguments for atheism, they need to show how established solutions to those problems can be used to reject anti-natalism. Otherwise, it's difficult to see why anti-natalism doesn't pose a unique challenge to theism.

The other set of arguments for anti-natalism that I didn't discuss in this chapter is often referred to as misanthropic arguments. They focus on the harm that humans often inflict on each other, nonhuman animals, and the rest of the environment. When one starts examining the magnitude of human destruction, it becomes increasingly difficult to justify creating more members of our species. But consider theists from the four major monotheistic religions in Judaism, Christianity, Islam, and Traditional African Religion. All four of these religions affirm the value of procreation and the value of the family unit. At the same time, however, these traditions also tend to embrace a self-sacrificial and other-centered ethic. Such an ethic would have individuals refrain from harming others when possible. But if the misanthropic arguments for anti-natalism are sound, they reveal that one way to greatly reduce the amount of suffering in the world is to stop procreating. This highlights a tension between two values typically affirmed by these religions (i.e., the value of reducing harm and the value of the family unit, which typically includes having children). Again, theists have conducted very little work to engage with this type of challenge.

I haven't claimed that any of the arguments for anti-natalism are in fact sound. Instead, I have tried to show that if they are sound, they present various challenges to certain aspects of theism, if not theism itself. I hope that in future work theists will take up this call to engage directly with anti-natalism.[13]

Notes

1 However, with talk of essences mostly falling out of fashion in the twentieth and twenty-first centuries, philosophers now seem to take existence to be morally neutral. It could be good or bad, but it is not inherently one or the other. But even putting the idea of essences aside, it's still coherent to ask whether humans should

be grateful to God for their existence. It's still possible to ask whether some, most, or all humans have lives that are worth starting and worth continuing. In light of this, much of my discussion will still apply to those who are sceptical of essences.

2. ST Ia.5.I and Ia.5.3.
3. The summary of the arguments in this section first appeared in my entry, "Anti-Natalism" in *Internet Encyclopedia of Philosophy* (2019) which is published open access.
4. See Parfit (1986) for discussion.
5. Consider parents who don't have children because they know beforehand that they would be born with a genetic impairment.
6. For some objections to the Asymmetry Argument, see Bradley (2013), DeGrazia (2012), Harman (2009), Metz (2011), Overall (2012). Benatar (2013) replies to some of these critics.
7. The Undeluded Gladness Argument has received far less attention in the literature than the Asymmetry but for challenges to it see DeGrazia (2012) and Harman (2009).
8. Notice that what position one takes regarding divine foreknowledge affects the impact of this argument on theism. Molinists about foreknowledge will say that God possesses epistemic certainty about the way her creation will turn out. Open theists will claim that while God does not possess epistemic certainty about how her creation will turn out, she possesses very strong predictive power regarding the outcome. There are clearly many more different positions on divine foreknowledge. I use these two as examples for the sake of simplicity. Likewise, what I say here will apply to other models of divine foreknowledge.
9. Of course, one problem for this view is that it is difficult to explain why people shouldn't procreate as much as possible. Benatar claims that his asymmetry thesis best explains why there is no obligation to create happy people.
10. See Davis (2008), Ch. 6.
11. Notice too that that (5) is true if even just one of the philanthropic arguments are sound.
12. One exception to this, albeit indirectly, is Kenneth Himma who argues that it is immoral for theists to procreate if they believe in the doctrine of hell (see Himma 2010 and 2016).
13. Thanks to Joshua Harris for extensive comments on a draft of this chapter.

References

Adams, Marilyn McCord. (2000). *Horrendous Evils and the Goodness of God*. Oxford: Oxford University Press.

Belshaw, Christopher. (2012). "A New Argument for Anti-Natalism." *South African Journal of Philosophy*, 31 (1): 117–27.

Benatar, David. (2006) *Better Never to Have Been: The Harm of Coming into Existence*. Oxford: Oxford University Press.

Benatar, David. (2013). "Still Better Never to Have Been: A Reply to (More of) My Critics." *Journal of Ethics*, 17: 121–51.

Benatar, David. (2015). "The Misanthropic Argument for Anti-natalism." In Sarah Hannon, Samantha Brennan, and Richard Vernon (eds.), *Permissible Progeny?: The Morality of Procreation and Parenting*, 34–59. Oxford: Oxford University Press.

Bradley, Ben. (2013). "Asymmetries in Benefiting, Harming and Creating." *Journal of Ethics*, 17: 37–49.

Davis, Brian. (2008). "Is God a Moral Agent?" In D. Z. Phillips (eds.), *Whose God? Which Tradition?*, 97–122. New York: Routledge.

Davies, Brian. (2011). *Thomas Aquinas on God and Evil*. Oxford: Oxford University Press.

DeGrazia, David. (2012). *Creation Ethics: Reproduction, Genetics, and Quality of Life*. Oxford: Oxford University Press.

Harman, Elizabeth. (2009). "Critical Study of David Benatar. *Better Never To Have Been: The Harm of Coming into Existence* (Oxford: Oxford University Press, 2006)." *Nous*, 43 (4): 776–85.

Harrison, Gerald. (2012). "Antinatalism, Asymmetry, and an Ethic of *Prima Facie* Duties." *South African Journal of Philosophy*, 31 (1): 94–103.

Himma, Kenneth Einar. (2010) "Birth as a Grave Misfortune: The Doctrines of Hell, Exclusivism, and Salvific Luck." In Joel Buenting (ed.), *The Problem of Hell: An Anthology*, 179–98. Burlington, VT: Ashgate Publishing.

Himma, Kenneth Einar. (2016). "The Ethics of Subjecting a Child to the Risk of Eternal Torment." *Faith and Philosophy*, 33 (1): 94–108.

Howard-Snyder, Daniel and Frances Howard-Snyder. (1994). "How an Unsurpassable Being Can Create a Surpassable World." *Faith and Philosophy*, 11 (2): 260–8.

Kraay, Klaas J. (2011). "Theism and Modal Collapse." *American Philosophical Quarterly*, 48 (4): 361–72.

Lougheed, Kirk. (2014). "Divine Creation, Modal Collapse, and the Theistic Multiverse." *Sophia* 53 (4): 435–46.

Mackie, J.L. (1982). *The Miracle of Theism: Arguments for and against the Existence of God*. Oxford: Oxford University Press.

Metz, Thaddeus. (2011). "Are Lives Worth Creating?" *Philosophical Papers*, 40 (2): 233–55.

Overall, Christine. (2012). *Why Have Children?: The Ethical Debate*. Oxford, UK: MIT Press.

Parfit, Derek. (1986). *Reasons and Persons*. Oxford: Oxford University Press.

Plantinga, Alvin. (1989). *God, Freedom, and Evil*. Grand Rapids, MI: Eerdmans Publishing.

Rowe, William. (1979). "Friendly Atheism, Skeptical Theism, and the Problem of Evil." *International Journal for Philosophy of Religion*, 59 (2): 79–92.

Rowe, William. (2004). *Can God be Free?* Oxford: Oxford University Press.

Shiffrin, Seana. (1999). "Wrongful Life, Procreative Responsibility, and the Significance of Harm." *Legal Theory*, 5: 117–48.

Singh, Asheel. (2012). "Furthering the Case for Anti-natalism: Seana Shiffrin and the Limits of Permissible Harm." *South African Journal of Philosophy*, 31 (1): 104–16.

Wykstra, Stephen J. (2012). "Foundations of Skeptical Theism." *Faith and Philosophy*, 29 (4): 375–99.

9

Thank *You*

William Desmond's Metaphysics of Gift and Ethic of Gratitude

Ethan Vanderleek

To think the gift of being is to delve into an immeasurably deep mystery. However frequently this path of thought is pursued, however brilliant an exposition offered, the question of being springs afresh. My own questioning down this path has been led by many others, especially William Desmond, to whom I refer freely and frequently later. My chapter here is an attempt to draw together what I have learned from them into a coherent line of thought which opens the mysterious gift of being onto the mystery of God-as-personal. Mystery—what we cannot fully master or know, that which we inchoately grasp as mastering and knowing *us*—confronts us throughout our lives, if we attune ourselves to hear, see, and know what lies beyond our hearing, seeing, and knowing.

The thesis I advance is that the being of finite existence is a gift from a personal giver, God. The appropriate, rational, and religious response is ethical gratitude in both particular actions and in life itself. Reason itself can move us toward this thesis, without recourse to any special, historical revelation. Of course, this path of thinking has emerged and developed very strongly within certain traditions, but such development is a *discovery* within these traditions. It is neither a mere invention of human thought nor a pure revelation with no point of contact in human reality as such. If this philosophical journey proceeds logically and reasonably, it does so by submitting itself to a common reality, not by depending upon revealed, historical facts of particular religious traditions (however much such traditions have had this reality revealed to and through them).

By finite existence I mean everything around us that we recognize, experience, and live with as constrained by space, time, and human capability. Finite existence has limits, boundaries, understood in any sense. A flower, a house, a distant star, a political ideology, a water molecule, a human person, and every other thing or entity we can encounter or even conceive of are all finite. Some of these things remain beyond human knowledge by virtue of inaccessibility, such as distant galaxies and the core of the Earth, some by the inscrutability and unpredictability of human behavior and action, such as political movements and personality. But these, too, are subject to limits: no distant star is infinite nor is any human reality (even if human reality can open *up* to the infinite). Other things, such as the location of objects in my room, objects which I know how to use and know something about, can be acted upon and talked about fairly easily. However, as we will see, even objects which I appear to totally control, like a pen or a pencil, initially give themselves to me with a power of self-presentation I cannot control or bring about.

Any finite existent, though, including the totality of finite existence—that is, everything that was, is, and will be—expresses a certain excessiveness or surplus. Careful reflection on anything we encounter leads to the recognition that within finite limits a surplus of self-expression issues from beyond the finite thing itself. The trees outside my window do not explain or provide their own existence; they are beneficiaries of being, not self-creations. The surplus is *being itself*. There is no finite existence "as such," because any finite entity does not contain its being within itself. All finitude is a window beyond itself to infinitude. All finite existence presupposes being, and being is not subject to the limitations of this or that finite thing. W. Norris Clark suggests that the existence of a thing is not reducible to what the thing is. He writes, the "inner act of existence is not reducible to an essence or mode of being, a *what*, nor a mere *static state* but a *dynamic act of presence* that makes any essence or nature to be real, to present itself actively to other real beings."[1] There is a dynamic self-expressiveness which shines through all limited, finite entities, but which is not reducible to any one or even the entirety of such entities. This tree exists, and my desk also exists; and so do countless other finite entities. They all share in being, by virtue of their actually existing, yet no particular thing exhausts the fullness of being itself. As William Desmond writes, "There is something surd about the 'that is it' of the 'to be': it just happens to be, and initially it does not explain itself."[2]

We can only encounter things in existence. Their existence is necessary for them to be present to us for whatever activity or analysis with may undertake with or on them. An infinite length of human activity or analysis in time would never touch or access the being of a thing. All of our activity and analysis depend upon things already existing. An exhaustive material, social, or any other determinate analysis of any finite entity, any community of such existents, or even the entirety of all finite existence, does not provide an explanation or source for its very being. All such analyses depend upon this self-presentation of being-already-there to provide their subject matter. Hans Urs von Balthasar suggests that the question of being as such "is not posed seriously by any [determinate] 'science' because science always presupposes its subject matter as objectively given thus."[3] Being is the absolute presupposition for all finite determination and negation.

It is impossible to act or to know without there *being something to act or know upon*. Our interaction with things in the orders of knowing and acting is derivative of something prior *to* our knowing and acting. And, further than just our activity, an entity's *own* existence is necessarily prior to it being this or that determinate thing. As William Desmond writes, "negation and determination originally presuppose this excess of being as a positive indetermination, the overdetermination of plenitude."[4]

What is this being that finite existence receives? Being is "in" all finite existence; if the self-expressiveness of being were not present or operative, then finite entities, as individuals or a totality of all individuals, would not exist, would not be at all. And yet, we can never pin down or grasp the being of a finite entity or entities. No amount of examination, manipulation, or time would help us arrive at the being of any finite entity; all such activities arrive too late, for being is necessarily metaphysically prior. As Khaled Anatolios writes, commenting on Gregory of Nyssa's epistemology, "Being . . . is a dynamic of active self-announcement that cannot be superseded by the knower's grasp and announcement of it."[5] While finite beings are immanently present to us in a certain sense, dynamically self-presenting to be known, encountered, and acted upon, no finite entity or even all finite entities will deliver their being, that dynamic act of self-presentation, over to our analysis or use. An exhaustive material analysis of a thing does not touch its being nor does a thorough submission of a thing to my will or our use.

Nor would a violent, destructive attack, or even the gentle slipping away of an entity with the passage of time; after destruction or dissolution, the past being of the thing still remains untouched. It *did* exist, and such existence was necessarily excessive of the thing itself. As Desmond writes, "the power of the negative is not on a part with this excess original power of being . . . negative work is always a modification of this original power of being."[6] All finite being is subject to what Desmond calls the "universal impermanence" and so will suffer such change, use, and eventually destruction or dissolution.[7] However, naming this impermanence does not at all explain the existence of finite being. It only draws the mind onward, deeper into the question: How it is that things exist at all? How does *anything* and *everything* exist at all?

Being is simultaneously immanent and transcendent to finitude. Being inheres so closely to finite existence that we are hard pressed to find words to describe this closeness and intimacy. Finite existence would not-be without being. Being is that-without-which-a-finite-thing-would-not-be, and so we always encounter something of being-as-such, even in a limited, finite expression. Being not only sustains finite existence; it is not merely an external condition or cause of finitude, but it somehow mysteriously inheres *in* finite being. When we encounter a finite entity, we encounter it *as* existing. So being is not an external cause, like a hammer blow that leaves a mark on soft metal. It inheres more intimately than that, more analogous to a mother carrying her unborn child.

And yet, being itself is also transcendent to finitude, because nothing in finite existence accounts for its own being. Everything that does exist will eventually cease to exist, in its emerging, changing, shifting, and eventual disappearance. Finite being participates temporally, locally, and finitely in infinite Being. Being-as-such is never exhausted, never even touched by the totality of finite existence in time and space. It remains impassably transcendent. As Balthasar says,

> although all existents partake in Being, yet—to whatever extent we were to multiply them—they never exhaust it nor even, as it were, "broach" it. In their individual finitude as fragments they can indeed form a greater, perhaps somehow even the greatest whole, which however hangs as much in the air (of Being) as a total configuration as do its constituent parts.[8]

One more or less finite entity, or even the totality of *all* finite existence, does not deplete this inexhaustible source, being itself. No quantitative amount can cross the qualitative chasm.

This simultaneous immanence and transcendence, or finitude and infinitude, of Being suggests that every encounter we have with finite being immediately invokes and depends upon the surplus and excess of infinite being. As David Bentley Hart says, "we can approach nature only across the interval of the supernatural."[9] At every moment we encounter both immanence and transcendence simultaneously. Our inevitable and necessary focus on immanent things, needs, and concerns only displaces transcendence from *our* perspective but does nothing to actually eliminate the transcendent source of finite existence, being itself. This source is never absent: any local concern for knowing or using being depends upon the over-and-above presence of infinite being offered to us through finite, immanent entities.

In naming this community of immanence and transcendence, we are pursuing a path indicated by Desmond in one of his early works, where he says that the aim in contemplating being as such "is not to ascend to being from becoming and leave becoming behind."[10] Becoming, or finite existence, subject to time, growth, and decay, *is*, and because it does not contain its principle of being within itself, it is necessarily in relation to transcendent being. Not containing its existence in itself, it receives it from beyond itself. Transcendence is not a static realm isolated from immanence; finite existence is not denied community with infinite being. Indeed, far from being denied, such community is necessary. Though there is *difference* there is no *opposition* between immanent existence and transcendent being. An image: a child can be helped by a parent toward a common goal that they both share, even in their difference, in contrast to enemies who pursue opposite and opposing goals. Transcendence aids, supports, and encourages immanence, rather than being opposed to it. Immanent existence depends upon and exists in relation to transcendent being. This being so, there must be a dynamism and relationality *within* transcendence, such that it can issue forth, ground, support, and enable finite being in its immanence. This dynamism and relationality suggest a personal giver who unites being and becoming, transcendence and immanence. I will return to this.

The perplexity and mystery deepen further when we direct our inquiry toward ourselves. Upon recognizing the excessiveness of being in other finite entities, I am brought to the realization that I, too, am finite. I, too, do not contain the reason for my existence within myself. I, too, am in relation to transcendence, that infinite source of being from which my finite being issues forth. We know this analogously in the complex network of relations which support our existence. I depend upon my father and mother for my existence, I depend upon a supply chain (a hot political/economic point of discussion these days) for the food and other goods which sustain me, and I depend upon community and friends for my relational, psychological, and spiritual health. Pushing this further, though, I see that all these relations of dependence, these various networks, are *themselves* lacking the reason for their own existence. Just as I necessarily depend upon these various finite relations, even more so is my very being sourced from beyond the entirety of the finite realm. This truth absolutely gives the lie to any project of complete human autonomy. Any autonomy I achieve is always immediately related to what is *not* mine, my very existence, given as a gift. Autonomy is derivative of heteronomy.

Because we do not have the principle for our own existence within ourselves, and yet we *do exist*, at every moment we are in relation with what is other than ourselves. When we love ourselves, we therefore also love what is not ourselves. Thus, proper self-love is also a love of being as such. For I am, yet I did not create myself. I love myself, I exist, yet my existence is not mine but is shared with all finite being, which is equally non-self-substantial. Desmond calls these two loves "first love," or love of self, and "second love," or love of others and otherness.[11] While first love is temporally prior, since it begins spontaneously in the infant, it is derivative of the more primordial second love, which is a love of being as such. We spontaneously affirm the goodness of all being when we love ourselves. True, first love can be distorted and retracted in either narcissism or self-hatred, but such distortion logically depends upon second love; there could be no distortion of first self-love if it were not rooted in the proper affirmation and celebration of being in the second other-love. First love matures and blossoms the more fully it realizes its dependence upon second love and the gift of being, our relatedness to what is other than ourselves.

But is being really a *gift*? Gift implies goodness and generosity. Does an analysis of first love and its derivation from second love merely explain how we *experience* being, but not how being is in itself? Do we see being as good simply as a projection of our own self-love? Perhaps being is not good, is not a gift, but is simply a neutral thereness. We place value on it because we must do this to survive, but such value is merely subjective projection; there is no objective ground for value. We might agree that being is an excess or surplus, not contained in an entity itself or even the totality of entities, but why should this mean being is a gift? Especially concerning the experience of evil, shouldn't finite being, derived from being-as-such, be understood in itself as neutral, to which we subjectively ascribe either goodness or evil?

The thought of neutral being is terrifying to us. We do not and cannot dwell with it for long, because we necessarily live in a world charged with value. We always belong to a valued world, what Desmond called "the ethos."[12] The question here is whether the valued world we live in is a subjective imposition or if our valuing activity encounters what is not simply *our* values. Do we value finite existence, are finite things capable of being valued, because being as such is inherently valuable or valued? At the very least, we must grant this: being is *hospitable to value*. We undeniably *do* value finite being. Even if we theoretically suggest that being is neutral, we live in a world where being is at least *capable* of being valued. But how can we account for this hospitality to our value? How is finite being capable of receiving our value if there is nothing inherently valuable about it? The hospitality of finite being to our valuing suggests that finite being has some mysteriously inherent value. We could not value finite being were it not receptive to such valuing.

Desmond will frequently point out that if finite being is ultimately valueless, then so are we; the values we create or impose have no ground, for we are completely a part of this community of finite being. If we want to give our valuing some foundation so that our valuing activity does not merely blow away with a light breeze, this activity must be grounded in a value that is not ourselves. As Desmond suggests, "the good for us presupposes a more primordial sense of the goodness of being."[13] We always do *trust* that our valuing is met by hospitality to value; does such trust intimate a nonsubjective source of value upon which our subjective valuing depends?

Regarding the question of evil, both human and nonhuman, our ability to recognize evil suggests that evil is derivative of such primordial value. We value finite being, and we recognize when that value is violated. We love someone and are appalled by their suffering. The hospitality of being to value allows us to value it and to recognize when such value is distorted. Finite entities cry out when oppressed; an important question is if we are capable of hearing and heeding such a call. Though we may treat the earth, for example, as simply neutrally there for our purely subjective valuing and use, the earth pushes back against distortions or valuing. Environmental degradation and our ability to recognize such damage point to an inchoate yet truly inherent value of finite being pushing back against our distortions. The same is true of the cry of the exploited human poor. In both cases—the earth and the poor—how could a cry of violation be issued or be heard if finite being were not itself a source of value, inherently valued by something or someone other than ourselves?[14]

In speaking of this "inherent value," I am not suggesting that value can easily and objectively be read off of finite being. The value or worth of finite being does not impose itself upon us. Finite existence, in its hospitality to our valuing, says something to the effect of "here I am. I am open to your love, your use, but also to your misuse and abuse." Being is offered through finite existence as a gift, capable of receiving our value, which may lead to celebration and elevation of such finite existence—for example, the grateful reception and use of grain for bread—but also to a twisting of finite existence toward our own, self-enclosed ends. As gift, finite being does not determine us, does not demand from us, even if a mature soul can recognize when the gift is being abused, when the gift-character of the gift is ignored, and when we treat finite being as merely manipulable material in service to ourselves.

Let me summarize the path I have followed thus far. Being as such is in excess to all finite existence. Every finite determination depends upon an excessive or overdetermined surplus which is not contained by finitude, even as finite existence manifests this surplus in a beautiful multiplicity of finite entities. Being suggests itself as a gift, since it does not naturally *belong* to any finite entity. But is it really a gift? Could it not be neutral, or even inherently evil? The fact that we live in a world of value, and that we necessarily *do* value finite being, means that being offers itself to our valuing through the finite entities we use (and often misuse). We can and do value and use the world around us. Finite being is hospitable to our value, to our saying "this is good," even if we frequently reduce finite being to "this is good *for me*." It is not a definitive argument but a suggestive one: How could finite being receive our valuing activity, if there were not some appropriate fit or belonging between that activity and the transcendent being shining through the finite entity so valued? And since both the being of the valued thing or entity and the being of the valuing entity, ourselves, do not belong to us, we are pointed to a giving source of both.

The movement of this line of reasoning pushes us to the thought of gratitude. If finite being, both our own and other being, is a gift, the rational response is gratitude. Gift summons and invites gratitude, but does not demand it. Gratitude is a posture of the whole person, which infiltrates not just discreet moments or feelings of thankfulness but may, at its most mature and developed, affect every dimension of the person's life. How is this so? If being itself is a gift to finitude, a gift to us, both in ourselves and what is other to ourselves, there is no dimension of our existence over which we could claim absolute ownership. Anything we can and do control is derivative of this more primordial gift-nature of being. The deepest gratitude, what Desmond calls "ontological gratitude," is fundamentally a spiritual disposition or attitude, which recognizes that everything is fundamentally *received*.[15]

Human existence necessarily depends upon a certain level of control, mastery, and autonomy. We must master our environment to feed and clothe ourselves, master ourselves to organize social relations. But the discipline and practice of gratitude involve a constant shift of perspective, which recognizes that these activities depend upon gift. Ontological gratitude affects the how and why of our mastering activity. Desmond frequently makes a distinction between the *passio essendi*, the passion of being, and the *conatus essendi*, the endeavor to be.[16] The *passio* is more metaphysically primordial, a fundamental receptivity of our finite being, always prior to our endeavoring activity. Gratitude consists in recognizing how the *conatus* is asymmetrically grounded in the *passio*. The *passio* is not similarly grounded in the *conatus*. Gratitude encourages the activity of the *conatus* to recognize and align itself with the *passio*. Though the *conatus* can and does run roughshod over the *passio* (as in the discussion of abuse, earlier), the cry of the earth and the cry of the poor suggest that the prior givenness of things to us in our *passio* can never be finally eliminated. An excess of *conatus* provokes a cry of protest. "Remember I am a gift! I am not simply or merely yours!" Our endeavor run amok will provoke an outcry, even if issuing from the quiet and lonely places of creation. Gratitude is a discipline of hearing, of attuning ourselves to these silent cries: Where is the gift-character of being suppressed by an absolute demand that everything serve me?

Ontological gratitude, the foundation of all more determinate modes of thankfulness, is the recognition of the gift of being. Gratitude is a posture of affirming and celebrating our receptivity to this gift. Gratitude is deeply and richly rational, for it is a response to the way things actually are: offered, given, received. I and my world are not self-creations. Gratitude for the gift of being is rational in being metaphysical, in responding to the gift of being in-and-through every finite thing, which would not be for us and would not be *at all*, if not for giftedness. Desmond writes that "metaphysical gratitude is not only a thanks for this or that, but in the this and the that its consent overflows the boundaries of determinate things."[17] If gratitude is called for by *being* itself—"that barest, most basic, more primordial of attributions"[18]—then all finite being cries out to be affirmed, celebrated, and given thanks for. "Ethics springs from gratitude."[19]

This link between metaphysics, gratitude, and ethics is demonstrated in Balthasar's beautiful fusing of metaphysics and ethics, at the culmination of his dense contribution to Christian and philosophical metaphysics in *The Glory of the Lord V*. "The Christians of today," he writes,

> are given the task of performing the act of affirming Being . . . an act which is at first theological, but which contains within itself the whole dimension of the metaphysical act of the affirmation of Being. . . . the Christian is truest to his calling when he finds himself in the presence of this poorest and smallest area of love's manifestation.[20]

Gratitude unites thought and action, mind and flesh. It is this celebration of finite being which encourages the metaphysician to necessarily also be an ethicist, affirming those dimensions of finite being which are neglected, seemingly silenced: the oppressed, the suffering, the abused, both human and nonhuman. In short, the poor in spirit, for theirs is the Kingdom of heaven.

One final move remains to be made, from the gift to the giver. If we are rationally to give thanks for the gift of being, to *whom* do we give thanks? To a meaningless void, which accidentally and impersonally supplied the gift? Can a gift be given without a personal giver from whom the gift issues? Can a gift be impersonal? The great twentieth-century Russian theologian Sergius Bulgakov recounts a moment in his conversion away from the atheism of his youth: while traveling toward a mountain range, he "[sees] them for the first time," recognizes their beautiful strangeness and givenness. This recognition suggests a personal source. "My soul had grown accustomed long ago," he writes,

> to see with a dull silent pain only a dead wasteland in nature beneath the veil of beauty, as under a deceptive mask; without being away of it, my soul was not reconciled with a nature without God. And suddenly in that hour my soul became agitated, started to rejoice and began to shiver: *but what if* . . . *if it is not wasteland, not a lie, not a mask, not death, but him, the blessed and loving Father, his raiment, his love?*[21]

The experience of beauty is enormously suggestive of the gift of being beyond our demands of usefulness.[22] Beauty is not useful but simply gives itself for our enjoyment and celebration. Bulgakov's experience of the given beauty of the mountains immediately provokes him to think the source of this gift, not as impersonal, but as *him*, "the blessed and loving Father." The giver of a gift is a personal *Thou*, not an impersonal *it*.[23]

The concept person, especially in a philosophical argument for God, seems to depart from the strictures of reason. Doesn't the notion of a personal giver of finite being stem more from individual, intimate piety and religion than from the impersonal universal scope of reason? Doesn't a personal God seem to restrict God to a finite being to whom people pray and find comfort, rather than the impersonal, awe-inspiring ground of being? A "personal God" seems ripe for Feuerbach's critique of Christian faith as a projection of human "personality" onto a "God" who only exists by that projection: "the object of any subject is nothing else than the subject's own nature taken objectively."[24] God, the object of human knowledge, is simply the nature of the human subject taken objectively. The human subject desires a personal God, and so God is personal: "Longing says: there must be a personal God, *i.e.*, it cannot be that there is not; satisfied feeling says: He is."[25] It appears to be a simple, logical step to conclude that a personal God is *merely* a human projection: "the divine being is nothing else than the human being, or rather, the human nature purified, freed from the limits of the individual man, made objective."[26]

But *is* this such a logical argument? Sebastian Moore has suggested that there is no reason to include "merely" as an adverb for the fulfillment of human desire in God.[27] If a personal God fulfills human desire to be known and personally loved, that is no argument against the existence of God. Now, many monotheistic traditions recognize that idolatry is a real problem, and that our gods are all-too-often human projections and so have some affinity for Feuerbach's analysis. But the critique of idolatry is paired with the revelation that idols are unable to meet our deepest desires; we are not so satisfied with subjective projection as Feuerbach suggests. What I long for is not just a projection of myself, which is ultimately *un*fulfilling, but rather a personal Other who loves and affirms me, whose love and affirmation is the very ground of my finite existence and also the finite existence of everything else that is.[28]

Thinking of God as a personal giver may seem to run counter to the richest reflections of the world's greatest philosophers and theologians. A personal God may be suitable for the masses, for those who, in their weakness, need their religion to offer comfort and encouragement. Surely speculative metaphysics is a far grander and more mature approach to God, which dispenses with the childish ways of God as "person" and instead ascends to the pure categories of being, goodness, truth, and beauty. But what I am suggesting in this chapter is that the line of metaphysical inquiry pursued here leads *precisely* to a personal God. Metaphysics pursued with Desmond may provide something of a philosophical rationale for the layperson's prayer life or other practices that are too easily dismissed as mere anthropomorphizing of divinity.

I certainly recognize the temptation to shrink God down to our size, and there is a sense of a "personal God" which does fall subject to a "merely" critique. God is not "merely" a comforting, personal friend, a nonjudgmental listener and affirmer. True, there is an analogy between God as person and the finite, human persons we are, know, love, befriend, marry, and so on. But the analogy must work to expand *our* notion of the human person toward the mysterious personhood of God, not to restrict God to a limited understanding of human person.[29]

The word "person" has roots in the *persona* of Greek drama; *persona* "was the enacted being, the presented identity of the character on the stage."[30] Drama provides an analogy with what is always going on in ordinary human relations. The mask of the actor incarnates and makes present the character, yet also hides the actor, suggesting a simultaneous presence and absence. The person is manifestly there, offered in their flesh and their communicative presence, yet that presence is never exhaustive of mysterious depths of character, personality, will, memory, desire, and so on. When we encounter another person, we do truly encounter them, for even a person who lies or deceives does so by distorting a more primordial truth or presence. But this truth and presence, even in the most trusting and nondeceptive relationship, is never without remainder. "Showing is always both showing and keeping in reserve";[31] personal manifestation is never complete.

Perhaps describing the human person in this way, as a finite manifestation of infinite depths, is a distinctive mode of being finite. As we have seen, nothing contains the principle of its own being. Finitude receives its being from outside itself, as a gift. But this opening beyond can take on different levels of intensity. An inanimate object and a living thing are both finite; both share a mysterious source of being. A living thing, though, manifests a greater complexity and diversity which inspires greater pause when considering its source of being. A rock might suggest a more static form of being (though even a rock suggests some dynamism in its communicable presence), but a plant or animal intimates more fully the dynamism, the relationality and self-transcendence of the origin of being. The human person deepens the mystery even further with even richer communicative capacity: For what is the mysterious source of these rich communicative powers of the human person?

The mysterious depths of the human person suggest that to ascribe personhood to God the giver of being is not to restrict God but to recognize how far beyond us God is. The personal is *more*, not less, mysterious than the impersonal. As Desmond writes, "To be is to be in relation: to be personal is to be in social relations, to be at all is to be in community. In that light, being as personal is ontologically richer than being as impersonal."[32] If we recognize that human personhood suggests this rich, mysterious depth, then divine personhood is no shrinking of God to a "merely" personal God. Rather, the "merely" critique would fall more appropriately upon an *impersonal* God. "Impersonal" suggests a God more static, more conformable to our knowing capacity. God-as-personal, on the other hand, pulls our knowledge and our action beyond our own self-sufficient capacity in a self-transcending movement toward knowledge and love of God.

If God is the creator of all that is, and if all that is includes human persons, then the source must be *eminently* personal, for no effect can outstrip its cause. As the doctrine of divine simplicity directs us toward naming God as the Good, True, and Beautiful, so too does it indicate that God is infinite Personality, Personhood as such.

Being is a gift to finite existence, and it is a gift from God-as-personal, the "thou" to whom our gratitude is directed. Does God, in giving this gift, give the gift of himself? Is God being as such, in whom all finite existence participates? Desmond suggests a tension be held between God as-being and God-beyond-being. If God is the cause of all being, then in some sense God stands beyond being. But if God is beyond Being, then what link connects the giver and the gift? Desmond's aphoristic response to Jean-Luc Marion's book *God without Being* reads: "God without being becomes being without God."[33]

The move toward God without being is to retain God's transcendence, refusing to encompass God without our schemes of organizing and knowing beings. God, as creator, is certainly not a being among beings. However, why should we grant that being as such is a static category, fixed to our human measure? Being is an excessive, personal gift, dynamically self-expressive. We can say that God is the fullness of being itself; God gives himself freely in and through immanent reality, transcendently self-offering himself through all that is. The gift is so total, so intimate, that most of the time we cannot even recognize it, for the world appears to us as already in existence, and quickly deteriorates, in our vision, into simply inert, impersonal stuff, that we manipulate and use. But if being is God-as-personal, then finite existence is meant to be elevated, returned to the fullness of personhood in God. Our use of the gift of finite entities, participants in being, must be a gratitude that personalizes finite being, gently bringing it into a human, personal sphere which respects the infinite personal depth that lies in each individual thing, never exhausted, never contained.

In *What Is Called Thinking?* Heidegger grounds thinking in thanking. Thinking is not repaying a gift with another gift, but "pure thanks is rather that we simply think—think what is really and solely given, what is there to be thought."[34] He enjoins a certain contemplative posture for thinking, thinking which "devotes its thought to what is to be thought."[35] But this remains abstract, impersonal. The thanks offered by thinking is simply offered up into a void. Who receives this thanksgiving of thinking? Heidegger does not broach this question.

Perhaps we could amend Heidegger's suggestion with "*prayer* is thanking"; prayer of thanksgiving is the foundation of thinking. There is an aspect of thinking which can tip into prayer. As Heidegger rightly notes, thinking submits itself to what is to be thought: "What calls on us to think, demands for itself that it be tended, cared for, husbanded in its own essential nature, by thought."[36] But prayer is addressed to a *thou*; it is an infinitely *personal* reality to whom prayer responds, to whom prayer pulls us. The gift of being to finite being summons forth gratitude and thankfulness, not vague and abstract, but directed toward a thou, to whom we can say "Thank *you.*" Again, personal thankfulness does not reduce God to a finite giver; an analogical chasm remains between our thankfulness for finite gifts from finite people and the ultimate gift of existence itself from God. Yet all finite gifts participate in the infinite gift of being as such, given to all finite being by the infinite giver. Prayer beholds finite being, whether of self or other, and perceives the personal gift which subtends all such finite existence. Prayer is a constant discipline of gratitude, a process of recognizing and celebrating our absolutely dependent existence upon an independent, loving, personal source. Our life itself can become a prayer. "Praying without ceasing" (1 Thess. 5:17) allows us to live out of gratitude, affirming things in their *gift* dimension, before they become subservient to my or our demands. And even when our prayer and gratitude falters, we can never escape the gift, for it is always present, always excessively above what we ask or imagine. Prayer is always possible, because the gift is always actual.

Notes

1. Norris Clark (2001: 79–80).
2. Desmond (2016: 205).
3. von Balthasar (1991: 613). Of course, metaphysics is the science of being *qua* being, but it is a different order of science from the science Balthasar refers to here. We might use vocabulary from Desmond to distinguish between "determinate" sciences, such as history, psychology, and biology, and the "overdeterminate" science of metaphysics.
4. Desmond (1995a: 292).
5. Anatolios (2011: 163).
6. Desmond (1995a: 291).
7. See chapter 7, "Creation: The Universal Impermanence" in Desmond (1995a: 267–97).
8. von Balthasar (1991: 618).
9. Hart (2015: 228).
10. Desmond (2014: 217).
11. See Desmond (1990: 188–9).
12. See Desmond (2001: 21).
13. Desmond (1995a: 512).
14. This paragraph is a metaphysical riff on the title of Leonardo Boff's liberation-eco-theology book, Boff (1997).
15. "Proper use is to use with ontological gratitude" (Desmond 1995a: 437).
16. This distinction recurs in many places in Desmond's writings. For an example, see Desmond (2008: 21).
17. Desmond (1995b: 258).
18. Hart (2017: 99).
19. Desmond (2001: 217).
20. Balthasar (1991: 348, 349).

21 Bulgakov (2012: 8).
22 See Desmond (2018), esp. chap. 1.
23 A distinction famously explored in Martin Buber (2004).
24 Feuerbach (1957: 12).
25 Feuerbach (1957: 146).
26 Feuerbach (1957: 14).
27 Moore (1983: 13).
28 Moore (1983: 18).
29 See Hart's discussion of "person" in a Trinitarian and anthropological context in *The Beauty of the Infinite: The Aesthetics of Christian Truth* (Hart 2003: 170): "Does not the burden of and promise of trinitarian thought lie now in its incompatibility with modernity's understanding of personality, and its ability, consequently, to expose that understanding [described by Hart earlier 'as isolated, punctiliar, psychic monad'] as a perverse and sinful fiction?"
30 Desmond (2008: 192).
31 Desmond (2001: 190).
32 Desmond (2008: 191).
33 Desmond (2008: 284).
34 Heidegger (1976: 143).
35 Heidegger (1976).
36 Heidegger (1976: 121).

References

Anatolios, Khaled. (2011). *Retrieving Nicaea: The Development and Meaning of Trinitarian Doctrine*. Grand Rapids, MI: Baker Academic.

Boff, Leonardo. (1997). *Cry of the Earth, Cray of the Poor*, trans. Phillip Berryman. Maryknoll, NY: Orbis Books.

Buber, Martin. (2004). *I and Thou*, trans. Ronald Gregor Smith. London: Continuum.

Bulgakov, Sergius. (2012). *Unfading Light: Contemplations and Speculation*, trans. Thomas Allan Smith. Grand Rapids, MI: Wm. B. Eerdmans Publishing Co.

Desmond, William. (1990). *Philosophy and Its Others: Ways of Being and Mind*. Albany, NY: State University of New York Press.

Desmond, William. (1995a). *Being and the Between*. Albany, NY: State University of New York Press.

Desmond, William. (1995b). *Perplexity and Ultimacy: Metaphysical Thoughts from the Middle*. Albany, NY: State University of New York Press.

Desmond, William. (2001). *Ethics and the Between*. Albany, NY: State University of New York Press.

Desmond, William. (2008). *God and the Between*. Malden, MA: Blackwell Publishing.

Desmond, William. (2014). *Desire, Dialectic, & Otherness: An Essay on Origins*, 2nd ed. Eugene, OR: Cascade Books.
Desmond, William. (2016). *The Intimate Universal: The Hidden Porosity Among Religion, Art, Philosophy, and Politics*. New York: Columbia University Press.
Desmond, William. (2018). *The Gift of Beauty and the Passion of Being: On the Threshold between the Aesthetic and the Religious*. Eugene, OR: Cascade Books.
Feuerbach, Ludwig. (1957). *The Essence of Christianity*, trans. George Eliot. New York: Harper & Row Publishers, Inc.
Hart, David Bentley. (2003). *The Beauty of the Infinite: The Aesthetics of Christian Truth*. Grand Rapids, MI: Wm. B. Eerdmans Publishing Company.
Hart, David Bentley. (2015). *The Experience of God: Being, Consciousness, Bliss*. New Haven, CT: Yale University Press.
Hart, David Bentley. (2017). "The Destiny of Christian Metaphysics: Reflections on the *Analogia Entis*." In *The Hidden and the Manifest: Essays in Theology and Metaphysics*. Grand Rapids, MI: William B. Eerdmans Publishing Company.
Heidegger, Martin. (1976). *What Is Called Thinking?* trans. J. Glenn Gray. New York: Perennial Library.
Moore, Sebastian (1983). *The Inner Loneliness*. New York: Crossroad Publishing Co.
Norris Clark, W. (2001). *The One and the Many: A Contemporary Thomistic Metaphysics*. Notre Dame, IN: University of Notre Dame Press.
von Balthasar, Hans Urs. (1991). *The Glory of the Lord V: The Realm of Metaphysics in the Modern Age*, trans. Oliver Davies et al. San Francisco: Ignatius Press.

Notes on Contributors

Michael Almeida teaches philosophy at the University of Texas at San Antonio. He is the author of *Freedom, God, and Worlds* (2012), *The Metaphysics of Perfect Beings* (2008), and *Cosmological Arguments* (2018).

Neal DeRoo is Canada Research Chair in Phenomenology and Philosophy of Religion at The King's University. He is the author of *The Political Logic of Experience* (2022) and *Futurity in Phenomenology* (2013), and has co-edited several works at the intersection of Continental philosophy and philosophy of religion.

Christina M. Gschwandtner teaches Continental Philosophy of Religion at Fordham University. She is author of *Reading Jean-Luc Marion: Exceeding Metaphysics* (2007), *Postmodern Apologetics? Arguments about God in Contemporary Philosophy* (2012), *Degrees of Givenness: On Saturation in Jean-Luc Marion* (2014), *Marion and Theology* (2016), *Welcoming Finitude: Toward a Phenomenology of Orthodox Liturgy* (2019), and *Reading Religious Ritual with Ricœur: Between Fragility and Hope* (2021), besides many articles and translations at the intersection of phenomenology and religion.

Joshua Lee Harris is Assistant Professor of Philosophy at The King's University in Edmonton, Canada. He has published in journals such as *Ergo*, *Res Philosophica*, *Faith and Philosophy*, *Philosophy East and West*, and *Journal of Social Ontology*. His research covers topics in metaphysics, medieval philosophy, and the philosophy of social science.

Kirk Lougheed is Assistant Professor of Philosophy and Director of the Center for Faith and Human Flourishing at LCC International University. He is also a Research Associate in the Department of Philosophy at the University of Pretoria. His latest monographs are *Ubuntu and Western Monotheism: An Axiological Investigation* (2022) and *African Communitarianism and the Misanthropic Argument for Anti-Natalism* (2022).

Thaddeus Metz is Professor of Philosophy at the University of Pretoria in South Africa. He is known for drawing on the African philosophical tradition analytically to address a variety of contemporary moral/political/legal controversies. Metz has had more than 300 works published, including recent articles on African philosophy in *Mind, The Monist, and Religious Studies*. His book, *A Relational Moral Theory: African Ethics in and Beyond the Continent*, appeared in 2022.

Graham Oppy is Professor of Philosophy at Monash University and a Fellow of the Australian Academy of Humanities. He has written nine books in philosophy of religion, most recently *Naturalism and Religion* (2018), *Atheism and Agnosticism* (2018), and *Atheism: The Basics* (2019). He has also edited several books in philosophy of religion, including *The History of Western Philosophy of Religion* (with Nick Trakakis, 2009), *Ontological Arguments* (2019), and *Companion to Atheism and Philosophy* (2019).

Catherine Peters is an assistant professor at Loyola Marymount University (Los Angeles, California). Her specialization is in medieval philosophy, with a particular focus on the thought of Thomas Aquinas and Avicenna. She earned her PhD from the Center for Thomistic Studies at the University of St. Thomas (Houston, Texas) in 2019. Her current research centers on the intersections of natural philosophy, metaphysics, and natural theology.

Brian Treanor is professor of philosophy and Charles S. Casassa SJ Chair at Loyola Marymount University. Like Les Murray, he is "only interested in everything." Consequently, his scholarship is interdisciplinary in its method and wide-ranging in its foci. He is the author or editor of ten books, including: *Melancholic Joy* (2021), *Philosophy in the American West* (2020), *Carnal Hermeneutics* (2015), *Emplotting Virtue* (2014), and *Interpreting Nature* (2013).

Ethan Vanderleek is a doctoral student in Theology at Marquette University.

Index

absolute explanations   112–17, 119, 120 n.9
actualization   38, 109, 111–12, 115–16, 119, 120 n.9
  of the world   109, 111–12, 115–16, 119, 120 n.9
adoration   31
affection (*storge*)   47
afterlife   90, 154
agape   47
agent   5, 14–15, 49, 96, 100, 105 n.41, 132, 134–6, 139
  as efficient cause   132
  God as   94–6, 135
  personal   5, 14–15, 94
Akan people   90, 94, 104 n.12
ancestors   92–4, 103, 104 n.16
angst   65, 80
anthropocentrism   58, 62 n.30, 63 n.46
anthropology   7, 66, 71
anthropomorphizing   173
anti-natalism   9, 101–2, 105 n.46, 143, 146, 148–51, 153–8
  arguments for   9, 143, 146, 149–50, 153–8
  and atheism   143, 155–8
  misanthropic arguments and   146, 158
  and the Problem of Evil   156–7
appraisal   45, 51, 53, 54
appreciation   2, 7, 14, 19, 22, 24–5, 27–8, 42, 45–57, 60, 61 n.10, 98, 103
  aesthetic   2, 49–52, 56
  gratitude and   19, 24, 45, 48–9, 51–2, 54–5, 57, 60
  love and   46, 50–1, 54, 57, 61 n.10, 62 n.29
  and pleasure   47, 49–50
appreciative-love   46–7, 50–2, 54–5, 57, 61 n.10, 62 n.29
appreciative-pleasure   47, 49–50
appretiare   51. *See* appraisal
appropriation   52

aquinas   4, 21, 23–4, 144–6
  existence and   144–6
  gift exchange and   21, 23–4
Aristotle   4, 46
art   5, 66, 72, 74, 99
  beauty and   5
Asymmetry Argument   6, 143, 146–9, 155–6, 159 nn.6–7, 159 n.9
atheism   5, 9, 16, 26, 56, 119, 143, 154–8, 172
  anti-natalism and   9, 143, 154–6, 158
  traditional   5, 119
Augustine   46, 74
Avicenna   5, 9, 123–40. *See also* Ibn Sīnā

beauty   5, 34, 36, 49–52, 54, 56, 57, 172–3
becoming   168
Befindlichkeit   80
being   8, 14, 55, 57–60, 61 n.10, 62 nn.28–9, 66, 70, 72–4, 80 n.1, 81 n.5, 82 n.21, 83 n.25, 83 n.36, 84 n.39, 85 n.60, 90, 92–5, 97–8, 101–3, 109, 111–12, 124–8, 130–3, 135–9, 141 n.10, 144–5, 147–9, 163–5
  alive   102
  artificial   140 n.7
  as-such   65, 166–8
  finite   9, 166–72, 174–5
  gift of   9, 163, 168, 170–2, 174–5
  giving and   66, 70, 73–4, 81 n.8, 91
  God's   111–12, 124, 126, 133, 157, 174–5
  great chain of   92
  horizon of   84 n.39
  human   7–8, 18, 24–6, 46, 57, 59–60, 63 n.46, 73, 93–4, 145, 172
  infinite   9, 166
  munificent   135–7
  mystery of   167, 174
  necessary   125–8, 130–1, 133, 138, 141 n.10

non- 58, 130, 133, 147
order of 93
other 57, 60, 76, 138
possible and impossible 126-8, 130-1, 133
potential 148
question of 66, 73-4, 163, 165
transcendent 166-7, 170
well- 1-4, 47, 54, 59, 97-8, 149-50, 163-75, 176 n.3
-with-others 80
belonging 48, 56, 168, 170
Belshaw, Christopher 153
Benatar, David 6, 99, 146-50, 159 n.6, 159 n.9
benefactor 3, 7, 13-16, 19, 22, 24-6, 28 n.1, 28 n.3, 29 n.14, 95-7, 99, 100, 103, 105 n.41, 134-5, 137
human 3
personal 13, 26
principal 7, 14, 26
universal 3
benefactor-beneficiary relation 27. *See also* gratitude, tri-polar structure of
beneficiary 6-7, 14-16, 19, 22, 24-7, 29, 94-7, 100, 137, 164
benefit 2, 6-7, 13-15, 21, 23, 25-8, 34, 41-2, 91, 94-5, 97-103, 105 n.41, 147-8, 151-2
from benefactor 7, 13-15, 25, 97, 100
gratitude and 2, 6, 13-15, 23, 25-6, 28, 34, 42, 91, 94-5, 97-101, 103, 105 n.41
pure 151-2
Bennett, Johnathan 112, 117
Bentley Hart, David 166
Bible 67-8
blessing 3, 102, 172
Buber, Martin 59-60, 177 n.23
Buddhism 5, 89
Bulgakov, Sergius 172

causality 79, 124, 126, 130, 132, 138-40
cause 20-5, 27-8, 38, 82 n.23, 123-7, 129-34, 136-9, 141 n.10, 141 n.14, 166, 174
efficient 131-3, 141 n.14

existential 125, 129, 132-3, 136-7, 139
final 131-2, 138, 141 n.14
first 138-9
formal 131-2, 141 n.14
indeterministic 38
material 131-2, 141 n.14
ontological 132-3
structuring 20-5, 27-8
triggering 20, 22
charity 23, 47, 75, 78
Christ 72-3
Christianity 68, 82 n.16, 89, 143, 158, 171-2
Clark, W. Norris 164
climate change 57, 62 n.30
colonialism 89
community 23, 34, 36, 60, 96, 164, 166-7, 169, 174
conatus essendi 170-1
confession 8, 74, 76
Confucianism 89
Conrad-Martius, Hedwig 65, 80 n.1
consent 22, 143, 150-2, 155-6, 171
extended 22
creation 4-5, 8, 40, 74, 79, 85 n.57, 85 n.59, 91, 93-4, 101, 109-14, 119, 120 n.9, 133, 141 n.16, 143, 146, 148-54, 156-7, 159 n.8, 164, 171
actualist accounts of 112, 119
contingent 113-14, 120 n.9
of contingent objects 110-11
divine 109-12, 119, 120 n.9, 157
as gift 74, 79, 85 n.57
necessary 113
self- 164, 171
theistic 8, 109-11, 119
creator 56-7, 74, 90, 92, 174-5
creature 4, 9, 29 n.11, 54-5, 57, 62 n.28, 85 n.59, 93, 124-7, 129-31, 133-40, 140 n.7, 140 n.10, 154
human 57, 62 n.28, 85 n.59, 126, 131, 154
culture 4-5, 7, 13-14, 24, 27, 48, 54, 89-90
African 89
economies and 4
existential gratitude and 7, 13-14

tribal 24
Western 27

Danken 66
Dasein 65–6, 80 n.1
death 28 n.4, 65, 67, 69, 72, 80 n.3,
    81 n.5, 93, 99, 151, 172
debt 23–6, 28, 78, 95, 99, 143
  legal 23–6, 28
  moral 23–4
Deluded Gladness Argument 143,
    149–50, 155–6, 159 n.7
democracy 67–8
Denken 66
Derrida, Jacques 8, 61 n.23, 66–70, 74–5,
    77–8, 81 n.10, 82 n.21, 83 n.29
  and the economy of the gift 8,
    61 n.3, 66–70, 74–5, 83 n.29
Descartes, René 73
desire 47, 49–51, 53, 55, 57, 97, 136,
    138–9, 150, 153–4, 172–3
Desmond, William 9, 163–6, 168–71,
    173–5, 176 n.3
Dillard, Annie 48, 52, 63 n.37
divinity 1, 3–4, 9, 68, 70, 73–6, 79,
    80 n.1, 82 n.21, 85 n.59, 91–4,
    96, 99, 109–12, 119, 120 n.9,
    137–9, 152, 154, 157, 159 n.8,
    172–4
duty 148, 152–3

Eckhart, Meister 66
economics 7–8, 24, 45–6, 52–4,
    61 n.23, 61 n.26, 66–71, 73, 75,
    83 nn.29–30, 167
  anti- 52
  circular 68
  earthly 68
  of exchange 7, 52–4, 66–71, 75,
    83 nn.29–30
  heavenly 68
  non- 45–6
embodiment 5, 93
emergent process 22–3, 25
emotion 13, 15–18, 25, 27, 29 n.10, 55,
    75–8, 80, 86 n.73, 95, 97
  founded 76
  founding 76
  gratitude and 13, 25, 27, 76–8, 95

interpersonal 76
moral 75–6, 86 n.73
religious 76
transcendent 15–18
energy 8, 91, 93–4
environment 7, 46, 48, 59, 65, 80 n.2, 93,
    158, 169–70
environmentalism 93
epistemology 165
essence 52, 58, 77, 80, 90, 111, 118, 125,
    130–6, 139, 140 n.9, 144–5,
    158 n.1, 164
  and existence 80 n.1, 103, 125,
    130–4, 136, 139, 140 n.9, 144–5,
    158 n.1, 164
  of the gift 52
  of gratitude 77
  highest 90
eternity 51, 99, 133
ethics 8–9, 65, 95–6, 126, 143, 151, 158,
    163, 171
  other-centered 158
ethos 168
etymology 13, 16, 18–19, 51, 69
Eucharist 72
evil 69, 82 n.18, 95, 118–19, 143–5,
    155–7, 168–70
  problem of 143, 155–7
evolution 34, 38, 62 n.28
excess 69, 72, 82 n.18, 164–9, 171, 175–6
exchange 3, 7, 18–19, 21–8, 52–4,
    61 n.26, 66–71, 75, 83 nn.29–30,
    88, 134
  economic 7, 52–4, 66–71, 75,
    83 nn.29–30
  of gifts 3, 18–19, 21–8, 52–4,
    61 n.26, 66–71, 75, 83 n.30
  property 67
  reciprocal 18, 52–4, 61 n.26, 66, 70,
    83 n.30
existence 1–4, 6, 8–9, 13–17, 26, 28,
    29 n.11, 39, 48, 58–9, 65–6,
    68–70, 73–4, 76–80, 80 n.1,
    81 n.5, 86 n.80, 87, 90–7, 99,
    102–3, 104 n.12, 109, 112,
    117–19, 120 n.6, 124–34,
    136–40, 140 nn.4–5, 140 n.7,
    140 nn.9–10, 141 n.14, 143, 150,
    152–7, 158 n.1, 163–70, 172–6

as benefit 6, 8, 147–8
contingent 4, 8, 79, 109
creaturely 4
finite 9, 163–70, 173–6
as gift 1, 4, 8–9, 15, 17, 26, 28, 74, 79, 94–5, 163, 167, 169, 174–6
as good 4, 8, 13, 16–17, 109, 143–7, 150, 154–5, 157, 158 n.1
gratitude for 2, 8–9, 13, 15, 26, 28, 48, 65–6, 68–9, 76–80, 91, 94–7, 99, 102–3, 109, 112, 114, 119, 124, 134, 137, 139–40, 143–4, 146, 148, 150, 152–4, 157, 159 n.1, 169, 176
as harm 6, 102, 146–50, 152–6
necessary 9, 124–33, 137, 164
non- 95, 118, 126–9, 140 n.5, 156
phenomenality of 79
possible 4, 9, 109, 124, 126–34, 136–8, 140 nn.5–6
existential gratitude 1–9, 13–19, 21, 24–8, 28 n.1, 28 n.4, 124–5, 134–7, 139
existential gratitude scale 2, 17, 28 n.4
experience 2, 3, 14–17, 26, 46–52, 54–9, 60 n.10, 62 n.32, 76, 79–80, 82 n.12, 86 n.80, 126, 137, 147–9, 153–6, 163, 168, 172
of nature 46, 49, 52, 55–6, 58
of pain 80, 147–8, 153–6
Exploitation Argument 143, 153–6
expression 1, 7, 31, 33–7, 39, 41–2, 46, 56, 69, 75, 78, 164, 166
asymmetry and 34–6
of gratitude 1, 7, 31, 33–7, 39, 41–2, 78
self- 164

Feuerbach, Ludwig 172–3
final value 8, 93–6
finitude 65, 141 n.14, 164, 166, 169–70, 174
forgiveness 48, 67–72
friendship (philia) 47, 69

Gegebenheit 70, 82 n.23
Gelassenheit 66
generosity 45, 66–70, 72–4, 76, 78–9, 81 n.8, 84 n.41, 168

genetics 147, 159 n.5
gift 1, 3–5, 8–9, 14–19, 21–8, 29 nn.13–14, 45–7, 49, 52–5, 58, 60 n.1, 61 n.23, 61 n.26, 66–79, 82 n.12, 82 n.16, 82 n.18, 82 nn.21–2, 83 n.30, 84 n.38, 84 n.57, 84 nn.64–5, 84 n.73, 84 n.79, 90–1, 93–5, 97, 99, 101–3, 104 n.4, 163, 167–72, 174–5
counter 67–8
economy 45, 52–4, 61 n.23, 61 n.26, 66–8, 83 n.30
and excess 69, 72, 82 n.18, 168–9, 171, 175–6
exchange 3, 18–19, 21–8, 52–4, 61 n.26, 66–71, 75, 83 n.30
-giving 8, 18, 22, 24, 47, 49, 66–78, 82 n.21, 86 n.79, 174
-love 47, 55, 60 n.10, 72, 75, 82 n.18
-object 70–1, 75, 77
receive a 3, 14, 22, 24–5, 29 n.13, 47, 52, 66, 68, 72, 74, 171, 174
return 22–3, 28, 53, 67, 70, 72, 77, 79, 84 n.49
symbolic 71
gift economy 52–3, 61 n.23, 61 n.26
givenness 8, 66, 69–74, 79, 81 n.7, 82 n.23, 83 n.25, 83 n.30, 86 n.78, 171–2
giver 4, 8, 18, 22, 24, 47, 49, 60–70, 81 n.8, 82 n.21, 84 n.38, 86 n.79, 134, 137, 151, 170, 174
giving 4, 8, 18, 22, 24, 47, 49, 60–78, 81 n.8, 82 n.21, 84 n.38, 86 n.79, 134, 137, 151, 170, 174
God 3–4, 7–9, 15, 18, 24, 26, 31–3, 36–42, 48, 56, 68, 70–5, 79, 82 n.23, 85 n.55, 85 n.59, 85 n.60, 90–7, 99, 101–3, 109–19, 120 n.9, 124–7, 129–40, 140 n.4, 140 n.10, 143–4, 146, 148–50, 152–8, 159 n.1, 159 n.8, 163, 172–5
Abrahamic 90, 92
African 90–4, 102–3
as-personal 163, 172–5
as benefactor 3, 15, 26, 95–7, 99, 103, 134–5, 137
creative activity of 8–9, 37–42, 74, 79, 85 n.59, 91, 93–7, 99, 101,

Index

102, 109–16, 119, 120 n.9, 134, 143, 146, 149–50, 152–8, 159 n.8, 174–5
  as dative object   15–16, 26
  existence of   73, 90, 117–19, 124, 126–7, 129, 133, 140 n.4, 155–7, 172
  as giver   8, 70–2, 74–5, 79, 90, 94–5, 103, 132, 137, 163, 172–5
  giving thanks to   4, 8, 90, 94–5, 103, 175
  gratitude and   7–9, 31–2, 37–42, 68, 91–2, 94–7, 99, 101–3, 109, 114, 119, 134–6, 139–40, 143, 146, 148, 150, 152–4, 157, 159 n.1, 174
  love and   56, 75, 172–4
  necessity of   125–6, 129–31, 133, 140 n.10
  resentment and   7, 32–3, 36–7, 40–1
  traditional   118–19
goodness   13, 16, 49–51, 55–7, 60, 93, 126, 144–5, 168, 169, 173
grace   4, 16, 23, 52, 57, 68, 82 n.16
gratefulness   2–5, 8–9, 14–16, 22–8, 28 n.3, 31, 33–4, 36–42, 48, 65, 68–9, 76–8, 91, 95–103, 105 n.41, 105 n.46, 124, 134, 137, 140, 143–4, 146, 154, 159 n.1, 169
  existential   2, 5, 8, 26, 28, 65, 68, 76, 78, 98–9, 101–3, 134, 137, 143–4, 146, 154, 159 n.1
  to God   9, 31, 37–42, 68, 91, 95–6, 101–3, 140, 143, 146, 154, 159 n.1
gratia   4, 18–19, 23, 27–8, 29 n.6, 26 n.9, 68
gratitude   1–9, 13–19, 21–8, 28 n.1, 28 n.4, 29 n.6, 29 n.12, 31–7, 39–42, 45–9, 51–4, 57, 60, 61 n.26, 65–9, 74–80, 81 n.8, 85 n.65, 86 n.78, 91–2, 94–103, 105 n.41, 105 n.46, 109, 112, 114, 119–20, 124–5, 134–40, 143, 146, 148, 150, 152–5, 157, 163, 170–1, 174–6, 176 n.15
  cosmic   1, 3, 11, 14–15
  dimensions of   7, 14, 19, 25–7, 29 n.6, 75, 78, 170, 176

  as discipline of hearing   171
  dispositional   2–3
  emotion and   1, 13, 15–17, 19, 25, 27, 75–7, 80
  epistemic dimension of   78
  ethics and   8, 9, 96, 163
  expressions of   1, 7, 31, 33–7, 39, 41–2, 78
  gratuitous dimension of   16, 29 n.6, 52, 67
  in-   78–9, 96
  as inappropriate   99, 101, 112, 114
  as interpersonal   4, 66, 74–7
  as intersubjective phenomenon   1
  metaphysics and   8–9, 102, 114, 124–5, 134–5, 137, 139, 171
  morality and   1–2, 5–7, 9, 23–8, 75–6, 78, 95–6, 103, 109, 153, 157–8
  ontology and   8–9, 170–1, 176 n.15
  as personal   3, 76, 175–6
  phenomenology of   8
  as a positioned phenomenon   14, 19, 21
  praise and   134–7, 139
  prepositional expressions of   7, 31–7, 41–2
  propositional expressions of   7, 31–7, 41–2
  proximate genus of   19
  psychology and   2, 4, 13, 18–19, 22, 24–7, 80
  religion and   1–4, 9, 13, 17, 24, 28 n.4, 32–3, 35, 76, 91, 102, 163
  spectrum of gratitude   3
  spirituality and   1–3, 5–6, 9, 28 n.4, 61 n.26, 170
  as spontaneous   23, 25, 49
  syntactical structure of   19
  as transactional   53, 134
  transpersonal   3, 14
  tripolar structure of   14–17, 19, 26–7
gratitude density   3
gratitude studies   2, 4
gratitudo   29 n.8, 51
gratuity   3, 5, 16–17, 29, 47, 52–3, 67
gratus   16, 18, 51
group identification   34–5

harm 6, 41, 99, 102, 118, 146–58
  existence as 6, 146–9, 152–5
  unjustified 151
Harrison, Gerald 151–3
Haslanger, Sally 7, 14, 19, 20, 22
Heidegger, Martin 65–6, 70, 73–4, 79–80, 80 n.1, 81 n.5, 81 nn.7–8, 83 n.36, 85 n.54, 175
Henry, Michel 74
hermeneutics 58
Holy Spirit 73
home 50, 56, 65, 67, 80, 80 n.2, 124
Homer 18
hospitality 67–8, 168–70
human 1–4, 6–7–8–9, 18, 24–7, 29 n.11, 35, 40, 46, 48, 55–60, 62 n.28, 62 n.30, 63 n.45, 63 n.46, 65–6, 73–4, 80 n.1, 81 n.7, 85 n.59, 89–90, 92–5, 97, 99, 104 n.16, 110, 118, 126, 131, 143, 145–6, 148–50, 152–8, 158 n.1, 163–4, 167, 169–75
  anti- 46
  in- 40, 46, 48, 62 n.29
  non- 7–8, 46, 58–9, 63 n.38, 158, 169, 171
  vocation 57
humanity 40, 62 n.28, 63 n.45, 73, 90, 92, 118
humiliation 78
humility 75–9, 85 n.72, 86 n.78
Husserl, Edmund 65, 70, 82 n.23
Hypothetical Consent Argument 143, 150–2, 155–6

Ibn Sīnā 4, 123. *See also* Avicenna
idolatry 74, 173
immanence 165–7, 175
indigenous 8, 24, 66, 89–90, 92, 104 n.9
  African culture 24, 92, 104 n.9
  philosophy 8, 104 n.9
infinity 9, 55, 111, 116, 164, 166–7, 174–5
institutions 2, 34
intentionality 14, 19, 22, 27, 79, 84 n.38, 94, 138–9
Islam 4, 89, 123, 158

Jankélévitch, Vladimir 69, 82 n.18

joy 2, 15–17, 24, 53–4, 79, 148
Judaism 89, 158
justice 14, 23–4, 34
  commutative 23
  in- 34

Kamm, Frances 99
Kierkegaard, Søren 46, 67
Kimmerer, Robin Wall 45–6, 52–4, 57–8, 60, 61 n.23, 61 n.26, 63 n.38, 63 n.45
Kohák, Erazim 59, 63 n.46

Lacewing, Michael 1, 13–19, 21, 26–8, 29 n.6
language 16, 33, 58, 63 n.38, 73, 82 n.21, 152
Leben 5, 26
Leibniz, Gottfried Wilhelm 37–8
Lewis, C.S. 46–7, 49, 51, 56
liberty 25
life 1–6, 8, 13–17, 24–6, 28, 42, 48–9, 54–7, 60, 61 n.10, 62 n.29, 69, 74–5, 79–80, 86 n.80, 90–103, 104 n.9, 104 n.16, 118, 123, 125, 147–50, 152–4, 163, 170, 173, 176
  bad 6, 91, 101, 147, 149–50
  as beneficial 6
  as burden 79
  civic 24
  future- 147
  as gift 17, 26, 28, 79, 90, 93–7, 99, 102–3, 104 n.9
  given by God 3, 90, 92–4, 96–7, 101
  as good 4, 54, 101, 150, 152
  grateful for 2–3, 5, 13–17, 26, 28, 69, 80, 96–9, 101, 163, 170
  human 6, 8, 48, 90, 93–4, 99, 104 n.16
  present- 147
  quality of 91–2, 96–8, 101–2, 149–50
  religious 2
  social 1, 24–5
  web of 57, 92
  worth continuing 147, 152
  worth starting 147, 150
life force 8, 89, 91–6, 98–9, 101–3, 104 n.16

ancestors and 92–4, 103, 104 n.16
final value and 8, 93–5, 102
gratitude for 8, 89, 91, 94, 96, 99, 101–3
linguistics 16, 33
literature 6, 9, 17, 29 n.7, 34, 42, 70, 103, 150, 156–7, 159 n.7
philosophical 6, 9
logic 15, 28, 69, 103, 110, 112–15, 117–20, 120 n.1, 121, 127, 154, 156, 163, 168, 172
logos 92
love 36, 42, 45–7, 50–7, 60 n.10, 62 n.29, 63 n.36, 70, 72–5, 82 n.18, 85 n.60, 97, 167–9, 171–4
dimensions of 70
first 168
gift- 47, 55, 60 n.10, 72, 75, 82 n.18
gift of 71–2
interpersonal 66, 75
modes of 47
need- 47, 50, 55, 57, 61 n.10
second 168

Magesa, Laurenti 90
Maimonides 4, 75
Manela, Tony 6, 32, 104 n.25, 105 n.39
Marion, Jean Luc 8, 66, 69–75, 81 n.10, 82 nn.21–2, 83 nn.23–30, 83 n.36, 84 nn.38–41, 84 n.48, 84 n.49, 85 n.55, 85 nn.59–60, 85 n.64, 86 n.79, 175
phenomenology of givenness 8, 66, 69–75, 82 n.22, 83 n.25, 83 n.30, 84 nn.40–1, 84 n.49
saturated phenomenon 70, 72, 83 n.27
Mauss, Marcel 21, 24–5, 29 nn.13–14, 66–8, 83 n.29
Mbiti, John S. 89–90
mercy 17, 75
metaphysics 4, 8–9, 59, 70, 73, 79, 84 n.38, 91–3, 96, 102–3, 109–10, 112, 114, 116–19, 123–8, 130–5, 137–9, 165, 170–1, 173, 176 n.3, 176 n.14
Avicenna and 123–8, 130–9
space and 116, 118–19
of theistic creation 8, 109–10, 112, 114

truth and 4, 173
modal collapse argument 8, 109, 112–13, 117
Molinism 38, 152
morality 1–2, 5–7, 9, 23–9, 60, 75–6, 78–9, 86 n.73, 90, 93, 95–6, 103, 109, 118, 143, 152–3, 155, 157–8, 158 n.1, 159 n.12

nation 34, 36, 54
Potawatomi 54
natural 5, 46, 58–60, 62 n.28, 123, 131–2, 140
beauty 5
beings 62 n.28
causality 132
philosophy 131
resources 58
sciences 123
substances 140
super- 166
un- 62 n.28
world 46, 59–60, 118
nature 5, 7, 26, 45–6, 49, 52, 55–8, 61 n.28, 62 nn.28–30, 63 n.45, 103, 172
beauty of 5, 49, 56, 172
as gift 58
as home 56
as object of love 55
otherness of 55, 59, 61 n.28, 62 n.29
personalist view of 46, 58–60
the Necessary Existent 4, 124–6, 129–30, 133–40, 140 n.7
Nietzsche, Friedrich 5, 26
No Best World Problem 143, 155, 157
No Victim Argument 143, 152–3, 155
Nyssa, Gregory of 165

object 3–4, 7–8, 14–16, 26, 28 nn.1–2, 35, 47, 55, 58–9, 63 n.38, 70–1, 73, 75, 77, 92, 110–12, 116, 119, 139, 164, 172
actual 110, 120 n.2
concrete 8, 92, 110
contingent 110–12
dative 14–16, 26, 28 nn.1–2
gift- 70–1, 75, 77
of gratitude 3, 4, 7, 19, 35

human as 73
inanimate 8, 174
land as 58-9, 63 n.38
of love 47, 55
ontology 92
possible 110-11
objectivism 97
obligation 23-4, 52, 66-9, 76-80, 93, 153, 159 n.9
offering 71, 78, 95, 175
offspring 150, 152
okra 94
ontological gratitude 9, 170-1, 176 n.15
ontology 8, 9, 62 n.28, 70, 73-4, 79, 85 n.54, 92, 96, 129-30, 132-3, 135-6, 170-1, 174, 176 n.15
causality and 130, 132-3
de- 96
force 92
object 92
optimism 149
other 31, 47, 54-5, 57, 65, 69, 72-80, 81 n.5, 124, 158, 164, 167-70, 173, 175
otherness 46, 55, 61 nn.28-9, 76, 168
ousia 71, 83 n.36
ownership 67, 170

panpsychism 59
passio essendi 170-1
perfection 98-9, 134-6, 138-9
personalism 58-60
personhood 58-9, 98-9, 101-2, 173-5
of God 173-5
phenomenality 66, 70-2, 77, 79, 83 n.25, 84 n.49
phenomenology 8, 65-6, 69-73, 75, 77-8, 80, 82 n.23, 83 n.25, 83 n.29
of givenness 8, 66, 70-3, 75, 82 n.23
of gratitude 8, 66, 77-8
philanthropic arguments 146, 154-9
philosophy 6, 8, 21, 23, 26, 34, 51, 58-9, 66, 73, 89-90, 93, 102, 104 n.9, 131
aesthetic 26
African 8, 89, 93, 102, 104 n.9
continental 51
French 66

metaphysical 73
natural 131
of religion 89, 90, 102, 104 n.9
Western 6, 21, 23, 58
Plantinga, Alvin 38, 156
pleasure 6, 32-3, 47, 49-50, 54, 60 n.10, 147-8, 152
appreciative- 47, 49-50, 60 n.10
dis- 33
need- 47, 49-50, 60 n.10
pluriverse 116-20, 121 n.9
poetry 46, 48, 66
politics 124, 164, 167
Pollyanna Principle 149-50
Potawatomi 54, 58, 63 n.38
prayer 9, 95, 172-3, 175-6
presence 48-50, 55, 72, 74, 84, 86, 145, 164, 166, 173-4
dynamic act of 164
Principle of Sufficient Reason (PSR) 113, 116, 120 n.6
procreation 143, 146, 148, 150-3, 156-8
prodigal son 71-2
psychology 4, 18-19, 21-2, 24-7, 29 n.9, 34, 40, 79-80, 149, 153, 167, 176 n.3
positive 2-3, 13
purpose 2, 28 n.4, 56, 132, 134, 136, 138
transcendent 2

reality 28 n.4, 45-6, 59-60, 62 n.28, 83 n.25, 92-3, 145, 163-4, 175
gift-nature of 45-6
as relational 60
transcendental 28
receiver 14, 22, 135
receptivity 65, 72, 84 n.38, 84 n.48, 170, 171
reciprocity 4, 7, 14, 18-19, 21-2, 24-8, 29 n.7, 29 n.9, 34, 36, 52-4, 61 n.26, 66-8, 70-1, 75, 78, 83 n.30, 87
circular 18, 27, 29 n.9
economic 4, 52-4, 66-8, 75, 83 n.30
gift-exchange and 18, 22, 24-5, 28, 52, 66-8, 71, 78, 83 n.30
relation and 24, 52-4, 58, 83 n.30
social 4, 14, 19, 21-2, 24-5, 34, 36
recompense 67-8, 134-6

relationship 1, 3, 7, 9, 24, 27, 31, 46,
    52–5, 58–60, 62 n.29, 67–8, 71,
    74–8, 81 n.7, 82 n.16, 83 n.30,
    96–7, 115, 126, 128, 135–6, 167,
    170, 173–4
  asymmetrical 24
  economic 54, 67–8, 71, 83 n.30
  interpersonal 74–6, 81 n.7
  I-Thou 59–60, 175
  of reciprocity 24, 52–4
  social 170, 174
religion 1, 3–4, 8–9, 13, 17, 24, 28 n.4,
    31–3, 35–6, 75–6, 89–92, 95,
    102–3, 104 n.9, 124, 141 n.23,
    158, 163, 172–3
  monotheism and 32–3, 35, 158
  nonreligious 17, 28 n.4, 76
  Traditional African 8, 89–92, 95,
    102–3, 104 n.9, 158
  tradition and 1, 13, 163
  world 4
repayment 23, 26, 29 n.106, 175
  proportionate 23
resentment 5, 6, 31, 33–7, 40–1
  prepositional expressions of 7, 33–7,
    41
  propositional expressions of 7, 33–7,
    41
reward 49, 52, 68, 154
Ricœur, Paul 68–9
Roberts, Robert C. 1, 13–19, 21, 26–8,
    28 nn.2–3, 32
Roberts-Lacewing debate 14–17, 19,
    26–8
Rowe, William 112, 117, 156–7

S5 theorem 110, 113–18, 120, 120 n.1,
    121 n.10, 121 nn.12–16
sacrifice 67, 70–2, 95, 98
  Abrahamic 67, 71
  Traditional African Religion and 95
Scheler, Max 46, 59, 65
Schopenhauer, Arthur 6
scientific realism 103
Sein 66
self 51, 72–6, 81 n.5, 83 n.25, 84 n.38,
    90, 92–3, 97–9, 101–3, 149, 158,
    164–5, 168–9, 171, 174–5
  -abandonment 72, 74
  -awareness 92
  -creation 164, 171
  disembodied 93
  -expression 164–5, 175
  -forgetting 81 n.5
  -givenness 72–6, 84 n.38
  -interest 97, 99
  -love 168
  my 49, 74, 76, 85, 103, 131, 134,
    167–8, 173
  -transcendence 174
Seneca 4, 18, 21–4, 26, 28
  gift-exchange and 21–2, 24
Simic, Charles 48–9
social-structural explanation 7, 14,
    19–28
sociology 71, 81 n.10
soul 25, 92, 123, 152, 169, 172
spirituality 2, 28 n.4
Steinbock, Anthony 66, 74–7, 79,
    81 n.7, 82 n.12, 85 n.64, 86 n.73,
    86 n.78
Steindl-Rast, David 14–15
Stoicism 1, 27
structuring causes 20–5, 27–8
subjectivity 1–2, 97, 149–50, 168–9, 173
  inter- 1
sub-Saharan peoples 89–90
suffering 2, 3, 28 n.4, 80, 148, 152–4,
    156, 158, 169, 171
suicide 69, 79, 95
sustainability 53–4, 61 n.26, 101, 166–7
  gratitude and 53–4
  life-force and 93–4, 99
Swinburne, Richard 112
systems 19, 40, 66, 120 n.1, 123, 125
  biological 19
  eco- 40
  economic 66

Tempels, Placide 93, 104 n.9
temporality 48–9, 51, 77–8, 86 n.78,
    110–11, 166, 168
  spatio- 110–11
thankfulness 14–16, 51–4, 86 n.78, 90–1,
    94–5, 99, 102–3, 170–1
thanks 4, 18, 22, 28 n.4, 47, 53, 57, 60,
    77, 92, 94–5, 98, 101, 171, 175
  give 57, 60, 171, 175

-giving 53, 175
to God 4, 92, 94–5
as response 18, 22, 47, 98, 175
theism 4–5, 7–9, 13, 15–17, 26, 32–3, 35,
 38–9, 41–2, 56, 89, 92, 109–12,
 114, 116–19, 120 n.1, 143–4,
 146, 149–50, 152–8, 172
 actualism and 8, 109–12, 116, 144
 anti-natalism and 9, 143, 146,
  149–50, 152–8
 classical 143–4, 146, 155, 157
 creation and 8
 existential gratitude and 13, 15, 26
 Judeo-Christian 143
 mono- 4–5, 32–3, 35, 41, 89, 92, 126,
  158, 172
 non- 13, 15–17, 26
 open 38
 traditional 118–19
theology 2, 4–5, 8, 68, 70, 72–3, 76, 90,
 95, 110, 115, 117–18, 120, 144,
 171–3, 176 n.14
 African 90, 95
 metaphysical 73
 philosophical 110, 115, 117, 120, 144
 Russian 172
 white 73
thrownness 65, 79, 80 n.2
time 50, 69, 71, 77, 100, 110, 153, 163–7
tradition 1, 5, 8, 13, 36, 46, 53, 58–9,
 89–92, 94–5, 102–3, 106–7,
 118–19, 131, 146, 158, 163, 173
 African 8, 89–92, 94–5, 102–3, 158
 atheistic 5, 119
 Mahāyāna Buddhism 5
 monotheistic 92, 172–3
 non-Western 1
 phenomenological 8
 of philosophy 58–9
 Potawatomi 58
 religious 1, 8, 89–90, 95, 158, 164
 theistic 118–19, 146
transaction 53, 134
transcendence 2, 15–17, 19, 28 n.4,
 82–83 n.23, 166–7, 170, 174–5
 being and 166–7, 170, 174–5
 self- 174

truth 4, 31, 60, 113, 115, 120, 143, 147,
 154, 157–8, 167, 173
 contingent 113, 115, 120 n.1, 147
 metaphysical 4
 necessary 113, 147

undeserved good 8, 13, 16–19, 27–8
universal impermanence 165
universe 2, 8, 37–9, 42, 54, 90, 93,
 110–11
 best 37–8
 as created 8
utilitarianism 53
utopia 153

valuation 7, 51, 53
Van Inwagen, Peter 8, 109, 112–15, 117,
 119
vital force 90, 92–4, 104 n.12
vitality 90, 92, 95–6
vocation 57
Von Balthasar, Hans Urs 165

welfare 97–9
Wesen 77
wonder 15–18, 47–8, 54, 56–7
Woolf, Virginia 51
world 4, 7–9, 15, 18, 36, 45–6, 48,
 54–60, 62 n.28, 62 n.30, 62 n.32,
 63 n.38, 65, 72, 75, 79–80, 89–
 92, 95, 100, 103, 103 n.1, 109–
 19, 120 n.2, 120 n.9, 121 n.11,
 121 n.15, 132–3, 143–4, 147–9,
 153–8, 168, 170–1, 175
 actual 8, 109–16, 121 n.9, 154
 alien 48
 ancient 18
 natural 46, 55, 59–60, 62 n.30
 necessary 109, 113, 115–16, 119
 nonhuman 63 n.38
 possible 109–12, 114–19, 120 n.2,
  120 n.9, 121 n.15, 144
 real 54
 states of affairs in the 111–19,
  121 n.11, 121 nn.13–15
 valued 168, 170
worldviews 89, 92

www.ingramcontent.com/pod-product-compliance
Lightning Source LLC
Chambersburg PA
CBHW061832300426
44115CB00013B/2353